MW00440130

THE
LAST
HEIR

The Triumphs and Tragedies
of Two Montana Families

BILL VAUGHN

University of Nebraska Press
LINCOLN

Library of Congress Control Number: 2021040740

Set in New Baskerville ITC by Laura Buis.
Designed by N. Putens.

For the reporters

Two households, both alike in dignity.
—*Romeo and Juliet*

CONTENTS

ILLUSTRATIONS

MAPS

PREFACE

The only thing the Herrins and the Burkes had in common was their Irish ancestry. Opposites in most ways, the families nevertheless personified two common threads in the history of Western America. As the owner of one of Montana's premier early twentieth-century stock-raising operations—what would later be famously named the Oxbow Ranch on the west shore of Holter Lake—Holly Herrin ruled with frontier violence and legal vehemence over a mammoth fiefdom of land, water, cattle, and sheep. George Burke was a real estate agent, a deputy sheriff, a game warden and a civil engineer in a family of professionals—newspaper editors, lawyers, and politicians, including a U.S. senator. The country-mouse Herrins voted Republican; the city-mouse Burkes Democratic. Both patriarchs, fighting with their fists and their lawyers, were active players in the far-reaching dramas and ludicrous comedies that shaped modern Montana.

While I learned much about the Herrins and the Burkes from newspaper articles, books, deeds, wills, pamphlets, and other public records such as court judgments, I drew essential primary material for these intertwined stories from two people. The first is my wife, Kitty Herrin—the great-granddaughter of Holly Herrin and the granddaughter of George Burke. And the second is her mother, Molly Catherine Burke Herrin. As a college-educated journalist, Molly felt compelled to warehouse most every document that came into her possession, from letters and photographs to canceled checks, tax records, journals, transcripts, union dues receipts, and pay stubs.

What follows from this research is the twelve-decade story of two clans whose fortunes would finally be married together. First up are the Burkes, followed by the Herrins. The narrative concludes with the fate of all empires, whether with a bang or, in the case of this one, with a whimper.

THE BURKES & THE HERRINS

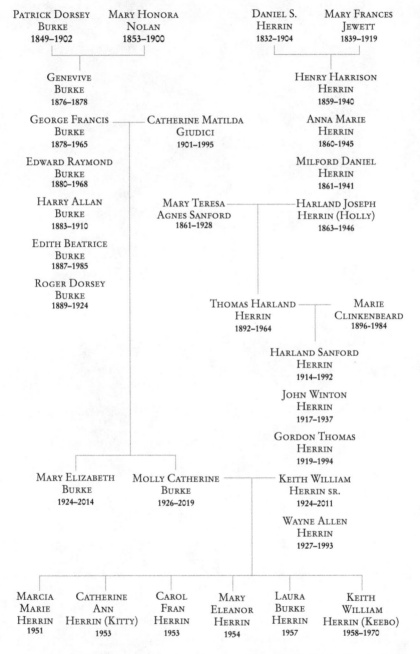

FIG. 1. Burke and Herrin family trees. Courtesy of the Molly Burke Herrin Estate.

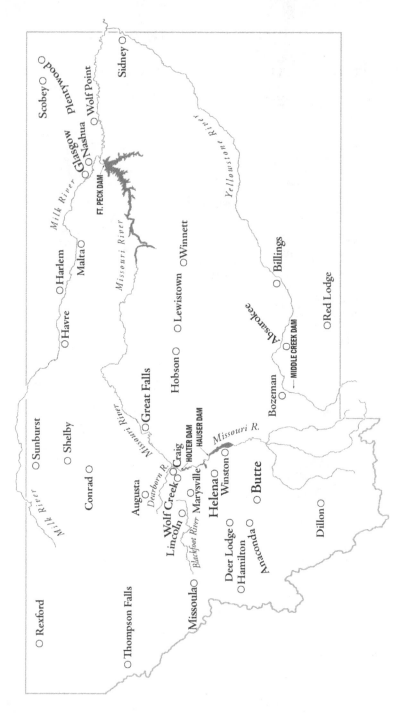

MAP 1. Montana. Created by author.

THE LAST HEIR

1

Without a Trace

On a frigid afternoon in February 1969 Molly Herrin and her ten-year-old son left the three-story brick slab housing the Montana School for the Deaf and Blind in Great Falls and walked toward the family's lumbering blue Travelall parked in the lot. As he tapped the sidewalk with his white cane she chatted with him about the nice lady who had just taught him this new skill. Driving into the setting sun, they crossed the Missouri on the Tenth Avenue South bridge and headed through West Great Falls toward Interstate 15, which wound upstream along the big frozen river to the Herrin Hereford Ranch ninety miles south in the Helena Valley. Settling down beside her in the front seat, Keith Jr.—his sisters called him Keebo—put on his earphones and turned the dial on his transistor radio until he found KUDI, the only rock and roll station in town. He loved the Beatles and the Rolling Stones and had lately developed a taste for Sly and the Family Stone, whose single "Everyday People" was topping the charts. When they entered the volcanic palisades of Wolf Creek Canyon and the station faded to static, he reached for his social studies book. In the dark he read the raised dots with the fingers of both hands.

Everyone on the ranch knew that the doctors had run out of options. But the painful subject of Keebo's health was not something his large extended family talked about much. The conversations tended instead toward fences and farm equipment and the weather. Molly and Keith Sr. were trying to work through problems in their marriage, so entrenched that they had sought counseling, a fact they kept secret because therapy wasn't something engaged in by Montana ranchers. Keebo's aunt and uncle, who lived on their adjoining ranch next to the Herrin place, had their hands full running both spreads, especially after Keith Sr. had become distracted by matters other than hay and cattle. Keebo's grandmother, a widow living in yet another ranch house, was busy with her garden club and her singing and volunteer work with the Daughters of the Nile. And his sisters were caught up in the social whirl that preoccupies popular teenage girls.

Walking to her house, Molly could see her breath in the ten-degree air. Inside, the girls were gathered around the dining room table. Keebo found his way to a chair and sat down.

"What's going on?" Molly asked.

Marcia, a senior at Helena High who was planning to study journalism in college, never minced words. "Dad left. He's not coming back."

"His rifles are gone," Carol said. She was Molly's third oldest, and Kitty's mirror twin. "So are all his clothes. And his saddles."

Although people in the community would be outraged when they learned that Keith had abandoned his family to run off with a married woman—who also betrayed her husband and children—Molly was neither surprised nor shocked. She had sensed for some time that the day would come when she and Keith would part ways. But she had hoped her husband would somehow muster the courage to stay on in this lifeless marriage, if for nothing else, the sake of his ailing son. The immediate problem caused by Keith's desertion wasn't the emotional pain her children would suffer or what the neighbors thought. It was money. She realized that, suddenly, she had been stripped of any financial stake in the ranch where she had lived and labored for two decades and raised a family. Without a dime in savings, plus mounting medical bills and no promise of an income, how in the world would she provide for herself, her six children, and their menagerie of cats, dogs, sheep, steers, and horses? And if her brother-in-law decided to evict them, where would they live?

In the morning, Molly's panic had turned to resolve. Cradling a third cup of coffee after the kids went off to school, she considered her options. In fact, like her hard-working parents, she had always found a way to earn a living. And she vowed that she would find a way to do so again.

FIG. 2. George Francis Burke, circa 1910. Courtesy of the Molly Burke Herrin Estate.

2

First-Generation Americans

Molly's father, George Francis Burke, was born in Milwaukee in 1878, the son of an Irish immigrant named Patrick Dorsey Burke. Patrick was born in County Limerick on the banks of the River Shannon on St. Patrick's Day in 1849 (the Irish pronounce the name *Bur-kee*). When he was fourteen he sailed from Ireland with a group of friends to Ontario, Canada. He later moved to Wisconsin, where in 1876 he married Mary Nolan. He was employed in railroad construction his entire life. Among the lines he helped build was the Canadian Pacific, working as superintendent of construction from Calgary, Alberta, Canada, westward to the Pacific Ocean. His family accompanied him from place to place. Two of George's younger brothers, Edward Raymond and Harry Allan, were born in South Dakota. Harry Allan, called "Allan" by the family, became an ironworker and was killed in an industrial accident in 1910 while employed by the Pittsburgh Plate Glass Company. Another brother, Roger Dorsey, was born in Sparta, Wisconsin. His kid sister, Edith Beatrice, was born in Calgary, Alberta. Genevive, who preceded him but died at the age of two or three, was born in Wilton, Wisconsin. At the time Edward was born in 1880, Patrick was employed by a railroad line as superintendent of a stone quarry. His last years were spent working for the Great Northern Railroad Company. He died in Great Falls, Montana, in 1902, outliving his wife by two years.

That's one published version of Patrick's life.[1] Another published version paints a more colorful portrait. In that narrative Patrick D'Orsey Burke, or "P.D." as they called him, was a younger son of a Catholic landlord in County Westmeath, Ireland. One day soon after the American Civil War he collected his father's rents and sailed off to the U.S. with the money. A "boom and bust" railroad contractor who was described as "dashing and arrogant," in 1891 he was drawing wages as a roadmaster on the Canadian Pacific, responsible for supervising the crews that maintained and repaired the tracks. That year his wife gave birth to Edith Beatrice in a room above the Calgary railroad station. Apparently worried for some reason about Indian attacks, he kept a steam locomotive on a siding whose boiler was constantly stoked in case he had to suddenly evacuate his wife and his children. P.D. went off to strike it rich in Alaska during the 1898 Klondike Gold Rush, where he died penniless. Molly's grandmother, Mary Nolan Burke, whose father had abandoned his farm in Ireland and moved to America during the 1848 Potato Famine, died in 1900 of cancer. It was thought that the disease was caused by an injury to her breast sustained when the trolley car on which she was riding in St. Paul turned over after hitting a cow.[2]

Molly was told yet another story about P.D. In that yarn, he stole the rents and fled Ireland because he hated his stepmother. In 1887 he was working on a section of the Montana Central Railway being built from Great Falls to Butte, Montana. This was the brainchild of tycoon James J. Hill, who, at the urging of the city's founder, Paris Gibson, intended his railroads to turn Great Falls into a hydroelectric energy and industrial hub. They succeeded, and boosters would later call this wind-blown burg on the Missouri "The Electric City." Somewhere along the line Patrick became an alcoholic. He abandoned his wife and five children to pan for gold in Alaska. The children were then raised by the Nolan family. In fact, according to the 1900 U.S. Census, the two younger Burke children, Edith Beatrice, then thirteen years old, and Roger (also erroneously recorded as being thirteen, although actually only eleven) were living in Sparta, Wisconsin, with their aunt and uncle on their dead mother's side, Albert and Julia Hoffman.

When he was in his early twenties George moved from the Midwest to the prairie town of Glasgow, Montana, located on a coil of the Milk River.[3] Originally called Siding 45, this first rough sketch of a town shared the origin of its new name with several other whistle stops along the Great Northern Railroad's right-of-way through the Montana counties bordering Canada, what is now called the Hi-Line. Railroad officials in St. Paul amused themselves by blindfolding one another, spinning a globe, and stopping it with a finger. The place where the finger came down became the name of the station; thus were born the towns of Malta, Harlem, Kremlin, Zurich, and others.

While it's not known how George made a living during his first years in Glasgow, he must have had some steady source of income because in 1902 a Methodist pastor officiated at his marriage in Havre, Montana, to Jennie Wise, a divorced woman seven years his senior. Also a Wisconsin native, she was the mother of a child from her previous union with a man named Decker. By 1910 the Burkes were living in a sizable house on Second Avenue South in Glasgow they bought with George's commissions as a real estate broker working for the Rundle Land & Abstract Company. Business was good. They rented out a room to a twenty-one-year-old wagon driver named Noah Jenning and employed a twenty-five-year-old live-in maid from Norway named Christina Erickson. Two years later they sold this house and bought another one at the corner of Chestnut and Sixth Street.

The county seat of Glasgow and the surrounding northeastern Montana farmland in remote Valley County were booming as thousands of hopeful farmers poured into the area from all parts of America and beyond, lured by a combination of free farms, bountiful rainfall, and relentless advertising paid for by the railroad companies. A series of Homestead Acts gave away federal land stolen from the tribes after they were defeated by the U.S. Army and impoverished by the decimation of the bison herds by hunters. This enormous transfer of ownership coincided with a period of wet weather that lasted from 1909 to 1917, in which annual precipitation rose to fifteen and even eighteen inches in a region that normally got only seven to nine inches a year. Images of the blooming prairie were played up in promotions and advertisements paid for by the railroads that painted Montana's grasslands as a fertile breadbasket growing lush fields of grain without irrigation.[4]

As a consequence, from 1900 to 1910 the county's population more than tripled. Glasgow rose on the prairie from a squalid collection of shacks to a thriving little berg with proper stone and brick buildings whose downtown, which straddled the tracks of the Great Northern, was dominated by banks and hotels, saloons and cigar stores. The town boasted a theater that showed all the latest silent movies, a library financed with a grant from Andrew Carnegie, a telephone exchange, a hospital, and a flour mill selling a brand called "My Flour." In just one day in 1904, two hundred city lots changed hands.[5] The first automobile appeared on the dusty streets in September 1905.

The social life of George and Jennie was a frequent topic in one of the local weeklies, the *Glasgow Courier*, as they attended various social events, including a surprise party in 1915 at the home of the mayor. They gave money to support the town's high school basketball team and explored Montana in their brand new 1915 Ford Model T Coupe.[6,7] In December 1915 George was among a party of Shriners that traveled on a special railroad car to the state convention in Helena, Montana's capital city, during which they initiated new members on board, described mysteriously by the *Glasgow Courier* as "Those who must suffer the torture of being the 'goats' and sip the camel's milk."

While continuing to work for Sidney Rundle's real estate company, George was hired as a deputy sheriff. There was plenty of work for law enforcement. Trains were being robbed. Posses were being organized to apprehend horse and cattle thieves. Runaway horses were dragging people to their deaths and wagons to their destruction. Because of the number of saloons in Glasgow, public intoxication and fights involving drunks and the occasional pistol duel in the street were fixtures of civic life. In one bizarre case, a man was killed by a shotgun on a road a farmer had rigged with a trip wire to eliminate deer that were eating his crops.[8] In April 1913 a mob lynched a Black man named J. C. Collins, who was accused of a double murder.[9]

This was the beginning of what George hoped would be a long political career, perhaps culminating in an elected office on the national level. In May 1912 Deputy Sheriff Burke was appointed secretary pro tem of a meeting held by the Valley County Democratic Party central committee to select delegates to the state convention in Butte on May 24, which would in turn send delegates to the national convention in Baltimore in June, where the Democratic candidate for president would be chosen. The meeting was officiated by a state committeeman named Col. E. D. Coleman, who had in mind an agenda for the meeting, which was held in his Glasgow home. However, the gathering soon degenerated into name-calling after Glasgow mayor John Dawson moved that a subcommittee of his choosing be tasked with the choice instead of the committee as a whole. George, who wanted to ingratiate himself to the bosses of the state Democratic Party, raised his voice against the scheme, inciting the insurgents to accuse him of behaving like a lackey for the sheriff's office instead of an independent citizen (curiously, the Valley County sheriff, James Stephens, was a Republican). The motion was passed, over the objections of a minority, which included George and two others. A list of delegates and alternates was drawn up by the subcommittee and approved.

As secretary it was George's responsibility to prepare credentials that the elected delegates would present in Butte. But according to the *Valley News*, he refused to do his duty.[10] While claiming that he was compelled to attend to official sheriff duties in the remote Missouri River country south of Malta, he instead traveled to Helena for a clandestine meeting at the Grandon Hotel with Col. Coleman. Meanwhile, the chairman of the central committee, a man named Barnes, was informed of the situation and promptly issued credential to the delegates. (What was apparently being fought over was not the delegation's choice for president. Like most of Montana's Democrats, the Valley County Democrats supported Champ Clark, a Missouri congressman and Speaker of the House. Clark received the most votes on the first ballot in Baltimore, but forty-five ballots later, Woodrow Wilson emerged as the party's candidate and went on to win the White House in November.)[11]

At six feet tall and 190 pounds, George possessed the physical stature that commanded respect, a useful trait for police work. But he was also a hothead. In August 1912 a fifty-four-year-old traveling salesman from Minneapolis named A. B. Fisk claimed that Deputy Sheriff Geo. F. Burke punched him while Fisk was in the lobby of the Shannon Hotel, sending him crashing through a glass cigar case. Fisk appealed to a Justice of the Peace named Evans for a warrant to arrest George. But instead, Evans referred the salesman to the County Attorney, who sent the man back to Evans. Fisk then went to another justice of the peace named Kampfer and filed a complaint. But before any action was taken George secured a warrant from Evans and had the salesman arrested for "interfering with an officer in the performance of his duty." On a motion from the county attorney the charges were dismissed. However, George was soon served with a warrant and appeared in Judge Kampfer's court. He was represented by an attorney who moved for a change of venue, claiming his client couldn't get a fair trial before Kampfer. Fisk's attorney didn't appear at the hearing, and the motion was granted. Fisk gave up and left town, telling anyone who would listen that because George worked for the sheriff the county attorney refused to prosecute the case. "As to the details of the assault," the *Valley News* concluded, "Deputy Sheriff Burke is telling his side of the story, and Fisk and four or five witnesses are telling the other side."[12]

By 1915 George was still working in law enforcement, but now his employer was the state, not the county. He had used his political connections to the Democratic governor, Sam V. Stewart, to win an appointment as one of the Montana's twenty-two deputy game wardens. The position paid $125 a month (about $3,000 today), although he was forced to finance some of his trips around the area out of his own pocket. But the position was one of the most visible operations of state government at a time when governments were much smaller than they are now. Although most of his duties consisted of selling hunting and fishing licenses to people who depended on wild game to get them through the long, brutal winters, he made several arrests of men charged with violating the game laws, including a trapper illegally taking beavers from Porcupine Creek.[13]

In the spring of 1915 George opened his own real estate office, incorporating the Burke Realty Company with a capitalization of $50,000. His wife, Jennie, was listed in the articles of incorporation as a partner in the venture.[14] Although he was no longer working for Sidney Rundle, he agreed to rent office space to his former employer—now his competitor—which was located in the Burke Building. The arrangement would continue until the construction of his tenant's new accommodations were completed in what would become a three-story brick edifice called the Rundle Building.[15]

As is sometimes the case with roommates, the arrangement became acrimonious. On the morning of October 19, according to Rundle, George entered the office of the Rundle Land & Abstract Company and demanded to know why the day before Rundle had ordered carpenters out of the space he was renting. Rundle replied that the partition the carpenters were building not only reduced the size of the area he was renting, but the noise of hammering and sawing made it impossible to work. If Burke no longer wanted Rundle in the building, why didn't he serve notice? "He said, 'I don't give a damn if you ever get notice,'" Rundle testified, "And he also said, 'I want you to understand if you get funny again I'll throw you and your stuff out in the street.'" The carpenters returned and push soon came to shove. According to Rundle, George suddenly sucker-punched him on the side of the head. Dazed, Rundle said he staggered into the front office. George pursued him and began punching him some more, landing a blow under Rundle's chin. One of the carpenters grabbed George's arms to restrain him. After the dust settled Rundle filed a complaint charging George with assault and battery.[16]

The matter went to Justice Court. Several witnesses testified for the prosecution and none for the defense. Judge L. P. Evans ordered George to post a $2,500 peace bond, meaning that if Burke was charged with any offense for a period of one year he would forfeit a sum that would be worth $60,000 today (the peace bond is still a legal remedy in Canada, but has been supplanted in the U.S. by the restraining order). In the criminal matter, Evans allowed a change of venue requested by the defense, and the trial was transferred to a justice of the peace just downstream on the Milk River in Nashua, Montana. This time George presented an explanation of his actions, was found guilty, and fined ten dollars.[17] In May 1916 a district court ruled that Justice Evans "was without jurisdiction to issue any warrant" for a peace bond because Burke had filed an affidavit disqualifying him due to prejudice. Evans was also compelled to pay for George's legal fees.[18]

Like many aspiring politicians, George advertised himself by endorsing conspicuous civic causes. As a member of the Glasgow Commercial Club—which would join the other clubs across Montana in 1918 and change their name to the Chamber of Commerce—he crusaded on behalf of settlers who had moved into neighboring Sheridan County to claim "surplus" land on the Fort Peck Indian Reservation that Congress had made available for homesteading in 1913. These were quarter sections that hadn't been claimed by the native people, the Sioux and Assiniboine, who took ownership of the most fertile land, located in the Missouri River floodplain, as part of the deal they made with the government to allow white settlement on the reservation.[19] His personal acquaintance with fellow Democrats Senator Henry L. Myers and John M. Evans, one of Montana's three congressmen at the time, played in his favor as he made the rounds at a street fair in 1915 in Nashua, introducing the dignitaries to homesteaders and local businessmen.[20] While he had the ears of Myers and Evans, he lobbied for legislation that would offer financial relief to reservation homesteaders, who were derisively called "Honyockers" by cattlemen.[21] A series of small laws resulted in some remedy, although they couldn't prevent the decade of drought, beginning in 1917, that put an end to the freakish era of dryland farming on the reservation and throughout most of Eastern Montana. Like a spring flood washing down the Missouri, the surge of Honyockers into Montana drained away as abruptly as it had risen, and with it the grateful constituency whose votes George would have counted on when he decided on the right time to run for office.[22]

To escape temperatures that in January 1916 dropped to −56 degrees, George and Jennie joined America's original snowbirds and spent the next winter in Southern California. The Los Angeles Chamber of Commerce issued a press release recounting George's visit to an exhibition of Southern California products.[23] Two weeks after they returned home, the United States declared war on Germany. George registered for the draft. That November he traveled to Seattle to take the examination for the aviation section of the Signal Corps, the branch of the military that would become the U.S. Air Force. The following month the military announced that he had passed the test with flying colors, turning in the best score ever recorded by the Seattle office. Despite that, he would not be airborne anytime soon because at the age of thirty-nine he was deemed too old to pilot anything but his Model T.

Although two other Glasgow men qualified for pilot training, George was assigned as a private first-class to the "non-flying section" of the Signal Corps. He was ordered to Kelly Field in San Antonio, Texas, and was enrolled in a school that instructed recruits the pedestrian tasks required of supply clerks. He received some additional instruction at a base in Atlanta, Georgia. In April 1918 he finished his training, was commissioned a second lieutenant, and returned home to Glasgow on a two-week furlough, a visit mentioned in the *Courier*, along with his first published photograph showing him wearing his trademark brown Stetson.[24] Then he spent the rest of the war at an old military installation called the Vancouver Barracks on the Columbia River in Washington State, where he lived on base for several months with Jennie.[25] His duties included command of a platoon that was part of a company of two hundred soldiers responsible for accepting supplies delivered to the base.

On the day of his discharge from the army in March 1919, George received a letter from the commander of the Air Service Troops expressing his regret that Second Lieutenant Burke had not been promoted to first lieutenant and then captain. A typical army screw-up, his commission did not go through because his name was inadvertently left off a list of those recommended for promotions. The oversight would have been corrected eventually by the War Department, but promotions were halted when the Armistice was signed on November 11, 1918 (on the eleventh hour of the eleventh day of the eleventh month).

Finally, after an absence of nearly two years, he returned to Glasgow. He left again in late 1919 with Jennie for the winter, financing their stay in California by managing an apartment building at 722 Hartford Avenue near what is now the Staples Center in downtown Los Angeles.[26] In the spring of 1920, soon after the Burkes returned from LA, George opened a brokerage office in Great Falls, Montana, and began selling stocks.[27] The real estate business, like most every other business in northeastern Montana, was suffering because of the drought. By 1920 the production of wheat fell to a fraction of what it had been in 1916. There was talk of consolidating Montana's entire wheat crop for sale under one contract in order to bail out the least fortunate farmers. Part of this massive crop failure was due to infestations of grasshoppers, wireworms, and cutworms, which resisted the efforts of Honyockers to poison them with arsenic. Because farmers had no money merchants didn't either. And no one was buying houses or land.

Despite whatever financial success George enjoyed as a stockbroker in the summer and fall of 1920, the landslide Republican Party victory in November obliterated his political ambitions. Democrats were driven from the White House, the Governor's Mansion, and the Valley County Courthouse. Not only was the sheriff's office captured by the GOP, so were the offices of the coroner, the auditor, the assessor, the surveyor, and the clerk of court. Still working as a deputy game warden employed by a state controlled by Democrats, George campaigned relentlessly for his fellow party members, including James M. Cox for president, Burton K. Wheeler for governor and Burton Watson for Congress.

For his efforts he was lambasted by the *Glasgow Courier.* "The stockholder-candidate manipulators have turned over the works to George and he has grabbed the wheel of this flivver with the same avidity he has shown in grabbing his warrant from the State treasury of $150.00 per month as deputy game warden. He used to get only $125.00 per month, but when he moved to Great Falls it was found that it cost something to enforce the game laws in Valley County by telephone, so his salary was increased." In the same editorial, published a week before the Republican landslide, the *Courier* gleefully quoted its rival paper, the *Valley County News*, which had laid down a considerable amount of ink five years earlier attacking George. "Governor Stewart and State Game Warden DeHart have a chance to elevate themselves considerably in the estimation of the people of Valley county and especially here in Glasgow. Will they do it, or will they continue to remain indifferent to the local menace to good government that they are supporting by a petty $125.00 per month salary from the state funds?"[28]

Meanwhile, George's kid brother, Roger Dorsey Burke, who had followed him to Montana, was attempting to counter the growing Republican juggernaut by publishing and editing a Democratic Party weekly called the *Scobey Sentinel.* At the time, Scobey was the largest, single wheat-loading center in North America, where entire trains on the Northern Pacific's Hi-Line were filled with grain.[29] Besides supporting Democratic candidates for office, Roger lobbied to create a new county with Scobey as its county seat. In that campaign he was more successful. The legislature created Daniels County on June 1, 1920, from parts of Valley and Sheridan Counties. The *Producers News* was not amused. A Nonpartisan League newspaper published in Plentywood—the county seat of Sheridan County and the town with the most to lose if Daniels County came into being—the *News* claimed that Roger was a lackey for the "copper crowd," the Democratic Party bosses in Butte, where most of the world's copper was being mined. "Green Ink Roger Burke," the paper wrote, ". . . is the moving spirit for the county divisionists and that as a reward for his labors he will be made Clerk & Recorder for the new county and the Scobey Sentinel will get the printing contract and that he will also have the transcribing contract." The paper also implied that Roger was guilty of voter fraud. "Mr. Burke will be remembered as the man who was Deputy Clerk & Recorder of Sheridan County at the time when the election returns were altered and Mrs. O'Grady was counted out of office and Mr. Redmond counted in."[30]

Whatever Roger's motives were in campaigning for a new county, the "plunder" cited by the *News* was probably not part of it. That summer "the genial editor of the Scobey Sentinel," as the *News* had called Roger seven months earlier for unknown reasons, sold the newspaper to local farmers and embarked in August on an automobile trip around western Mexico to investigate the opportunities for starting or buying a newspaper south of the border. The *Sentinel* began publishing as a Nonpartisan League paper.[31]

A year later, Roger was back in Montana editing and publishing the *Wolf Point Promoter* on the Fort Peck Indian Reservation. According to the *Glasgow Courier*, "He is known as a good newspaper man and a brilliant writer."[32] In August 1922 he was promoted to editor and manager of the *Sidney Herald*, the leading paper in Richland County, a position he worked at for a year.[33] During his career as a Montana newspaperman he also worked for the *Carbon County Chronicle* in Red Lodge and lastly the *Sheridan County Farmer* in Plentywood. Although he had been "badly crippled by a railway accident" several years earlier, he was ambitious and energetic.[34] While it might appear that he could not keep a job, in fact it was known among newspapermen that he was adept at riding in on a white horse to rescue newspapers that were struggling to get on their feet.

George's foray into the world of investing was short-lived and not as lucrative as he hoped it would be. In 1920 he turned his attention to the next big thing in Montana—oil. In late 1919 the Frantz Oil Corporation of Denver struck crude in what would be called the Cat Creek Field in Central Montana. By 1921 several companies had bought leases on acreage in the area around Winnett, saving a few Honyockers from ruin. At its zenith more than sixty wells were pumping from a large reservoir of crude that established Cat Creek as the first commercially successful oil field in Montana.[35] George got a job with Ohio Oil and set about learning the business. Meanwhile, his marriage to Jennie had deteriorated for reasons it can only be speculated was complicated by the couple's financial challenges.[36] At any rate, after two decades of marriage, they divorced and went their separate ways.

In summer 1921 George parlayed his political connections to Thomas Arthur in order to get a job with the Mutual Oil Company. Arthur was chairman of the Montana State Democratic Central Committee, and an oilman who was the Montana representative of the Texas Company (also known as Texaco).[37] Working from offices in Lewistown and Billings, Arthur was a shaker and a mover who enticed a sizable flow of venture capital into the state from investors betting on the extraction of a sizable flow of crude.[38] On a Christmas trip back to Glasgow, George told readers of the *Courier* that "oil men the country over are now turning their eyes to northern Montana, and more particularly to the Bowdoin field."[39] He was being optimistic. The underground geologic feature called the Bowdoin Dome near Glasgow never lived up to the expectations of the crude oil industry.[40] After his visit George returned to work in the Cat Creek field. In January 1923 he was promoted to field superintendent for Mutual Oil's wells, staying nights and weekends at the two-story, twenty-four room Schmidt Hotel in Winnett.[41]

One evening, as he read a newspaper in the lobby, he was struck by lightning. Glancing up, he saw a fetching young woman descending the hotel's spiral staircase. Catherine Matilda Giudici was a nineteen-year-old fifth-grade school teacher who looked like she had sprung from the canvas of an Italian Renaissance portrait.[42] After growing up on a ranch in Beaverhead County with four brothers and four sisters she had graduated in 1922 from what was then called Montana State Normal College in Dillon ("Normal" schools were two-year institutions that taught people how to be teachers).

He would spend the rest of his life by her side, as she followed him from one job to another in the oil fields, military installations, and infrastructure projects of America.

FIG. 3. Catherine Matilda Giudici, high school graduation, Kalispell, Montana, 1918. Courtesy of the Molly Burke Herrin Estate.

3

The Migrants

In November 1923 George Burke was transferred to the burgeoning oil town of Corsicana, Texas, where he and Catherine were married.[1] A year later their first child was born, Mary Elizabeth. That same year Roger Burke was driving one October night with two other men near Plentywood when their car crashed. One man was uninjured, the second suffered broken ribs, and Roger was killed instantly when the vehicle rolled on top of him.[2] It's unclear who was at the wheel.

Meanwhile, their kid sister, Edith Beatrice, graduated from St. Vincent's Academy for girls on Catholic Hill in Helena, then spent a few years in a convent in La Crosse, Wisconsin, called the Sisters of Perpetual Adoration. She abandoned the Sisters for some reason, heading back to Helena to work as an au pair for a British gold assayer and his wife. She next attended Beloit College in Wisconsin, from which her older brother Edward would graduate in 1906 and go on to achieve fame or, depending on one's politics, infamy as a politician. She then returned to Montana to teach in one-room schoolhouses in mining camps. Her next adventure was graduating as a dietician from Miss Farmer's School of Cookery in Boston, where Fannie Farmer taught young ladies the importance of food to help sick people get healthy. Edith then worked as a dietician for the U.S. Army Hospital in Hot Springs, South Dakota. In 1911 she married a Montana rancher's son named John Sexton James, who had played on his college football team in Bozeman.

By spring 1925 the Burkes were living at the Lorraine Apartments in Tulsa, Oklahoma, where George was working for a pipeline company moving crude from the enormously productive Glenn Pool oil field to refineries on the Gulf Coast. In May 1926 Molly Catherine was born in Conrad, Montana, where the Burkes had moved, yet again, after oil was discovered under the prairie between Kevin and Sunburst, Montana.

After the stock market crash in October 1929 George's fortunes in Montana evaporated, along with much of the wealth of America. Remembering the balmy winters he spent with Jennie in Southern California, he moved his family to Long Beach. They rented a bungalow at 216 Santa Cruz Street, two blocks from the beach and not far from the famous Rainbow Pier, an enormous circular breakwater jutting from Seaside Boulevard that was built by the city of Long Beach to attract tourists to the business district. An amusement park called the Pike attracted thousands of visitors, many of whom came to ride the famous Cyclone Racer, a dual-track roller coaster built out on pilings over the water.[3]

Traveling south to live with the Burkes for the winter was Catherine's mother, Amanda Grant Giudici, who was born in Sweden. In 1892 she had married Isadoro Giudici, who was the son of an Italian family in Giornico, Switzerland. The couple bought 480 acres of grain and grazing land in Beaverhead County, Montana, and set about begetting four sons and five daughters, one of whom died as an infant. In 1910, when Catherine was nine years old, Isadoro died of throat cancer. The family employed several hired hands, and the boys pitched in with the ranch work. (Amanda did not allow her daughters to spend time in the sun, believing as did many white people that a peaches-and-cream complexion was a signpost of wealth, and tanned skin meant you were common.) By 1928 her mother and her older brother Carl were running the ranch. To make ends meet during the Depression they would be forced to lease it to neighboring ranchers. In 1939 the family would finally lose the ranch, and the children would scatter in the wind.[4]

Although George had considerable experience in the oil patches of the West, there is no indication that he ever found work in the Long Beach oil field, a prolific pool of crude five miles square that spawned a forest of oil derricks in the Signal Hill area of Los Angeles, and is still producing.[5] In the 1930 census he listed his occupation as a "millwright" who worked in a "plant." The plant was Long Beach Assembly, a brand-new production facility that built one of George's favorite things, Ford Model A automobiles. The job of millwrights in this plant was to maintain the machinery that assembly line workers used to fabricate these cars.

In 1933 Molly was attending first grade after being held out a year because of her chronic nose bleeds and ear infections. During the dinner hour on March 10, Long Beach was struck with the most devastating earthquake in its history. People fleeing brick-and-mortar buildings during the terrifying ten seconds of severe tremors were hit by falling glass and masonry, which killed 120 and injured more than 500. If the quake had struck during school hours, the toll would have been much higher. All twenty-eight schools in Long Beach were either destroyed or badly damaged, including Seaside Elementary, which the Burke girls attended, a fact that compelled local governments to enact much stricter building codes. Broken gas lines sparked fires. Water mains burst. The electric grid was knocked out. Oil derricks were uprooted. Pavement and sidewalks cracked and crumbled. For days after the quake, the Burkes, like most residents, lived outdoors in tents, afraid to enter their homes because of a relentless series of aftershocks. Those who could, cooked outdoors and built bonfires from scavenged lumber for heat. Those who couldn't, stood in food lines under the palm trees next to Long Beach City Hall or bought prepared food from enterprising vendors. Merchants displayed their wares on the sidewalks. The Burke girls remember the days after the quake as a time of adventure and high excitement (and why not—with no schools left to attend every day was a play day). Citrus growers piled mounds of oranges on the streets, free for the taking.

When the quake struck, George Burke was in Helena, looking for work. Although phone service to Long Beach had been disrupted, he somehow managed to get a call through to Catherine. She assured him that although their bungalow had suffered some cosmetic damage, she and the girls and her mother were safe and sound. After a sleepless night, George got on a National Parks Airways flight to Salt Lake City, where he caught another flight to Los Angeles. Friends in LA had been stopped at a roadblock before they could reach the Burkes in Long Beach, but George bulled his way through. Although he was relieved to find that his family was indeed healthy, after looking around at the destruction he ordered them to pack their things. They were driving home to Montana, where it was safe. So he thought.

Two weeks after the earthquake George got the job he had left his family in California to pursue: working for the Montana Railroad and Public Service Commission as an inspector in the oil and gas fields of the southern half of the state. This was a political plum arranged by his Democratic friends in state government. (Frank Cooney, a Democrat, had moved a week earlier into the Governor's Mansion at Sixth and Ewing after appointing the previous governor, John E. Erickson, to the United States Senate to replace Thomas J. Walsh, who died of a heart attack at the age of seventy-three on his way by train to the inauguration of FDR.) Among Burke's typical tasks was his inspection of an oil well being drilled near Hobson in October 1933. His job was to ensure that operations such as this conformed to Montana's rather lax regulations about safety and management practices in her oil fields. When the rig hit a depth of 1,232 feet, it hit a small reserve of oil and gas and pumped out twenty-five barrels of salty, radioactive water before it was decided that the well had been sunk too close to a fault, and was started over in a new location. Burke expressed his high expectation that the new wildcat would soon be pumping many barrles of crude. (As it turned out, the Hobson field was a bust, although a strong artesian well had been tapped in the search for oil.)

Now that the Burkes felt they had some financial security, they celebrated with a brand-new car. This was a 1935 four-door, six-cylinder silver Terraplane they bought from the Roberts Motor Company in Helena for $565.[6] Adding to a list of their many addresses during the Depression, the Burkes lived briefly at the Giudici ranch in Dillon. Then, while George worked out of his car and an office in Billings, the Burke family lived in a cabin outside the town of Absarokee, forty miles west. That summer he was transferred again, this time to Shelby, where he was put in charge of oil and gas inspections for the northern half of Montana. He and Catherine stayed in a fleabag hotel next to the tracks. The girls remained that summer in Absarokee with a woman named Mrs. Nitche. (In their letters to Catherine, written in pencil on lined school paper, they described a party at the cabin and their funeral for a "little chicken." Molly called Catherine "mamma" and Mary called her "mother.") Next stop was Helena, where they lived briefly in the Grandon Hotel. The girls were enrolled in Central School for three weeks before the family rented a house on Ninth Avenue and the girls transferred to Jefferson School. In 1935 the family moved into the posh Blackstone Apartments downtown. Molly and Mary were enrolled in Hawthorn School and joined the Camp Fire Girls.

The Burkes figured they had found a safe haven in Helena. But late on the night of October 18, 1935 the city was ravaged by a powerful earthquake. It was almost as strong as the Long Beach quake, but the resulting damage was much less severe. Two people were killed by falling bricks, and two masons were killed while removing a brick tower during the strong aftershock that hit two weeks later, on Halloween. Helena High School was destroyed. This was a brand-new building, but it wasn't designed to withstand a quake. Also collapsing was the Lewis and Clark County Hospital. St. Vincent's Academy, the Catholic, girls high school, was so badly damaged it had to be demolished, as did the orphanage, St. Joseph's Home. In all, two hundred chimneys were ruined, and there was widespread damage in the business district, which was built largely of brick and masonry that was not reinforced.[7,8] The Hawthorn School was deemed unsafe, so the girls attended classes at the Episcopal Church. The following year their classes were moved to the YMCA.

Because Burke's appointment was political and not bound by any civil service rules, he served at the pleasure of the chairman of the Railroad and Public Service Commission (RPSC), Thomas E. Carey. A former president of the Anaconda Mine, Mill and Smeltermen's Union, and a janitor at Carroll College and the State House, Carey had been elected in 1932 as a Democrat to the RPSC for a six-year term and promptly became its chairman. Created by the legislature only twenty years earlier, the commission had been given broad powers to set the prices consumers paid for water, heat, light, railroad and highway transportation, sewers, and telegraph and telephone service. As a consequence, it had made corporate enemies. The RPSC had especially angered the Montana Power Company, whose board of directors was intertwined with that of the Anaconda Copper Company, which had spawned the utility in 1912.

Montana Power had waged a failing campaign to block the 1934 election of a RPSC commissioner named Jerry O'Connell, a fiery advocate of reducing electricity and natural gas rates to households as the Depression deepened. In 1930, at the age of twenty-one, he had been elected to the state House of Representatives. Montana Power enraged its detractors by placing negative articles and editorials about O'Connell in the biggest newspapers, which were owned at the time by the Anaconda Company. These included the *Missoulian*, the *Helena Independent*, the *Billings Gazette*, the *Anaconda Standard*, and the *Butte Miner*, what one scholar calls the "Copper Chorus."[9] Critics charged that the company was passing on the costs of this smear campaign to already-burdened consumers. In a collateral effort to discredit the RPSC, its opponents orchestrated the arrest of Thomas Carey on October 22, 1934, two weeks before the election. He was charged with molesting a fifteen-year-old boy, a felony. Carey posted $1,500 in bail and was released. He denied the "vile charge" and hired attorneys to defend him in what would be a loud and raucous trial the following May.

However, dirty politics turned out to be useless against the New Deal juggernaut. O'Connell won a landslide victory and immediately began voting to set lower rates for vital utilities. In February 1935 he and Carey ordered Montana Power to drop its minimum $1.25 monthly fee for natural gas—charged to residential consumers whether they used any gas or not—and invited the company to make up for significant lost revenue by raising the rates on large commercial consumers. They slashed the rates consumers paid for water in Butte and Thompson

Falls. In doing so they overrode the third commissioner, a corporate lackey named Andrew Young, whom detractors accused of wearing a "copper collar." Montana Power challenged the gas ruling in court, claiming O'Connell was "prejudiced" because he had promised during his campaign to eliminate the charge. In the end, relief for the company from the courts was denied.[10]

Meanwhile, Tom Carey was ferreting out what he perceived as disloyalty among the RPSC's employees. On January 4, 1935, he fired eleven of them. Burke and a stenographer were spared, apparently Carey's only trusted loyalists. Burke not only survived Carey's Friday afternoon massacre, but he was also appointed the commission's new chief engineer. Like most "engineers" of his generation, he had no college training.[11] But he had learned enough fundamentals of the profession from working for the oil companies, the Ford plant in Long Beach, and as the RPSC's oil and gas inspector to pass himself off as an engineer. His claim to this professional title was affirmed in October 1936 when he was nominated for membership into the Montana Society of Engineers.[12] He joined fifteen other men, including Archie Bray, a ceramic engineer and patron of the arts whose Helena-based Western Clay Manufacturing Company supplied the high-quality brick used to construct hundreds of buildings across the state in the 1930s and 40s.[13]

Burke performed poorly at his first public appearance as chief engineer. Testifying in a hearing in Missoula to determine whether Montana Power should lower the rates it charged consumers for water, he said his estimation of the value of the water system was $251,000, apparently trying to lowball a price that would make the municipal purchase of the privately owned water system more attractive to taxpayers. He said his estimate was based on a report commissioned by the city of Missoula in 1933. Under cross-examination by company lawyers, who questioned Burke's qualifications to appraise water systems, he was informed that in fact the study he cited pegged the figure at $625,000 (the figure was actually $843,000).[14]

Unlike most of the towns in Montana, Missoula's water system had always been privately owned. The first proprietor was a Flathead Indian named One-Eyed Riley, who delivered buckets of water in 1870 on a donkey cart to the few homes and saloons that had been thrown up in what was then not much more than a trading post. William A. Clark, the notorious Copper King who tried to buy a U.S. Senate seat in 1899 by bribing state legislators, bought what would be called the Missoula Light and Water Company in 1905 and sold it in 1929 to Montana Power. At the time, the water mains were pine planks coated with creosote. A 1933 effort on the part of city officials to create a municipal utility by wresting ownership of the water system from Montana Power was a failure. A crowd organized by the Missoula Taxpayers Association filled a judge's chambers and demanded that the city cease its efforts, arguing that it would lose significant property tax revenue if Montana Power's water system became a government facility; and they asked that if this publicly owned system couldn't offer lower rates than Montana Power what was the point?[15] In 1979 a hostile takeover attempt on the part of Missoula to acquire what was then called Mountain Water was nixed by the Montana Supreme Court. Finally, in 2015 Missoula was granted eminent domain to take ownership of Mountain Water from the Carlyle Group, a global hedge fund, which had refused to sell. The city argued that under the ownership of various out-of-state equity firms, Mountain Water had allowed the system to deteriorate. The price was set at $84 million plus some $14 million in legal fees, and Missoula joined the other 128 towns in Montana that own their own water.

Before Carey's guilt or innocence could be determined by any court, a legislative committee condemned him by voting for a resolution calling for Montana Attorney General Raymond T. Nagle to remove him from office for reasons of "malfeasance, incompetence, and neglect of official duty." In addition to the morals accusation, a House committee alleged that Carey had been absent from his office for two months, and had employed the services of the RPSC's stenographer to aid in his legal defense. The late-evening, closed-door debate, according to the newspapers, "was freely punctuated with displays of disorder and near-physical combat." The author of the Carey "investigation," a loud-mouthed Democratic legislator from Lewistown named Herbert Haight, was the recipient of an unsigned, typewritten letter the last line of which read: "May Satan give you your just desert and here's hoping your life will be very short-lived." In addition, a bill was introduced in the House that would abolish the RPSC. But it went nowhere. During the debate Representative E. R. Ormsbee of Mineral County rose to accuse the corporations of fabricating the charges against Carey in order to defeat O'Connell, and of poisoning the minds of other progressive legislators with their propaganda.[16]

The *Helena Independent* published a copy of a written "confession" allegedly signed by Carey in October of 1934 after his arrest, in which he admits to allowing several young boys to enter his room at the Grandon Hotel in Helena and there to "take hold of and play with his private parts."[17] Coming to Carey's defense was Lewis Penwell, well-known lawyer, stockman, and U.S. collector of internal revenue for Montana. As the publisher of a small, rabble-rousing weekly called the *Western Progressive*, which railed against the corporations and the "copper collar" editors of their captive newspapers, Penwell had joined ideological forces with Carey and O'Connell in an attempt to leash Montana Power. In a statement published in a special edition of Penwell's paper, Carey claimed that the confession was a forgery. "Every word in that statement is untrue, the entire statement is a malicious falsehood and a vicious lie. I have never at any time spoken, uttered or written one single word contained in that document." He accused "predatory utility interests" of orchestrating the charges against him because he had joined Jerry O'Connell "in his fight to reduce exorbitant utility rates and save Montana from the plunder of the power trust."[18]

On May 16, 1935, Carey's trial began in Lewis and Clark District Court with testimony from a fifteen-year-old boy who claimed that the man invited him into his hotel room, where he made "indecent gestures." The boy said he "broke away" and "took a swing" at the defendant before running from the room. The boy further testified that on previous occasions Carey had sat down beside him in a lunchroom and slapped his leg. Defense attorneys countered with a sworn affidavit from the boy in which he admitted never having been invited into Carey's room nor ever being accosted by the defendant. Testifying for the prosecution, the boy said he signed the paper while he was surrounded by defense attorneys. One of them shook his fist menacingly, the boy claimed, declaring that unless it was signed the boy would bring disgrace upon his family and perhaps a jail term for himself. The prosecution trotted in several young boys who claimed to have been in Carey's hotel room. Carey responded that the boys invited themselves in because they liked Carey to read them the "funny papers" and help them with their homework. He denied the accusation that he had given the boys cigarettes. During the proceedings the attorneys shouted loudly, gesticulated wildly, and interrupted each other repeatedly. There were frequent references to the law books cluttering the large counsel table.[19] Relative peace returned after Judge George W. Padbury Jr. ordered the twelve-man jury to disregard the commotion.

Following final arguments, lasting until late in the evening of May 22, the jury retired at 10:45 p.m. from the packed courtroom to deliberate. Ninety minutes later they returned to a courtroom that was nearly empty because no one had expected such a speedy decision. "We find the defendant not guilty," the foreman announced. The verdict enraged Montana attorney general Nagle. He vowed that Carey would face new charges. On June 17, 1935, Carey was again accused of lewd and lascivious conduct involving a minor. Again he plead innocent and, again, was compelled to post a $1,500 bond. The case was set twice for trial, but both times the court declined to hear it. Finally, on November 27, 1936, after Carey had endured more than two years of legal and political harassment, the county attorney determined that there was not enough evidence to prosecute, and the vendetta was abandoned.[20]

The Railroad and Public Service Commission embarked on a rate-slashing spree. Water charges in Missoula were cut by 20 percent; in Butte the figure was one-third; electricity rates in Baker and Forsyth were cut, as were the rates in twenty-six towns in northeastern Montana. "Our fight to win utility justice for the people of Montana," Commissioner O'Connell proclaimed, "continues unabated." Commissioner Young was consistently outvoted and complained bitterly to the press.

Alarmed by the onslaught, Montana Power threatened lawsuits, but in the end determined that it would be cheaper to negotiate with Carey and O'Connell than to fight them. On November 8, 1935, it announced that cuts to *all* Montana consumers would go into effect the following week. Residential consumers would pay 22½ percent less for electricity; commercial consumers 17 percent less. Missoula and Hamilton water rates were reduced by 20 percent. Consumers of natural gas in Montana would henceforth pay the lowest rate in the United States. In all, the cuts would deprive Montana Power of $550,000 a year ($10.5 million in today's dollars). The agreement was a huge victory for the RPSC and for Montana consumers besieged by the Depression.[21]

Failing to remove Carey from the RPSC, his enemies turned their sights on Jerry O'Connell again. In January of 1936, after he had announced his candidacy for the U.S. House of Representatives, a reporter for the *Helena Independent* claimed that O'Connell was bugging the office of Leonard Young in the Capitol Building. Young said he'd found a Dictaphone hidden near his desk connected to wires that led to O'Connell's adjoining office where, it was alleged, resided a similar device enabling O'Connell to eavesdrop. Late one Saturday evening, when O'Connell and Tom Carey were away on RPSC business in Billings, Young and a reporter from the Helena newspaper secured a key to O'Connell's office. But when the reporter attempted to open the door he was "assaulted" by a number of "belligerent and tyrannical" RPSC clerks and a bouncer for a local bar, all allegedly summoned by O'Connell with telegrams. A fistfight ensued. The newspaper claimed one of these "gangsters" was carrying a gun. Attorney General Nagle was alerted. He called the governor, Elmer Holt, who rushed from his bed to the scene. After he arrived the key could not be located. The attorney general and the governor removed a glass partition between the offices and crawled into O'Connell's office. According to the newspaper, "Inside they said they discovered that a device had been torn off the wall above O'Conner's desk and the wires leading to Young's office had also disappeared." When they saw that one of the windows had been thrown open, they theorized that someone had crawled along a ledge from a window in

Tom Carey's office and ripped out the offending device during the commotion in the hallway.[22]

That afternoon Governor Holt ordered that all offices in the Capitol Building be searched for bugging devices. Meanwhile, the bouncer, whom the *Helena Independent* falsely described as a former welterweight boxing champion of the world, was evicted from his room at the Mitchell Hotel, charged by the owner with failure to pay his bills. The newspaper published a photo of Young holding the device he claimed he had discovered concealed in his office. O'Connell vehemently denied the accusations and pointed out that no Dictaphone had ever been found in *his* office, and that such a device never existed. "Deer Lodge," he said, in reference to the state prison, "is full of men without influence who, in the dead of the night, have jimmied their way into private offices; and I have asked my attorneys whether Will Campbell, editor of the copper-controlled yellow rag, the *Independent*, his son and reporter and their willing tool, Leonard Young, are possessed of any special immunity or are in any different category when, in their midnight madness, they broke into my private office to which the people of Montana have elected me. . . . What they actually wanted in my office was not the alleged dictaphone [*sic*], but my files and my records in an endeavor to hamper me in the hearings which are to be ordered today against the Montana Power Company and the Telephone company on light, gas and telephone rates all over the state of Montana."[23] Over the decades, squabbling and backbiting among commissioners would become endemic. In 2020 they accused one another of stealing emails and publishing them on the internet. Commissioner Roger Koopman called what had become the Public Service Commission (so named after its jurisdiction over railroads was transferred to another agency) "diseased and dysfunctional."[24]

Voters saw through the ludicrous attempt to discredit O'Connell. On November 3, 1936, he was elected to Congress from the First District in a landslide that awarded him more than 63 percent of the vote. But the tide that washed in a huge Democratic majority in Congress that year began to wash out in 1938. One factor was the recession of 1937 that undercut FDR's claim that the Depression was over. Another was Roosevelt's unpopular attempt to pack the Supreme Court by adding six new justices, presumably favorable to the New Deal (his leading critic was Democratic Senator Edward Burke, George's big brother). One of the casualties of this backlash was Jerry O'Connell, a staunch New Dealer who had become a moving target. He lost his seat to a Republican by the margin of 54 percent to 45 percent. Before the election, in May 1938, he was barred from giving a pro-labor speech at a rally in Jersey City, New Jersey, by the mayor, who accused him of being involved with "Reds, Radicals, and Communists."

Much more damaging politically was the public roasting in Helena of O'Connell by Francis E. Townsend, the founder of the influential Townsend Clubs that began springing up across America in 1934. In response to the hard times that had thrown millions of older Americans out of work, and in some cases out on the streets, the Old Age Revolving Pension Plan, called the Townsend Plan, would levy a 2 percent national sales tax to fund a federal "pension" that would grant $200 a month to every American over the age of sixty. The scheme required that the recipient must be retired, free from "habitual criminality," and must spend his monthly stipend within thirty days in order to stimulate the economy (it was never clear how the federal government would prevent hoarding and verify this spending). At the time of his epiphany, which he shared with the largely retired readers of the *Long Beach Press-Telegram*, Townsend, sixty-seven, was a soft-spoken, out-of-work physician and a failed real estate salesman and a dry ice manufacturer. The idea, he claimed, came to him in 1933 after he saw three old women eating from garbage cans in an alley (a story he likely fabricated).

Townsend's vision was marketed by a Long Beach real estate developer named Robert Clements, who saw it as a surefire way to make a buck. The 3,400 clubs the partners organized across the United States, by 1936 boasted a membership of three million and paid an estimated $3.6 million in dues to the national organization. The organization's newsletter, the *Townsend National Weekly*, was pulling in a quarter million dollars a year in advertising from the manufacturers of geriatric products, such as constipation remedies. There were Townsend Clubs in almost every community in Montana. They organized dances, dinners, and picnics; the Great Falls chapter staged a three-act play at the Masonic Temple called *Dreamers Triumphant*, which told the story of the ideals and ideas of the movement.

In Helena, George and Catherine Burke attended meetings most every week. The old-age pension scheme not only meshed with their belief in the slogan "from each according to his ability to each according to his need," one of the Townsend Plan's conspicuous supporters was Jerry O'Connell, George's boss. Because the plan had been attacked as "socialist" and a cult, Catherine kept their membership a secret from the upscale residents of the posh Blackstone Apartments, where she and George and the girls had moved in 1935. While the internecine warfare at the RPSC raged, George continued to travel around Montana in his capacity as chief engineer. In March of 1935, he attended rate hearings in Thompson Falls and Superior. In 1937 he was in Rexburg to see what could be done about that community's water system, which froze solid every autumn and didn't thaw out until spring, compelling its denizens to man bucket brigades and finally to truck in water tanks.

The rapid growth of the old-age pension movement encouraged Townsend to leverage club membership into political power. Soon, instead of asking for the support of politicians, he began demanding it. The strategy's first victory came during a special 1935 Congressional election when he personally stumped for a Republican candidate in Michigan named Verner Main, who had pledged his support. Main demolished his GOP rivals in the primary and then buried his Democratic foe. Like the Nonpartisan League, the Townsendites supported any politician, left or right, who supported them (in fact, they tended to support far more Republican candidates than Democratic). To the many politicians who had dismissed the plan as economically illiterate and dependent on a regressive sales tax that wouldn't raise enough money to fund its goals, Townsend had a message: "Whoever supports the Townsend Plan we will elect. Candidates will accede to our demands—or stay at home." He predicted that after the 1936 election the Townsend movement would determine the outcome of all the races west of the Mississippi, and would soon control Congress.

Franklin Roosevelt was beginning to feel the heat. More than 50 percent of Americans over the age of sixty were living below the poverty line. In August of 1935 he signed into law the Social Security Act, which used mandatory contributions from workers and their employers to set aside money for the unemployed and retirees 65 and older. In early 1935 Congressman John S. McGroarty sponsored a Townsend Plan bill, but it failed in the Ways and Means Committee, whose members grilled Townsend and ridiculed him mercilessly. (McGroarty was also California's poet laureate; from 1896 to 1901 he was an executive with the Anaconda Copper Company in Butte, Montana.) However, because Social Security payments to old people maxed out at only $30 a month and the first check would not be mailed until 1940, the Townsendites doubled down on pushing their plan through Congress. After some tweaks, it was introduced as HR 4199 in 1938, the General Welfare Act. Although it had more support than the original bill, this one also fizzled. In 1939 the final nail in the Townsend Plan coffin was hammered home when the House voted 302–97 to kill it. Townsend vowed to push for a Constitutional Amendment, but in the end the Townsend movement suffered a lingering death. The last Montana club petered out in Butte in the late 1950s.[25]

O'Connell had supported Townsend's ideas and spoke widely on their behalf. He was endorsed by the movement in his first run at office. And he was endorsed in his second run by the *Townsend National Weekly*. But a week before the general election of 1938, Francis Townsend himself flew to Butte to deliver a statewide radio broadcast in which he denounced O'Connell and endorsed his GOP rival, Dr. Jacob Thorkelson, a Norwegian immigrant and a political unknown. A crowd of eight-hundred had gathered in Helena's Consistory Shrine to hear Townsend's address broadcast on local station KPFA. In it, Townsend disavowed his publication's endorsement and alleged that O'Connell's claim of support from forty-two Montana clubs was fabricated. He called O'Connell a "dangerous" ringleader of the cabal in Congress supporting a rival plan and then abandoning it when they received little support from their colleagues. "This substitute bill of O'Connell's and his group," Townsend said, "would have utterly destroyed the entire purpose of our organization and all that it stood for."[26]

O'Connell expressed amazement at Townsend's reversal. In fact, the Revolving Old Age Pension movement had become splintered as Townsend's growing messiah complex compelled him to take political positions that had nothing to do with retirees. His demand that the clubs support his condemnation of FDR's 1937 plan to pack the Supreme Court cost him many thousands of followers. Plus, he had been one of the organizers of the populist Union Party, which won a dismal 2 percent of the vote in the presidential election of 1936. One of the other organizers was Charles Coughlin, a rabidly anti-socialist Catholic priest whose widely broadcast radio shows voiced his antisemitism and support for fascist regimes in Europe. After the Union Party's defeat, Townsend backed away from his public condemnation of FDR, and the Townsend movement went through a leadership shake-up, shifts that enticed many members to return. In the 1938 election, Townsend endorsed scores of Republicans hostile to FDR, including W. C. Husband of Montana, who lost in the Second District, and Jacob Thorkelson in the First. Jeanette Rankin, who in 1916 became the first woman elected to Congress, would defeat Thorkelson in the 1940 GOP primary after his incendiary insertions in the *Congressional Record* denouncing Jews and extolling the virtues of fascism (she would go on to defeat O'Connell in the general election). Columnist Walter Winchell called Thorkelson "the mouthpiece of the Nazi movement in congress" and put him on his list of "Americans We Can Do Without."

For George and Catherine Burke, O'Connell's 1938 defeat was a disappointment. But the failure of another one of their favorite politicians was a catastrophe. Tom Carey, the man who hired Burke as chief engineer, finished third in a field of three Democrats on the primary ballot. When a new administration at the Railroad and Public Service Commission took charge, George lost his job.[27]

However, because of his experience and the fact that he had friends in high places, he would land on his feet. For the automobile-loving

Burkes, the solution to any problem was simple: road trip. George and Catherine packed the girls in their silver Terraplane and headed east to Washington DC where another younger brother, Edward Raymond Burke, was serving as a United States Senator.[28] Born in 1880 in what is now South Dakota, Edward graduated from Beloit College in Wisconsin in 1906, taught school for a couple of years, then graduated with a law degree from Harvard University in 1911. He was admitted to the Nebraska State Bar and served as a second lieutenant in the Air Service during World War I. In 1927 his political career was launched when he was elected president of the Omaha Board of Education. In 1930 he ran for Congress but was defeated. Two years later he ran again and won, defeating the man who had beaten him in 1930. In 1933 he was elected as a Democrat to the Seventy-Third Congress and served one term before running for the Senate in 1934, winning with more than 55 percent of the vote. By 1938 he had become a vocal opponent of Franklin Delano Roosevelt and his New Deal policies, charging that these programs eroded the self-reliance of Americans. He often voted with other conservative Democrats and southern Republicans against the White House. In 1940 he vigorously opposed FDR's nomination for a third term.[29] Although he was voted out of office by seventeen percentage points in the 1940 primary against Nebraska's popular governor, Edward would accomplish at least two things: first, he would cosponsor the Selective Training and Service Act of 1940, also known as the Burke-Wadsworth Act, which was used to conscript young men to fight in World War II. Second, he would land George a federal job as a civil engineer with the Public Works Administration.

George Burke's first assignment was to inspect the construction of the earth-filled Middle Creek Dam fifteen miles south of Bozeman, whose construction began in July 1939. He moved his family into a tent house with a wooden floor near the excavation site in Hyalite Canyon. As Molly's ninth school year began, he drove the girls into Bozeman weekday mornings so they could attend Gallatin County High School. A heavy snowstorm in early October snapped limbs off trees, so George immediately moved the family to a motel cottage in town.[30]

In 1940, when delays in construction became endemic, he was assigned to inspect aspects of the final phases of construction of Fort Peck Dam, the largest earth-filled impoundment in the world. Begun in 1933, Fort Peck was sold to taxpayers as a way to control flooding on the lower Missouri, which routinely jumped her banks all the way from Bismarck to her confluence with the Mississippi, causing heavy damage, especially in Kansas City. Another benefit, FDR promised, was its role in aiding downstream navigation. But its real purpose was the employment of ten thousand out-of-work men during the darkest days of the Depression. (It was only after Pearl Harbor that the government decided to install generators to produce electricity for the war effort.)

The Army Corps of Engineers and several private contractors were in charge of construction, which was administered by Burke's employer, the Public Works Administration. Instead of building a dam with poured concrete, the corps pumped sediment from under the Missouri and reinforced it with rocks and gravel along a four-mile embankment. In 1938 a portion of the upstream side of the embankment collapsed into the gathering pool. Eight workers were killed; the bodies of six of them have never been recovered and are thought to be entombed inside. Because of this disaster, Burke joined a legion of inspectors dispatched to monitor the placement of the top layer of fill on the massive dam 250 feet high, and the final grooming of the slopes along the long earthen wall. While working, he stayed at the fifty-five-room hotel built in the new government town of Fort Peck to house federal employees, those deemed in "positions of responsibility" whose dependents were left at home. Home for the Burkes in 1940 was the Park Avenue Apartments in Helena, where George and Catherine lived in c-2 on the third floor. Molly and Mary lived in a-2, their own apartment on the first floor, which their parents rented for them because the Park Avenue offered only one-bedroom units. (Responding to a knock on the door at a-2 on April 15, thirteen-year-old Molly assured the census-taker that she was, indeed, the head of the household.)

Soon after the United States declared war on Japan, Germany, and Italy in December of 1941, George was assigned to work on the water treatment system at Fort Lewis, the burgeoning army complex outside Tacoma, Washington, that grew from seven thousand troops stationed there in 1940 to thirty-seven thousand by 1944. When he arrived, a massive hospital complex was under construction that would include almost three hundred buildings, creating space for some 2,500 beds to treat the grim parade of maimed soldiers sent home from war in the Pacific.[31] The project was overseen by the Federal Works Agency, which absorbed a welter of bureaucracies created by the New Deal (the Public Works Administration would hang on until 1944). George's experience with pipelines would serve him well in his new job. He moved the family to the town of Lakewood, a few miles south of Tacoma and just northwest of that part of Fort Lewis that is now McChord Air Force Base. Molly and Mary were enrolled in the Clover Park Junior and Senior High School (Go Warriors!). Mary as a junior and Molly as a sophomore; they didn't distinguish themselves by joining clubs or competing in sports or other extracurricular activities.[32] They most likely figured there was no point in getting too involved in one school because George would probably move them again to another. And, of course, he did.

4

The Home Front

This time the Burkes headed twenty-five miles north to Bremerton, Washington, where George had been assigned to help construct a two-thousand-foot expansion of the municipal sewer lines. On the eve of Pearl Harbor, the town had been a greasy, threadbare navy burg of fifteen thousand. But by spring 1943 the population had more than quadrupled as workers poured in from all over the United States to build and repair warships around the clock at the Puget Sound Naval Shipyard.[1] A tall, leggy high school junior living with Mary and their parents in the East Park section of Bremerton, Molly spent her mornings at Bremerton High School (Go Wildcats!), whose enrollment had swollen to two thousand packed into a building designed for nine hundred. The flood of students compelled the school board to schedule classes in half-day shifts. Seniors and juniors such as Molly and Bill Gates Sr., the junior class president, attended in the morning, freshmen and sophomores in the afternoon. Dancing elbow to elbow, the mob that crammed into an auditorium for the junior prom, whose theme was "Hawaiian Nights," danced to the music of a twelve-piece band crammed into a grass hut. Around school, it was joked that driver's education and sex education were taught in the same car. As a consequence of the population boom, every day at 11:30 a.m. Molly found herself with time on her hands. Like most of her classmates, she decided to find some part-time work.[2]

With so many men leaving the civilian workforce for the military there were plenty of jobs to go around. Some of the boys at school found half-time employment at the yard, making one dollar and twenty-six cents an hour, more than four times the minimum wage. One fifteen-year-old classmate of Molly's dropped out of school altogether and drove around the yard on his Harley Davidson delivering messages. The same kid, Brian Corcoran, also worked as a sports reporter for the *Bremerton News-Searchlight,* and covered an American Legion baseball game in which he also played second base. A few of the girls went to work in the naval yard, as well, after attending a class in shipboard terminology, covering such topics as *port* and *starboard, forward* and *aft.* Some of them became gophers fetching tools and matériel, and others were issued hardhats, goggles, and grinders, which they used to remove the tops of rivets, so damaged steel could be replaced. They helped repair ships nearly destroyed at Pearl Harbor, such as the USS *West Virginia* and USS *California.*

But most of the Bremerton High girls who wanted to work looked for after-school jobs elsewhere. Few of them had to look for very long because the labor shortage was so acute a girl could stroll around downtown and get job offers right on the sidewalk. Many of these jobs were in the entertainment venues catering to the flood of sailors and ship-building families pouring into Bremerton, sixty to seventy new shipyard hires every day. There were a half-dozen movie theaters within a few blocks of one another that needed ticket takers, concessionaires, and usherettes, including the Admiral, a fifteen-hundred-seat emporium built the year before on Pacific Avenue that would cost $4 million today. There were roller skating rinks, bowling alleys, cafes, ice cream parlors, soda fountains, and six dance halls, most notably Perl's Pavilion and del Marco's Dance Pavilion, which stayed open into the wee hours to accommodate workers finishing the swing shift. Before they were shut down by an ambitious young county prosecutor named Scoop Jackson, there were a dozen thriving brothels, although there's no evidence that any Bremerton High girls worked in one.

Molly and Mary had talked about going to work in the shipyard. Although it was segregated from the city by armed guards and an imposing cast iron barrier, the hum and bustle of workers coming and going like army ants twenty-four hours a day was exciting. Welders, chippers, caulkers, drillers, riggers, mechanics, painters, and shipfitters were all laboring at a frantic pace toward the common goal of sending America's damaged fighting ships back into the fight. Although their father didn't doubt that his daughters could do this sort of industrial labor, he and his wife were leery of allowing them to work alongside grown men. So instead, Molly took a job as a sales girl at Sears and Roebuck, which had just opened on Fourth Street in the heart of the city's raucous downtown (although the municipal police force had expanded considerably since Pearl Harbor, the inevitable street brawls among sailors were often allowed to proceed to the final round). She was issued a social security card, which she carefully preserved in plastic (and would keep close her entire life). Happy to be earning fifty-eight cents an hour, she worked twenty or more hours a week after school and on Saturdays selling affordable men's clothing to working-class shoppers.[3] Between January and May 1943 she earned $213, and paid her fair share of the Victory Tax levied to finance the war—ninety cents.

On sunny school mornings Molly and Mary rode their bicycles to school. It was a good thing they didn't have vertigo, because to get there they had to cross the Manette Bridge, a long, two-lane wooden span looming eighty feet above the deep water of the Port Washington Narrows dividing the east side of Bremerton from the west. On rainy mornings, which were the norm on the Kitsap Peninsula, where the precipitation exceeds fifty inches a year, they hopped on a green navy bus with other students bound for school and workers headed for the day shift at the yard. The Burkes' rented home in East Park was part of a development quickly built by the Bremerton Housing Authority to address the acute need for shelter in what had become one of the most critical West Coast cities in the war against the Japanese.[4] Before the construction of East Park and several other housing projects, hundreds of people were forced to find shelter in shacks, garages, and tents. Cots that went for fifty cents a night filled the gym at the downtown Army-Navy YMCA, and all the chairs in the lobby were occupied around the clock. But the Burkes were more fortunate because of George's job. They paid fifty dollars a month in rent for their two-bedroom house, and four dollars and fifty cents for utilities, plus they took advantage of the garden space, lawn mower, and central laundry room that were provided.[5]

As their bus headed along Wheaton Way, across the bridge and into the downtown area, the girls couldn't avoid being reminded that the city expected a Japanese attack at any moment. Antiaircraft facilities had been installed on the roofs of buildings and in the playgrounds of schools. Tethered to barges in the Sinclair Inlet and any open area around the yard were enormous blimps inflated with air and hydrogen. Called barrage balloons, they had been invented by the British during the Blitz to confound the Luftwaffe as it tried to destroy London. In Bremerton, the sixty-foot-long balloons were secured to the ground by quarter-inch steel cables coiled around winches set in concrete. The theory was that once the balloons went aloft in advance of an attack, the cables would snap off the wings and otherwise maim Japanese aircraft diving down to bomb or torpedo ships docked at the yard. Or maybe the grenades attached to the cables would find an unlucky target. There were also occasional days when the smudge pots encircling the yard were fired up for a test. These devices belched clouds of black smoke that obscured the yard and the ships docked there.

Like most of their classmates, Molly and Mary did their patriotic best by buying war bonds and stamps and recycling aluminum foil. But most of the time it wasn't hard to ignore the war because there were so many ways in Bremerton for a teenager to have fun. They loved to roller skate and go to movies. In the first months of 1943 they saw dozens of films, from *Casablanca* and *The Song of Bernadette* to *They Came to Blow Up America* and *I Walked With a Zombie*. Big name performers and their bands played Bremerton throughout the war, including Tommy Dorsey, Lionel Hampton, Louis Armstrong, and Bob Crosby and his Bob-Cats (older brother of Harry Crosby, better known as Bing). Like most Americans during the heyday of radio, they also gathered around the set with their friends and families to listen to comedians such as Jack Benny,

Bob Hope, Fibber McGee and Molly, and Charlie McCarthy slinging insults at W. C. Fields. There were dramatic shows such as *Lux Theatre* and scary shows such as *Inner Sanctum*, in which the creepy screech of a creaking door introduced each episode. Because Molly stayed home from school and work from time to time with earaches and nose bleeds, she got to listen to soap operas such as *Ma Perkins* and *Back Stage Wife.* Although Bremerton didn't have its own radio stations, those in Seattle, fifteen miles east across the Sound, came in loud and clear. It was from one of these stations that the girls first heard a bouncy, patriotic toe tapper called "Rosie the Riveter," which was recorded by several bands, including Kay Kyser's, and a wildly popular singing group from St. Louis called the Four Vagabonds.

> She's making history, working for victory
> Rosie, brrrrrrrrrr, the riveter

Before Molly finished her junior year the Burkes packed up again and moved seventy-five miles north to Oak Harbor on Whidbey Island, where George was assigned to work at the U.S. Naval Air Station. That summer, before her senior year, Molly learned that they were going to have to relocate yet again, this time back south to Seattle. They moved into a duplex on a circular lane called Abelia Court in Rainier Vista, a new Seattle Housing Authority development built by the federal government to house war industry workers. Some three thousand of these residential units were built in Seattle during the war. Like the other projects nearby, such as Holly Park, Rainier Vista's planners were guided by the "garden city" concept pioneered in Great Britain to alleviate the deadening brick architecture of gridded row housing built for workers who swarmed into cities such as Manchester during the Industrial Revolution. Located in the Jefferson Park area of Beacon Hill, Rainier Vista was built on curving streets and cul-de-sacs named after trees and shrubs. The houses were clustered around green spaces. The project included a community center, a childcare center, a club room, and a central laundry.[6]

In order to finish high school in Seattle, Molly would have to enroll in Cleveland High, an intimidating fortress built in 1927 in the neo-Georgian style. Because Mary had graduated from Bremerton High and would no longer share her days with Molly, it was determined at a family meeting that the kid sister would not have to serve out her senior year. The girls wanted to join the war effort. Not only had they been listening to the unavoidable renditions of "Rosie the Riveter" on the radio, everyone was talking about the illustration on the cover of the May 29 *Saturday Evening Post*. While the girls had formed their own pictures of what Rosie looked like, Norman Rockwell's painting altered those images by giving her flesh. Muscled and big-boned, cradling a massive air-powered riveting gun on her lap, she's nonchalantly munching a meat sandwich while propping her penny loafers on a trampled copy of Adolf Hitler's *Mein Kampf.*[7] A family council concluded that the girls could go to work for Boeing, with one stipulation: their mother must join them on the production line.

Beginning in June of 1943 most every workday for the Burke women began the same way. Before dawn they dressed in their work clothes. This might be a Boeing slack suit—a belted, pleated, blue cotton coverall with breast pockets, slightly padded shoulders, with the Boeing logo sewn on one of the short sleeves. Sometimes one of them wore a siren suit—a one-piece, belted garment with breast pockets that zipped in front, named after the easy-on, easy-off garment Londoners wore to the air-raid shelters during the Blitz. Or they might go with bell-bottomed slacks and a blouse. Because leather was rationed, they wore fabric shoes with low heels. Like Rosie, they tied their hair back with a scarf. After a quick breakfast they packed their lunch boxes with sandwiches and fruit, filled their thermoses with coffee, and got on a Boeing bus that would take them the three miles from Rainier Vista to Boeing's Plant Number Two, on the right bank of the Duwamish Waterway in South Seattle. When they got there, workers were streaming toward the gate for the day shift, which began at 6:30 a.m. At the gate their lunch buckets were checked by a security guard (sometimes they didn't bring in lunch, choosing instead to eat in the factory commissary). They punched their time cards; put on their goggles, ear protectors, and gloves; and headed out onto the factory floor.

It was here that thirty thousand workers laboring round-the-clock in three shifts produced only one product—the B17G heavy bomber. A mammoth four-engine, propeller-driven airplane, it was dubbed the "Flying Fortress" after a *Seattle Times* reporter who saw it for the first time. It weighed eighteen tons, was seventy-four feet long, had a wingspan of more than a hundred feet, and the roof of its cockpit loomed twenty feet above the tarmac. Its nose turret was made of reinforced glass, and it was armed with thirteen .50-caliber machine guns designed to point in every direction so the crew members could defend themselves against enemy fighters. It carried up to eight thousand pounds of bombs and enough fuel to give it a range of two thousand miles. Although it was never used to bomb mainland Japan because of this limited range, it was largely responsible for the destruction of many German cities in the last years of World War II.[8]

Molly and Mary had been hired as "C" grade riveters, part of the army of so-called soldiers without guns, the labor force of the armaments industry. They were paid ninety-two cents an hour. The job was simple and repetitive. Working as a team, one riveter stood on scaffolding outside the bomber's aluminum skeleton, or on a wing, while the other stood inside. There were only three objects involved. The first was the rivet, a small aluminum shaft with a round head on one end. The outside riveter inserted a rivet into predrilled hole. The inside riveter pressed a hunk of heavy metal, called a bucking bar, against the shaft of the rivet while the outside riveter used a pneumatic hammer to flatten it into a head. Then they moved on to the next hole and the next rivet. In this manner they attached the airplane's aluminum skin firmly to its skeleton in pieces. Why not use screws instead of rivets? Screws can come loose and cannot be made flush with the skin, which means they would create drag when the craft is in the air.

Meanwhile, Catherine Burke, whose job description was "mechanic," spent her workday bolting together various metal parts and attaching them to the airplane. The Burke women promptly joined Local 751 of the Aeronautical Mechanics Union and were assessed one dollar and fifty cents per month in dues. In September 1943 Molly was formally initiated into the union at the Eagle's Nest, a grand ballroom in downtown Seattle.[9] She worked for the Boeing Aircraft Company from the summer of 1943 to October 1944, earning $1,111.42 in 1943 (about $16,000 in buying power in 2018) and paying $155.21 in taxes that year. During this period she and her fellow workers churned out three hundred Flying Fortresses every month, an industrial onslaught the fascists couldn't counter, after their coal and petroleum transportation systems were ruined.

The girls were constantly reminded of the war because, if for no other reason, the entire Plant Number Two was camouflaged in an attempt to hide it in plain sight from Japanese bombers. A Hollywood set designer was hired to create what from the air appeared to be a residential neighborhood on the twenty-six-acre roof of the plant. Fake houses made from plywood were constructed along fake streets with signposts identifying them with names such as Synthetic St. and Burlap Blvd. Fake cars, also made of plywood, were parked on the "streets." Fake trees, shrubs, and lawns were fabricated from chicken wire, fabric, and dyed feathers. Eerie photographs commissioned by Boeing show women "sunbathing" in their "yards." The plant was never bombed, but the camouflage served to remind Molly and her fellow workers that the work they were doing was a critical effort to protect their country.

A milestone for the company and its workers at the Number Two Plant was achieved on May 13, 1944. Scores of employees put the finishing touches on the five thousandth Flying Fortress built by Boeing since the attack on Pearl Harbor. It was dubbed the "Five Grand." Molly and Mary and Catherine lined up along with thousands of other workers to paint their names on the fuselage and wings of the plane. Then, instead of being towed out of the plant onto the tarmac by a truck, it was pushed out by a crowd of jubilant workers. Three weeks later it bombed Nazi gun batteries in Holland just before the D-Day invasion of France, still tattooed with thirty-five thousand names.[10] Although building bombers appealed to her sense of patriotism, Molly had something else in mind for her future.

5

Girl Reporter

At night Molly attended classes in order to earn her general education diploma. And she took a correspondence course in history offered by the University of Washington in Seattle. On June 9, 1944, Bremerton High School awarded her a diploma. That fall she and Mary enrolled as full-time students at UW (Go Huskies!). But after one semester, George, yet again, was transferred, this time back to Helena. The Burkes again moved into the fashionable Park Avenue Apartments, at the corner of Placer and North Park.[1] Molly got a job as a typist with Stinson of Montana, a manufacturing company whose business office was housed only five blocks from the apartment in the original Helena High School building, which had somehow survived the 1935 quake, and had been built on the grounds of the city's first cemetery.[2] Having learned to type at night school in Seattle, that summer she earned $433.13—about $6,000 in today's dollars—and paid $61.50 in income tax. That fall Molly and Mary transferred their credits earned at the University of Washington to Montana State University (which was later renamed the University of Montana). Molly moved into New Hall, a dormitory for upper-class women, which would later be renamed Brantley Hall, and enrolled in the School of Journalism. She told friends that for her, journalism would be the easiest course of study. After all, she said, there couldn't be much to it. You observe an event and ask people to comment on it, then you write about it.[3]

In 1945 the Missoula college, huddled in a picturesque setting at the base of five-thousand-foot Mount Sentinel, which the university owned, had a small student body of less than three thousand students, but would grow rapidly as soldiers returned from the war to attend school on the GI Bill. Many of these men and their young families lived in temporary prefab housing thrown up on and around campus by the federal government. The girls enjoyed renting horses from the stable on campus and riding them up into Pattee Canyon a couple of miles away in the mountains. Their mother insisted that they send their clothes to Helena for her to launder, because, she told them, no one else could do it correctly. So once a week they packed their dirty garments into a steamer trunk, took it by taxi to the Northern Pacific railroad depot at the north end of Higgins Avenue downtown, and shipped it to their mother, who washed their clothes in the laundry room at the Park Avenue Apartments. Then she loaded the clothes back into the trunk and shipped it to her daughters. Once, during finals, Molly wore the same outfit for ten days and was so ashamed of its condition that instead of sending it to her mother she threw it away.

Extracurricular activities at the university in the 1940s were not significantly different from those eighty years later. Every spring, freshmen hiked up Mount Sentinel to whitewash the enormous "M" that was formed in concrete on the west-facing slope of the mountain. At homecoming, choral groups entertained alumni with their traditional "singing on the steps" of old Main Hall. Eight fraternities and seven sororities dominated the social scene, although neither Molly nor Mary joined. As it is today, the focus of the campus was sports (Go Grizzlies!). Unlike today, in the 1940s this included an annual boxing and wrestling exhibition in the Old Gym. And no one gave a second thought to the four white boys in blackface singing at a music school fundraiser called "Plantation Days." While the century-old Forester's Ball is still a highlight of the winter social season, the Sadie Hawkins Day dance; the annual barn dance; and the Barrister's Ball, sponsored by the law school, are relics of the past.

Molly lived in New Hall her entire college career. In 1948, her senior year, she was elected dormitory president. Although men were required to live on campus for only their freshman year, a woman could only move out of the dorms if she was a senior, married, or had turned twenty-one. This rule would change in 1970 after Marcia Herrin, Molly's oldest daughter and an eighteen-year-old sophomore, relentlessly and publicly pestered the university president, Robert Pantzer, demanding that women be granted the right to make the same choices as men about where to live. After a couple of months Pantzer relented.[4]

In 1948 Mary was in her final year of law school, one of only three women in a class of thirty. The grades earned by the Burke sisters were so stellar that they were inducted into Kappa Tau, an exclusive scholastic honor society. Previously, in 1946, Molly had been inducted into Alpha Lambda Delta, a scholastic honor society for freshmen. Both Molly and Mary were awarded scholarships for the 1946–47 school year that paid their tuition and other fees in full for three quarters. Molly was awarded the Dean Stone Scholarship in 1947, named in honor of the founder of the journalism school, Arthur Stone. Finally, just before she graduated in 1948, she was inducted into Sigma Delta Chi, the professional journalism fraternity, for ranking in the upper 10 percent of her graduating class. She was chosen to give a speech at a Hotel Florence banquet welcoming Helen Kirkpatrick, a celebrated war correspondent invited to share her experiences with the university and the community.[5] Molly's dean, James L. C. Ford, wrote her several letters of praise during her college years (and another one congratulating her the day Marcia was born).[6]

She excelled at the core curriculum of journalism—reporting and editing—skills which would help her land a prestigious job when she graduated. Some of the other courses required for the degree were of no use to a reporter whatsoever. Two of these—typography and advertising—are no longer taught at Montana. (Molly's second daughter, Kitty, would use her self-taught knowledge of these arcane crafts to start a typesetting, design, and advertising business in 1976.) Before Molly graduated she was offered several jobs, including a position working as Dean Ford's assistant in the J-school, and another one working for a regional publication in Washington State called the *Pacific Northwest Cooperator* with a circulation of seventy thousand (the starting weekly pay of these jobs was only forty dollars).

But during the summer after her graduation she landed a job with United Press in Helena. This was at a time when very few women were being hired by the wire services. As Dean Ford wrote to her: "As you realize, it's unusual for a girl to have a position with a press association, but I, personally, have no qualms as to your ability to do a thoroughly satisfactory job." She quickly discovered that her occasional reporting and copyediting for the *Montana Kaimin*, the student daily, had not prepared her for the brutal midnight deadline and relentless pace of work in UP's Helena office, which was housed in the *Independent Record* building downtown. At one point she asked Mary, who was living in Helena with the family after graduating from law school, to help her write headlines for the stream of Montana-based stories that went out on the wire to UP's subscribers all over the world. Dealing with the men in the newsroom added to the challenges. They were typical journalists—cynical, skeptical, thick-skinned, and foulmouthed. Plus, they treated her like a secretary, ordering her to bring them coffee. Still, she persevered. Her determination was finally rewarded—sort of—although the recognition she received came for her role in reporting a tragedy.

It began the summer of 1948 when heavy rains drenched what was then called the Gates of the Mountains "Wild Area" along the Missouri River in the Big Belt Mountains.[7] The wet weather nurtured an unusually abundant growth of brush and grass the following spring. During the first week of August 1949 temperatures climbed into the high nineties and the humidity dropped. On the afternoon of August 4, a lightning storm that passed over the area sparked several small wildfires. Four of these in a steep, brushy canyon called Mann Gulch were quickly extinguished by rangers. But another one was a "sleeper" that smoldered, undetected. An airplane was dispatched from the Helena airport on August 5 to check for such sleepers, but the observers reported seeing no more fire activity. A cautious district ranger asked a recreation guard to conduct a survey on foot. The guard, James O. Harrison, was a twenty-year-old former smokejumper attending the university in Missoula who quit jumping because his mother thought it was too dangerous. He left the guard station at nearby Meriweather Canyon and hiked into Mann

Gulch, where he spotted the sleeper and began battling the growing six-acre blaze with a hand tool called a Pulaski. He had left a note on the door of the station: "Gone to fire. Be back at 3:00 p.m., Jim."

After smoke from the fire was seen by a spotter in a lookout tower thirty miles away, a crew of twenty-five firefighters soon joined Harrison. By 3 p.m. the fire was moving downhill through sparse grass and had burned about sixty acres. It appeared to the firefighters as a routine blaze. About 2:30 p.m., a C-47 took off from Missoula's Hale Field (now the site of Sentinel High School and Playfair Park), carrying sixteen smokejumpers. The temperature in Mann Gulch had climbed to ninety-seven degrees. The wind was beginning to whip up. At around 4 p.m. the smokejumpers dropped into Mann Gulch at an elevation of about 1,200 feet. They repacked their parachutes, gathered the equipment pushed from the plane on its last passes over the area, and went to work.

By 6 p.m. Harrison and the smokejumpers realized that they were in trouble. The wind had shifted 180 degrees and began gusting to forty miles per hour. They were ordered to drop their tools and packs and retreat to the river. But the fire had ignited the crowns of the trees, starting spot fires that caused the blaze to jump ahead of them, cutting off their route to the water. It was now moving through the highly flammable grass understory straight at them, driven by winds in the one-hundred-degree heat that were pushing a wall of fire twenty feet high. They turned around and began retreating up the slope, heading for safety on the rocky north ridge of Mann Gulch. Most of them never made it. Harrison and twelve of the smokejumpers suffocated to death before the fire charred their bodies. One man survived by setting a backfire in the grass that consumed the fuel and allowed him to create a sanctuary from the superheated air. He called to the others to join him in the blackened circle he had created. But because of the roar from the inferno, apparently, no one heard him. Two others made it to a crevice in the rimrocks and then into a field of huge boulders that shielded them from the inferno.

The following day, a Saturday, Molly went to the district forester's office in Helena to interview two of the survivors, Walter Rumsey, twenty-one, from Lawrence, Kansas, and Robert Sallee, seventeen, from Willow Creek, Montana, who had taken refuge in the boulder field. When she asked them to explain what happened they "sat in shocked silence," she reported. "Finally, one broke the silence to utter painfully, 'It was terrible.'" At the time, the fate of two of the smokejumpers was still not determined, and the survivors were hoping their comrades might have reached the kind of rocky sanctuary they had been lucky enough to find. "But as the fire pressed onward Saturday night," Molly wrote, "hope for the safety of the still-missing parachutists dimmed at headquarters here."[8]

Molly's interview was sent out on the United Press teletype all over the world. It was a three-hundred-word article. As was the custom among subscribers to the UP wire, some newspapers published her byline above her work, but most didn't. And some papers combined her reporting with that of fellow "Unipresser" Charles H. Turner, whose byline was published several times in connection with the articles about the tragedy.

For Molly, the Mann Gulch fire was a professional challenge. But it was also a personal loss. The previous month the Burkes had trailered their horses to a spot above Meriwether Canyon, where they joined other people belonging to a club called the Helena Trail Riders for an overnight camping trip down into this scenic backcountry valley. During the night two of the Burke horses managed to get loose and by first light had disappeared. George appealed for help from the recreation guard, Jim Harrison, who managed to find the horses two days later and return them to the family. Good-looking, personable, and fit from his summers working outdoors, Harrison soon had Molly's full attention.

But for another young man on that ride, it was Molly who commanded all the attention. This was Keith Herrin, twenty-five, the son of an old Montana ranching family that operated a thousand-acre cattle operation in the Helena Valley. His girlfriend at the time would enroll at what was then called Montana State College in Bozeman, and leave Keith back on the ranch. Just nine weeks after the Mann Gulch disaster, Keith and Molly were married in Helena by a Presbyterian minister. Molly had resigned from her United Press job two weeks before. She would never write another word as a professional.[9]

6

Lighting Out for the Territory

Two years after Molly and Keith were married, their first child was born. Marcia Marie Herrin increased to fifteen the population of the Herrin Hereford Ranch, a thousand acres of flat, fertile, and well-watered land in the Helena Valley on Prickly Pear Creek ten miles west of the Missouri River. In addition to Marcia's parents, the other residents included her paternal grandfather and grandmother, great-grandmother, two aunts, two uncles, four cousins, and Herman, the hired hand. Living in three houses and one cabin, the clan was completely dependent on the income it earned selling beef, Hereford bulls, and crops. But the postwar economy was booming, and the cattle business was good. For four generations the Herrins had been successful farmers, dairymen, and stockmen, extracting wealth from a high, dry country which, although nurturing the tribes for at least twelve thousand years, had defeated hundreds of settlers who weren't as skillful, as tenacious—or as lucky—as the Herrins.

In 1870 Marcia's great-great-grandfather Daniel S. Herrin was making a living of sorts on a small farm four miles east of the Kennebec River in Canaan township, Somerset County, Maine. His land straddled a swell of high ground now called Chase Hill, which was a six-mile ride down rutted, muddy roads to town. He and his wife, Mary, were bringing up four children under the age of twelve—Henry Harrison, Anna, Milford, and Harland Joseph—and were also responsible for the care of Daniel's widowed, seventy-two-year-old father, Henry.[1] Although trying to extract an income from crops and a few cows on land that was better suited for apple orchards, which would one day become a mainstay of Maine's agriculture industry, they could afford a domestic servant, the twenty-five-year-old daughter of a neighbor.

An 1860 business directory of Canaan Village listed "H & D. S. Herrin" as "Dealers in Stock & Country Products." That year marked a population peak in Canaan Town of 1715 residents, of whom two were lawyers, two were physicians, seven were merchants, and twenty-eight were farmers. By 1870 some of the farmers had given up and moved to the Midwest, where the soils were more fertile. The population of Canaan steadily declined for the next six decades, reaching a low of 714 residents in 1930 before slowly growing again. The pine and maple forests, which had been cleared to make way for farms, quickly grew back, leaving little trace of the Herrins. A map of the township drawn in 1860 shows the location of the farms owned by Daniel and that of Henry, nearby. Another map, this one drawn in 1883, reveals that the Herrins were no longer landowners in Canaan. For one reason, Henry had died in 1873. And for another, in 1877 Daniel and Mary Herrin sold the farm and moved to Clancy, Montana, a village a few miles south of Helena in the valley of the upper Prickly Pear Creek.[2] They bought a large, rambling house and turned it into a stagecoach stop that offered meals, lodging, and stabling to travelers heading south from Helena to Butte.[3] Like many merchants, they also raised a few cattle.[4]

In 1880 Daniel began buying land two miles south of Lincoln, Montana, where he built a house and moved his family. This was a desirable expanse of grasslands and timbered hillsides, watered by Humbug Creek, a dawdling tributary of the nearby Blackfoot River. A mile east along what is now called the Herrin Lake Road were a pair of large, boggy ponds, now called the Herrin Lakes. The area was perfectly suited for grazing, and still is. Daniel set about with his sons, Harland Joseph and Milford Daniel, to build up a herd. In 1883 he formed a legal partnership with them called Herrin & Sons. While many homesteaders took advantage of the 1873 Timber Culture Act to acquire land, the Herrins preferred paying cash to planting trees.[5,6] By 1887 the family had acquired almost a thousand acres.

Like people living on the land since humans first began domesticating the natural world, they relied on their clan for their livelihood, welfare, protection, primary education, and even most of their health care. And like the Joads in the *Grapes of Wrath*, members of the Herrin clan didn't stray very far away from one another. Benjamin F. Herrin, Daniel's younger brother by two years, had abandoned Maine, as well, and was granted a homestead patent in summer 1889 on 160 acres four miles west of the Herrin Lakes. A month earlier, Daniel had been granted a patent on the same amount of land in the Willow Creek valley bordering his original ranch.[7] In 1879 Daniel's nineteen-year-old daughter, Anna Maria, married a neighbor, Abel Dallas, who filed a homestead claim on 160 acres four miles east of the Herrin place along Humbug Creek. Although Henry Harrison Herrin, the oldest of the brothers, did not venture west, in 1898 he contributed his daughter, Annie May, to the Montana union of Herrins and Sanfords by blessing her marriage to John Sanford, Mary Teresa's brother.

These early stockmen shared little in common with the melodramatic picture of Montana cowboys popularized by works of fiction such as *Lonesome Dove* or the paintings of Charles M. Russell. First, the Herrins didn't take advantage of free forage by driving their herds across the vast sea of grass on the fenceless open range. And they didn't manage huge herds of half-wild longhorn cattle that had been brought north from Texas. They raised dairy cows, so-called shorthorn cattle originally trailed to Montana from Oregon, and not that many of them, since their experience was limited to the small collection of cows they owned in Maine. Shorthorns, developed in County Durham in the northeast of England, were used for both milk and meat. They were better suited to the woods and valleys of western Montana than longhorns, most of which didn't survive the brutal winter of 1887, when arctic blizzards and minus fifty-degree temperatures killed 90 percent of the cattle on the open range. The customers who demanded Herrin beef and milk were the denizens of the camps that had sprung up around the gold mines in Last Chance Gulch and Marysville.[8]

May Day 1888 was a busy day for Herrin & Sons. First, Daniel gave public notice that he intended to submit final "proof" of his homestead claim with the U.S. Land Office in Helena.[9] Witnesses to the fact that he had lived on the land for five years and had "improved" it included Abel Dallas.[10] On the same day Herrin filed his intent, Dallas filed his own notice on 160 acres four miles east of the Herrin place along Humbug Creek.[11] This was also the day Daniel and his boys publicly declared that Herrin & Sons was dissolved.[12] The estate was divided equally between the three partners. Milford and his father formed a new partnership, which continued until Daniel's death in Chicago in 1904 at the age of seventy-two.

Harland's share of the partnership was 325 acres, fifty-three head of cattle, and a dozen horses.[13] One possible reason for the breakup of Herrin & Sons was Harland's marriage in 1887 to Mary Teresa Agnes Sanford, an event that may have compelled him to strike out on his own with her by his side. She was born in 1861 in Devonshire, England, the daughter of a well-off farmer's son who brought his family to Michigan in 1869, and then moved them to Montana two years later. One thing is certain: "Holly," as his family called him, was much more ambitious—and far more ruthless—than anyone else in his family. In 1892, for a sum of $3,870, he sold his 320 acres of forest and pasture, which in 2020 would be valued at around $100,000. He used the money to buy a comparably sized spread near the booming mining camp of Marysville, for which he paid Fred Lindevidel $3,500. That was the year Thomas Harland Herrin was born, the couple's only child. Harland raised hay and cattle and ran a butchering business on the side. In 1891, for unknown reasons, he retired from H. J. Herrin & Co. and turned over his accounts to Sanford Bros., a ranching and gold mining partnership formed between his wife's father and uncle, Thomas and William. In 1896 he returned inexplicably to the meat business for two years, delivering beef by the wagonload to miners.[14]

In 1898 he sold this ranch to a Marysville rancher and former livery operator named Charles Winstrom for $6,500.[15] With this sizable profit, the next year he bought 1,364 acres from the Great Northern Railroad Company, land that straddled the Missouri River near the village of Wolf Creek a day and a half by horseback due east of his family's ranches. The river at this point, carving its bed through the Big Belt Mountains, ran clear and cold and wouldn't begin to color with the silt that earned it its "Big Muddy" moniker until exiting north through the mountains and onto the plains. Over the next few years, he added another 1,120 acres to his estate, buying most of this expansion of his holdings from the Northern Pacific Railway Company. This was some of the most productive land in the state, well irrigated, with thick, fertile layers of topsoil called basin fill that had been deposited over the course of thousands of years. Holly grew hay and grain, planted vegetables, and maintained a sizable herd of cattle. He grazed them on his own land, but also took advantage of the unfenced open range, which he willingly shared with other cattlemen, and reluctantly with the sheepmen who were beginning at the turn of the century to try their luck in Montana.[16] At the same time, Holly took on a business partner in the cattle operation, a lawyer named Albert J. Galen.[17] He would soon need Galen's legal advice to help keep him out of prison.

FIG. 4. Harland Joseph "Holly" Herrin, circa 1910. Courtesy of the Molly Burke Herrin Estate.

7

Wild and Wooly

Montana at the turn of the twentieth century was still a rough frontier where drunken men regularly fought in the streets with their fists and sometimes their guns. On Christmas Day 1904, while visiting Wolf Creek in his horse-drawn buggy, Holly found himself in the middle of a commotion caused by a saloon owner named M. H. Bray. After sampling his establishment's refreshments, Bray decided to celebrate the holiday by firing shots over the heads of a group of men who had gathered around Holly to chat, after he had drawn up to a hitching post. Suddenly, one of Holly's horses leapt into the air and fell down dead, a bullet in its brain.[1]

Three years earlier, in October 1901, Holly threw himself into a public brawl on Main Street in Wolf Creek with a pair of itinerant ranch hands named Arthur L. Green and Calvin C. Devois. According to a local report, Holly "knocked out Davis in the first round" and knocked out Green in the second. To show that he harbored no hard feelings Holly invited the young combatants into the Blue Bird Saloon for a drink, but they declined his offer.[2] (Harland Herrin was enormously strong and barrel-chested. According to an unverified family story, at an annual gathering in Wolf Creek he was the only man who lifted a five-hundred-pound keg of nails from a loading dock into a boxcar without spilling a single nail.)

On Christmas Eve of that year several fires broke out on Herrin and Galen's ranch, destroying two barns, two sheds, three corrals, four haystacks, and one straw stack, property valued at $8,000 to $10,000. Neighbors who rushed to the scene and doused the flames spared Herrin and Galen of even higher losses. Because of the nature of these multiple blazes it was believed they were intentionally set. A week later Green and Devois were arrested and accused of second-degree arson. Their bonds were set at $5,000 each, and they were remanded to jail in Helena until the following Monday, when they returned to court and entered pleas of not guilty. Because no evidence was presented at this hearing, an attorney tried to get Green released on a writ of habeas corpus, but the judge denied the request.[3]

In May 1902, following an eight-day trial, a jury deliberated Green's fate for three hours and returned a guilty verdict on the charge of arson.[4] During the trial the judge dismissed the charges against Calvin Devois, citing the state's lack of evidence, and he was set free. Green, however, was sentenced to six years in the state penitentiary at Deer Lodge. A self-described former schoolteacher born in Stratford-upon-Avon— William Shakespeare's hometown—Green had served a year in prison in 1894 after pleading guilty to a burglary in Fort Benton.[5] And several witnesses testified that he had publicly vowed to get even with Herrin. In February 1903 Calvin Devois sued Herrin and Galen for malicious prosecution, seeking damages of $10,240.[6]

While Green began serving his sentence, his attorney, E. A. Carlton, was preparing to file a motion for a new trial. In August 1902 he submitted six affidavits to district court in Helena that described misconduct on the part of witnesses for the prosecution and four of the jurors. These were firsthand accounts of Herrin engaged in friendly conversations with jurors at the Grand Central Hotel in Helena, where he was staying during the trial, and palling around with the prosecution's witnesses, some of whom were his employees.[7,8] A reporter described in breathless tones what happened next:

> Last evening, just before the scores of steel bolts shooting to their places in cell doors filled the long corridors with harsh noise and

announced the hour of bedtime, Green received a telegram which means a speedy good-bye to the prison and another chance for freedom which he thought lost. Judge Henry C. Smith of the district court signed an order to-day granting him another trial, and E. A. Carlton, who defended Green at his former trial, sent the message announcing the fact to the convict. 'Judge Smith made you a Christmas present of a new trial,' the message read.

Green was accused of arson by Herrin. The case was hard fought. Neighborhood enmities of long standing figured strongly on the outside. The evidence was circumstantial. The court holds that it was not strong enough to justify a conviction, but strong enough to raise suspicions against the defendant. The evidence in point concerns alleged threats made by Green against Herrin, who had previously beaten him. It also relates to his whereabouts last Christmas night. He claimed he was in a cabin. Another witness, so says Judge Smith's order, raised doubt as to its absolute truth. The fact that Green had threatened the victim of the fire and had in his threats talked of fire; that he had, after the fire, made other statements which would tend to cast suspicion upon him, these should not have, in the opinion of the court, led to a conviction.

Green will now be brought back to the county jail. His lawyer says that he will try to get the man's former bail reduced from $10,00 to a much smaller figure. If successful in obtaining a reduction, Carleton says he will be able to procure the sureties.[9]

After Green had languished behind bars for eighteen months, a second trial commenced in Helena. Green "does not look the bronzed and sunburned rancher he did when tried before," a reporter observed. "Instead he is thin and his face pale."[10] Two weeks later, on its second vote, a unanimous jury acquitted Green of all charges, and he was released from custody. "The Green case," a reporter noted, "was one of the most famous of its kind ever tried in this county."[11]

By 1903 Holly Herrin's net worth in today's economy would make him a millionaire several times over. Not bad for an indifferent student who never finished high school. But sometimes what makes one man rich makes another man poor. On a Saturday night in August 1903, Holly and eight other Wolf Creek area cattle ranchers, along with twenty to thirty of their neighbors and hired hands, armed themselves and covered their faces with bandanas. Under a full moon they rode north along the Missouri. Around midnight the gang invaded a 1,450-acre sheep ranch on the Dearborn River owned by Henry Nitsche, a forty-nine-year-old immigrant from Germany.[12] They tore down corrals penning some 2,500 head of sheep, and drove the animals through heavy brush, injuring fifty head. At gunpoint, they captured Nitsche's French-Basque sheepherder, Adelaire Des Genaise, put a rope around his neck, and took him several miles away before warning him to abandon Nitsche's sheep camp forever or they would hang him.

The incident was the latest battle in a war that pitted cattle ranchers against sheep ranchers over the issue of grazing on the open, unfenced range. The cattlemen saw sheepherders as invaders whose animals destroyed common pastures by cropping the grass down to the nub. They believed that the odor of sheep repelled cattle. They didn't like the Mexicans, Scots, Mormons, and Basques who herded sheep, believing them to be "un-American." (Although by 1910 Holly would hire numerous foreign-born men to work for him.) On the Montana-Wyoming border in 1902 some two thousand head of sheep were driven over a cliff by cattlemen, who bludgeoned to death those that survived the fall.[13]

In the "informations" filed against Holly and his neighbors in Lewis and Clark County District Court, he and eight others were charged with criminal conspiracy for the acts of August 8 that constituted what was known at the time as "whitecapping."[14] If convicted, Holly could end up in the state prison at Deer Lodge. (Whitecapping was a crime, primarily committed in the rural areas of the southern United States, but occurring in all parts of the U.S., of violent acts against drunks, criminals, the shiftless, minorities, those deemed immoral, and people whose businesses or occupations were perceived as threats to those carrying out violent acts. Vigilantes in Montana and the Ku Klux Klan in the Deep South are two strains of the phenomenon. Most whitecappers went free, because of their code of silence and because they often had support among the community and the legal establishment. In addition to the Dearborn attack there were several instances of whitecapping in Montana during the first two decades after the territory became a state.)[15]

Not surprisingly, the charges against the Wolf Creek ranchers were thrown out by a judge in Helena, and the accused were ordered released from custody. According to District Judge Henry C. Smith, it seemed unfair that these nine prominent ranchers should face such serious accusations without a preliminary hearing by a justice of the peace in Wolf Creek, their home district. He said that even if the defendants were found innocent, the charges against them could appear on their permanent records. Although the county attorney declined to pursue the matter, the victims fought back.

Nitsche and Des Genaise filed separate lawsuits against the ranchers. Nitsche claimed that the attack had put him out of business, forcing him to sell his holdings at a loss, and depriving him of an annual profit of $1,500. In addition to the loss of income, he cited $3,000 in "financial damage" plus $25 for the destruction of his "provisions," bringing the total to $4,525 in restitution demanded from the whitecappers (around $130,000 in the purchasing power of 2019). Des Genaise demanded $5,000 for his treatment at the hands of Holly and his gang, plus $250 to compensate him for the cost of moving to a safer place in Montana. The defense presented thirteen witnesses who verified the alibis of the defendants, all of whom claimed to be somewhere other than Nitsche's sheep ranch the night of August 8. One of them was home in bed, another was forty miles away, a third was spending the night at a neighbor's. And so on.

But the jurors didn't buy this testimony, especially after hearing from S. W. Mosher, a neighbor of Nitsche's and himself a sheepman, who identified two of the masked marauders.[16] In the end the jury ruled in Nitsche's favor, and awarded him $716.25. The defendants immediately asked for a stay of judgment and a new trial. They based their pleading on seven grounds: "Irregularity in the proceedings by which the defendants were prevented from having a fair trial; misconduct of the jury; accident and surprise which ordinary prudence could not guard against; newly acquired evidence; excessive damages appearing to have been given under the influence of prejudice; [and] the insufficiency of evidence to justify the verdict."[17] The judge, J. M. Clements, granted the motion. Two weeks earlier Des Genaise asked for a change of venue, citing Clements' "bias and prejudice" as reasons why he believed he could not get a fair trial, and was granted his request.[18] Because of a procedural error, Nitsche's request for a change of venue on the same grounds was thrown out. Des Genaise's lawsuit and Nitsche's second attempt at a legal remedy were moved to district court in Great Falls. What were called the "Augusta whitecapping cases" languished there for more than two years before the cattlemen finally settled with the sheepmen out of court for undisclosed sums.[19]

It was during this period of stress brought on by his legal problems that Holly, in 1906 at the age of forty-three, divorced Mary Teresa Sanford, citing her "desertion" as the grounds for the breakup.[20] The following year he married Mary Ellen O'Connell, the twenty-five-year-old daughter of Irish descent who had settled in Marysville, Montana, after coming west from Michigan. She moved into Holly's "home ranch" on the left bank of the Missouri, along with her ten-year-old brother, Brian O'Connell, and her sisters, Bernice, eleven, and Mabel, four. They had been orphaned in 1905 when their father, a fifty-year-old miner named Thomas, died of what the newspaper called "a lingering illness" as his children gathered around his death bed. His wife had died several years earlier.[21] But their deaths provided Holly with another achievement—a daughter—when he adopted Mabel four years later. These upheavals in his family life followed a radical change of course in his business life that would have struck him as incomprehensible during his assaults against the flockmasters.

8

A Man of Means

In 1905 Holly Herrin decided to turn his considerable energy to raising sheep. This wasn't a decision guided by the notion that if you can't beat them, join them. Instead, it was based solely on the profit motive. His first consideration was the low prices paid to stockmen for their cattle. In the first years of the twentieth century the cost of beef to the consumer rose inexorably, while the money earned by stockmen such as Harland Herrin remained static. In 1907 Holly was getting 4½ cents per pound on the hoof for the cattle he raised; Montana butchers were getting twenty-five cents per pound for porterhouse steak, which commanded prices of one dollar and seventy cents to two dollars per steak in two Butte restaurants. Demand grew steadily during these years as the economy prospered and wages rose. The average American was spending 7 percent of his income on beef. Someone was making a lot of money in the cattle business, but it wasn't Holly.

In 1904 Congress ordered an investigation to see if the disparity was the work of a corporate trust that was conspiring to fix prices. A year later President Theodore Roosevelt released a report by the secretary of Commerce and Labor concluding that the meat packing industry—which was dominated by six large companies, including Armour and Swift—shared no ownership in common and was not making profits that would justify accusing them of price fixing.[1] The report was widely criticized.

But whatever the reason for the low prices, Holly realized that using his ranches to produce wool was a better use of his grazing lands. Sheep needed much less water than cattle and they ate weeds cattle wouldn't touch. They needed very little attention—apart from protecting them from predators—and unlike beef, the wool they produced year after year never spoiled. By 1900 sheep raising had surpassed cattle as the leading agricultural industry in Montana and Wyoming.[2]

By 1907—less than four years after the raid on the Dearborn—Holly had built one of the largest flocks of sheep in Montana. These were Rambouillets, a breed developed in France by King Louis XVI, who bred Spanish Merinos with long-haired English sheep to produce garment-quality wool that was not only very fine (in contrast to the coarse wools that are used, say, in carpets) but also three or more inches long. This made it relatively easy to spin into yarn, which was then strung on a loom to produce cloth.[3] Adding sheep to Holly's business plan made economic sense. In Montana successful flockmasters were making huge profits selling wool, which was a valuable renewable resource high in consumer demand, especially across the frigid northern tier of the United States. On top of that, the era of open cattle ranges was coming to an end as young families flooded into Montana, especially after the Enlarged Homestead Act of 1909 made 320 acres of formerly common land available. Many of the newcomers promptly threw up barbed wire fences around their new private property.

The rush to enclose land in the Wolf Creek area was inspired by the stock management practices of Holly and some of his neighbors. In November 1910, for example, one of his herders, George Buderences, was arrested for moving a flock of Herrin woolies across land owned by Albion McDonald, a Wolf Creek rancher and saloon keeper.[4] During the summer McDonald had erected a half mile of barbed wire around this parcel, but when he went to investigate how Herrin's sheep got there, he discovered that his fence had been torn down. Not only were the posts pulled from the ground and tossed beside the wire, the post holes had been filled in. The man who freely admitted to this charge of malicious mischief was a native of England named John Trodick, said to be a veteran of the 1853–56 Crimean War in what is now the Ukraine. A constable was dispatched from Helena. The newspapers were amused that Trodick, ninety-two, was possibly the oldest man ever arrested in Montana.[5] He posted a one-hundred-dollar bond and argued before a justice of the peace that the land in question belonged to him, and not McDonald. The charges against him were dismissed after Trodick produced documents showing that the U.S. Supreme Court had seen enough merit in his claim to review a lower court decision that had gone against him. The following May, McDonald and his neighbors were shocked to learn that, indeed, the Supreme Court in *Northern Pacific Railway Company v. Trodick* not only awarded the old man ownership of the land under McDonald's doomed fence, but also the entire village of Wolf Creek, including the parcel under McDonald's saloon.[6]

In 1913 Holly perceived that his growing fortune was threatened by what he considered an insidious, harebrained geopolitical scheme. Civic boosters in the town of Cascade had organized a campaign to create a new county called Dearborn, which would be carved from portions of Cascade and Lewis and Clark counties. To Holly's great alarm, his ranches would lie within the southern border of this brave new land. The county seat, of course, would be Cascade, a sleepy burg of four hundred souls with no electricity on the left bank of the Missouri thirty miles downstream from Holly's home ranch. Cascade's merchants had formed a "county club" and pooled together $3,000 to finance the effort. Montana law dictated that the borders of any new county must enclose property whose assessed value was at least $3 million. Because their first map fell $400,000 short of that figure, the boosters were compelled to redraw it.

They contracted with a Scottish immigrant named Dan McKay to organize hucksters to convince 51 percent of the property owners to sign a petition asking the legislature to declare their independence from Helena and Great Falls. What they thought they would be getting were lower taxes, more responsive government, and less distance traveled to transact business with the new county. In fact, for years their taxes would have escalated for what seemed to Holly and the Lewis and Clark

County commissioners an obvious reason: a new county requires a new courthouse, a new jail, new schools, and all of the expensive employees required to run a new government.

At first it appeared that the County Club had won the day. Although they needed the signatures of only forty-four assessed property owners on their petition, they had managed to collect fifty-five. Upon closer examination it was determined that nine of these signers owned no property, and their names were stricken. Before the petition was submitted, Holly and the owner of the fifty-four-thousand-acre Gillette Ranch on the Dearborn River jumped on their horses and made a frantic dash from one ranch to another warning that "The taxes are coming!" They convinced thirty-two other stockmen to revoke their signatures. But McKay and his men went on the offensive again, turning thirteen of these revocations around. It wasn't enough. In the end the County Club could only come up with twenty-seven valid signatures, and the measure went down in flames.[7]

Like many prosperous men, Holly dabbled in politics. In August 1904 he was chosen to represent his Wolf Creek precinct as a delegate to the state Republican Convention, which was held a few days later in Billings.[8] It was there he applauded a speech by George Irwin, the convention's chairman, who railed against the Democratic Party. Repeating Horace Greely's claim that "not every Democrat is a horse thief but every horse thief is a Democrat," Irwin reminded his audience of the other party's historic support for slavery and current support for free trade, which he claimed produced prices for commodities ranging from wheat to copper that weren't even high enough to pay for the cost of their production. The GOP had opposed slavery, advocated protective tariffs on imports competing with American-produced goods and commodities, and adopted the gold standard, which tied the value of paper currency to the federal government's gold bullion reserves. Among the GOP's many accomplishments, Irwin crowed, were the purchase of Alaska, free rural mail delivery, the defeat of Spain and the liberation of Cuba and the Philippines from "autocracy," and the "perfection" of the public school system. Not only that, he continued, the GOP has "encouraged the worship of God, elevated the people to a high moral standard, [and] civilized the native Indians, educated them and made of them thrifty and deserving citizens."[9]

Four years later Holly was nominated for Sheriff, along with two other men, as the Lewis and Clark County GOP held its convention at the Auditorium in Helena.[10] On the first ballot it was Higgins, ninety-one; Travis, fifty-eight; and Herrin, forty. Holly was handed his hat after the second ballot when he received only 20 votes to 110 for Higgins and 59 for Travis.[11] Still a loyal Republican, Holly served as a county election judge for the Fifty-First Precinct the following November, when Martin L. Higgins won the sheriff's race.

In 1912 Woodrow Wilson won the White House. And his fellow Democrats swept most of the elected offices in Montana. Joseph M. Dixon, the incumbent U.S. senator and a member of Teddy Roosevelt's Progressive Party, was beaten by Thomas J. Walsh, a Democrat elected with a plurality of the votes cast in the Montana Legislature (this was a year before the Seventeenth Amendment mandated that senators be chosen by direct vote). Unfortunately for Holly, that was the year he finally saw his name on a ballot, as he ran in a crowded field for one of the five seats representing Lewis and Clark County at the thirteenth session of the Montana House of Representatives. He stressed his respect for majority rule by pledging to vote for whichever U.S. Senate candidate won Montana's otherwise meaningless popular vote. And he parroted the Republican support for protective tariffs.

In the end, however, he finished eleventh in a field of twenty. Although he polled better than most of the five Socialist and five Progressive candidates, he got fewer votes than one of the Progressives. Because the Montana Legislature meets every two years in January, serving in the session has always appealed to politically inclined farmers and stockmen. Winter is their slowest season, and spending three months in the hotels, restaurants, and watering holes of the capital city, with its many legislative capers and intrigues, was far more appealing than enduring a long, tedious, and snowbound winter on the farm. Still, Holly would never run for any kind of office again.[12]

To operate Holly's burgeoning agricultural empire he employed twenty-one men, all of whom lived on Herrin land. These were immigrant farm workers from Scotland, Romania, Germany, and Belgium, plus Americans hailing mostly from the Midwest. Due to electrification, improved farm machinery, and custom crews employed on a contract basis to shear sheep and harvest grain, by 1920 Holly needed only six men, one of whom was a fifty-two-year-old Chinese servant named Won Young, hired to help Mary around the house. Another man, Dan George, a Romanian sheepherder, had been working for Holly for more than a decade. But Holly would lose him as well.

George was arrested in early May 1921 for attacking a fellow sheep-herder named Charles Ortman with a hammer in one hand and a hatchet in the other on Holly's Holter Lake ranch. After he knocked Ortman unconscious he was restrained by Holly's other men. George was charged with first degree assault and thrown in jail. At his trial on May 18 in Lewis and Clark District Court, George testified, through a Romanian interpreter provided by his court-appointed attorney, that Ortman started the fight, and that he, George, was simply defending himself. Ortman showed the jury the scars still healing on his head. Holly testified for the prosecution. Although the twelve jurors were presented with testimony from several eyewitnesses, they remained dead-locked after thirty hours of deliberation (as was the custom at the time, their names were published in the *Helena Independent*). After Judge A. J. Horsky ordered them to try again, they came back after dinner on May 22 with a verdict of guilty. George was sentenced to six months in the county jail and fined $150.

The *Independent* reported George's attack as not an isolated event, but as part of a pattern of "Romanian blood lust." As proof of this "thirst for gore" the newspaper cited the case in July 1920 of a Romanian sheep-herder who killed a herder from another outfit on Granite Butte, twenty miles west of Holly's spread, in a dispute over grazing. The Romanian, Mike Berzan, thirty, was accused of body slamming Tom Miley, between sixty and seventy years old, then jumping on his ribs until breaking most of them and forcing the fractured bones into the older man's lungs and

The Oxbow Ranch

Land holdings in 1921,
when it was called the Holly Herrin Ranch

N

ONE MILE

Sentinel
Rock
Ranch

Wolf Creek

Little Prickly Pear Creek

Lyons Creek

to Helena

MAP 2. Oxbow Ranch, 1921. Created by author.

outward through his skin. Berzan was "a young giant in strength" and Miley weighed 102 pounds, or maybe 125, according to whichever newspaper account you read. Miley apparently fought back, causing bleeding wounds to Berzan's scalp. Berzan reportedly held these dripping wounds over Miley's face, ordering him to open his mouth. "Since you tried to kill me you must drink my blood," Berzan reportedly exclaimed. (Romania, of course, was the home of the Transylvanian vampire, Count Dracula.)

A jury found Berzan guilty of manslaughter and sentenced him to six months to a year in the state penitentiary at Deer Lodge. The newspaper called it a "creampuff penalty" that encouraged Dan George's Romanian rampage. "When the news got spread around among the 'silent sentinels of the hills'—as a susceptible poetess from the east was inspired to describe sheepherders—the Rumanians [sic] were lifted up in their zeal to emulate the traditions of their country across the Atlantic, and started to cut, slash, shoot and bludgeon at will." The paper went on, without citing any evidence, that the violence became so extreme some of the flockmasters in Lewis and Clark County armed themselves with shotguns and ordered their Romanian sheepherders off the range.[13] There's no indication that Holly was one of them.

The animus toward Romanians in particular and immigrants in general increased after the war as Americans circled the wagons and tried to cut themselves off from the rest of the world. High tariffs on foreign goods were just one result of this burgeoning xenophobia. The Immigration Act of 1924 barred immigrants from Asia and put quotas on the rest of the Eastern Hemisphere based on 2 percent of the U.S. population from each country as recorded in 1890. As a result, this legislation penalized Italians, Jews, Poles, Romanians, and other Slavs, resulting in an 80 percent reduction of immigrants arriving before World War I. The provisions of the act were so restrictive that in 1924 more Italians, Czechs, Yugoslavs, Greeks, Lithuanians, Hungarians, Poles, Portuguese, Romanians, Spaniards, Chinese, and Japanese left the United States than arrived as immigrants. There was marginal congressional opposition to the bill. Montana's two senators and two congressmen voted for it, and it was supported by both the trade unions and the Ku Klux Klan.[14]

Fear of foreigners had been growing in Lewis and Clark County years before the much-publicized depredations of "Rumanian" sheep-herders. In July 1917 an Afghani restaurateur named Khuja Khan was arrested on suspicion of arson after several buildings in Holly's home village of Wolf Creek burned to the ground on a hot night in July. The Wilson Hotel & Saloon, the American Hotel & Grill, another saloon, a barber shop, and a pool hall went up in flames. After fire broke out in the woodshed adjoining the American Hotel, a rooming house that Khan was leasing from the Holter Dam Company, it quickly spread to the six upstairs bedrooms of the two-story wooden structure. Although every room was occupied, there was only one fatality—an unidentified "foreign laborer" whose charred bones were found the next morning in the rubble. As the fire raced up the stairs to the second floor, a waiter named Ernest Blix was awakened by cries of "Fire!" from down in the street and realized that he was trapped. Passed out drunk on the floor of the room he shared was a Holter Dam construction worker from Austria named Matt Saberine. As fire began consuming the door of their room, Blix dragged Saberine to the window and threw him out, saving his life but fracturing the man's pelvis. His face blistered by the flames, Blix then followed Saberine out through the window. As the fire jumped to the other buildings on Main Street a bucket brigade of forty people tried to contain the inferno. Women waded up to their knees into Little Prickly Pear Creek and handed buckets of water to men on the bank. The general store was saved because one hundred comforters from the shelves were soaked with water and spread out on the roof.

For some reason Blix was also arrested and thrown into jail with Khan. A bartender had accused Khan of starting the fire because he held a grudge against the whole town and had threatened to "clean up the place" some days before the fire. In fact, Khan was disliked by at least some of the denizens of Wolf Creek. In denying that he had anything to do with the fire, he claimed this animus stemmed from the fact that he was a "Mohammedan" and an "Afghanistan" and was making too much money. He also claimed he had been warned to get out of town, and told by friends that some townspeople wanted to kill him. "What for I want to set fire to house," he pleaded from his jail cell, "when all I own is there?" In fact, he had owned a tamale restaurant in Helena that burned down the previous September, netting him a sizable sum in insurance. However, this money was used to rebuild the restaurant, which he was also managing at the time of the Wolf Creek fire.

Two days after his arrest, Khan was released from jail on a $500 bond put up by two Helena friends. One of the reasons he had been arrested was a rumor that before the fire he had shipped all of his personal belongings from Wolf Creek to Helena. In fact, the bill of lading showed that this shipment contained wieners, bread, and produce left over from the enormous Independence Day celebration at Wolf Creek, where he had sold food to the partygoers from the kitchen of the rooming house. He also discounted questions about why he had been at large on Main Street shortly before the fire broke out by claiming that he had gone into the American Hotel's garden to shoo away a cow that was eating his radishes.

No one ever appeared in court on charges of arson, and the case remains unsolved to this day.[15]

Back in August 1910, Holly had sold twenty-five thousand pounds of wool for 16¾ cents per pound to Elsemann Brothers, merchants at the wool market on Summer Street in Boston, netting him $4,000 (almost $100,000 in 2019 currency).[16] The price of wool over the next decade would make Holly a very rich man. While reinventing himself as a flockmaster, instead of using violence as a business tool, he began to use the courts instead. In 1911 he filed suit in Judge Henry C. Smith's District Court against Sieben & Grimes, a neighboring sheep ranching operation. Between October 5, 1910, and May 12, 1911, Herrin claimed, the defendants repeatedly pastured bands totaling five thousand sheep on land he had bought from the Northern Pacific Railroad despite repeated warnings to cease the practice. In his complaint he alleged that when Henry Sieben and Thomas Grimes drove their woolies to public pastures in the area five miles south of Wolf Creek, he crossed Holly's land—portions of seven-and-a-half sections totaling five thousand acres—consuming $2,000 in "grass and herbage." Sheep, of course, do not respect private property rights, and eat most any plant they might come across. Holly had hired a surveyor to mark the section lines around his property with stakes. During testimony he claimed to have seen three bands of Sieben-Grimes sheep grazing on his land at the same time. Holly's ranch foreman, Roy Wood, gave precisely the same account. During cross-examination the defendants' attorney, E. A. Carlton, accused the plaintiffs of collusion. "You and Mr. Herrin have talked this over in advance a number of times and decided upon what both of you would say, have you not?" Wood, who appeared confused during Carlton's aggressive line of questioning, denied the accusation.[17]

The twelve-man jury ruled in Holly's favor. He was awarded $1,200 in actual damages and $100 in exemplary damages, which are intended to deter others from repeating the act that led to the lawsuit. And the jury granted his request for a permanent injunction to prevent Sieben & Grimes from ever trespassing again. Sieben & Grimes appealed. A year later in *Herrin v. Sieben* the Montana Supreme Court modified the lower court's rulings. In an opinion written by Chief Justice Theodore Brantley the justices cut in half, to $600, the district court's award, recognizing that although Sieben's sheep had caused some "depasturing," this had resulted in no permanent damage. As for the injunction against Sieben & Grimes, the supreme court ordered the district court to find a way for the defendants to cross Herrin's property in order to reach the public grazing land they customarily were entitled to use.[18]

The court's decisions grew out of the open range doctrine, adopted by the Montana Territorial Legislature in 1865, which recognized the importance of free-roaming cattle to the economy of the territory. Under English common law the owners of livestock were required to prevent their animals from damaging the property of others by fencing them in. But in the vast and sparsely populated Montana Territory, this Old-World tradition was turned on its head. Territorial law decreed that if you wanted to keep your neighbors' animals off your property it was your responsibility to fence them out. It was reasoned that because most of the territory was open range, a commons available to everyone, where in theory you could become wealthy raising cattle even though you owned no land, it would be much less expensive for homesteaders and small landowners to fence their places than to erect fences around the open range. (Lawmakers chose to ignore the fact that in the largely treeless eastern and northern parts of the state where timber was scarce, small landowners couldn't afford fencing.)

Although the doctrine could have been applied to Holly Herrin, the court implicitly recognized that it would be impractical for him to fence the enormous tracts of land he began buying in 1907 from the Northern Pacific Railroad, along with his partner, Albert Galen. In addition, although there were forests on this land that could be converted to posts, and the price of barbed wire had dropped significantly since its introduction to Lewis and Clark County in the 1880s, much of the land was mountainous and carved by deep gulches, terrain which made building miles of fences an engineering feat that in 1911 was too expensive, even for Holly. Later, however, he would be compelled to string miles of barbed wire around his property.

The judgment in *Herrin v. Sieben* was riddled with contradiction. It awarded Holly damages for Henry Sieben's trespass and concluded that even though Herrin's land wasn't "inclosed" Sieben should have made himself aware of the property lines. But the court also decided that Sieben had a right to access public land by trespassing on Herrin's land. The problems addressed by this strange ruling were created in the 1860s when Abraham Lincoln, a former railroad attorney, proposed rail lines that would connect the Atlantic states to the Pacific states ("our distant possessions," he said in his third State of the Union address). Lincoln signed the Northern Pacific Railroad charter on July 2, 1864. Unlike the 1862 charter for the Union Pacific Railway, which received 6,400 acres and as much as $48,000 in government bonds for each mile it completed, the Northern Pacific opted for incentives that excluded government money but included forty-six million acres of Federal real estate stretching along its rails from Duluth to Bismarck and on to Oregon. The NP was awarded every other section, usually the odd-numbered sections in townships within a forty-mile corridor on either side of its railroad tracks. In order to pay the line's construction costs, the company sold this land east of the Missouri River for four dollars an acre and west of the river for up to two dollars and sixty cents an acre.

It was the resulting checkerboard pattern of ownership that caused the confrontation between Herrin and Sieben. Holly had purchased the odd-numbered sections 15, 23, 25, 29, 31, 33, and 35 of the hilly forest and grasslands in Township 14 North, Range 4 West, which straddled the Little Prickly Pear Creek.[19] The federal government retained ownership of the even sections abutting these odd sections. Sieben & Grimes owned sections adjacent to both Holly's land and the government's (see map 2). In creating this peculiar and environmentally untenable pattern of land ownership, the federal government failed to grant itself an explicit right-of-way allowing its agents to move between its retained sections by crossing sections it had granted to the railroads.

Theoretically, a federal agent—or Henry Sieben—could have stepped over the northwest corner of a government section, for example, onto the southeast corner of another government section without trespassing on private property. However, in the era predating GPS devices and extensive fencing, he would have to know precisely where this corner lay. Plus, the agent would be forced to violate the air space above this junction. (Montana trespass law is now codified to prohibit "corner-crossing" from one piece of public land to another.) And it's unlikely Sieben's sheep could have been trained to make the leap. (Ownership of the airspace would be at the core of a later Montana Supreme Court decision involving, yet again, the relentlessly litigious Harland Herrin.) Subsequent court rulings have defined "cornering" as an act of trespassing.[20]

In *Herrin v. Sieben* the court recognized the common law tradition whereby a "grantor has no means of access to other lands owned by him except bypassing over the lands granted, a way of necessity is impliedly reserved in his grant." In other words, because access to the public lands was impossible without crossing some part of the odd-numbered sections, an understood "easement by necessity" was reserved by the United States. This easement operated not only in the interests of the government, but also in the interests of citizens who wanted to enter the public land for settlement, timber development, mineral exploration, and grazing. Any contrary view, in the words of the court, would grant to the railroad (and subsequently to Herrin) "a monopoly of all the public lands within the limits of the grant."[21] At first glance this view seems reasonable, according to one analysis, and ignoring the impact of what would be called "the Herrin rule" on long established property rights, the logic is appealing. The public lands in the checkerboard scheme are, after all, completely surrounded by private land, and the private landowner may easily deny the public access. However, other justices in other times disagreed.[22] Several state supreme court decisions reversed and then reinstated the doctrine of easement by necessity. But most jurisdictions have based their decision to uphold Holly by voiding the "Herrin rule" on a landmark U.S. Supreme Court ruling in 1979, *Leo Sheep Co. v. United States.*[23]

Some of the sections of land involved in *Herrin v. Sieben* have reverted from Holly's possession to that of the federal government. They are now controlled by the Bureau of Land Management. As for Henry Sieben, he would prove that living well is the best revenge. He became one of the most successful and accomplished stockmen in Montana, whose heirs are still prominent ranchers, while Holly's fortunes and his family life, as we shall see, would wither.[24]

9

Wool Mania

By the time the United States entered World War I in April 1917 it had become more and more difficult to move around the Upper Missouri River Valley without stepping foot on land that Holly Herrin owned. His empire stretched along the serpentine left bank of the Missouri from the Gates of the Mountains downstream for almost twenty miles toward the village of Craig. It sprawled west from the river for several miles to encompass the last mile of Lyon's Creek. And he also owned the Sentinel Rock Ranch, a stretch of flat, rich bottomland straddling four miles of the Little Prickly Pear Creek from the village of Wolf Creek to the Missouri. This expanse of territory encompassed more than twenty-five thousand acres, nearly thirty-five square miles. Family lore claims that during the height of his sheep operation Holly owned thirteen thousand head. He employed a couple dozen full-time and part-time men to run this huge operation, a workforce that eventually drew the attention of organized labor.

The membership of the Industrial Workers of the World had steadily grown in Montana since it began attempting to recruit copper miners in Butte in 1905. In 1909 it won a free speech fight in Missoula. "One Big Union" socialists and anarchists, who were known as Wobblies, descended on Missoula from all over the country to challenge the Garden City's ordinance prohibiting public speaking on the streets. IWW "jawsmiths" such as Helen Gurley Flynn and Frank Little stood on soapboxes yelling Wobbly slogans and singing Wobbly songs until they were arrested.[1] Radicalized loggers and civil engineers took their places to read from the Declaration of Independence and the Bill of Rights, and they were likewise arrested. Missoula's jail became increasingly crowded and filthy. The prisoners were offered clemency in the mornings, but they refused and demanded jury trials. Finally, after several weeks of this constant agitation, the city council caved, struck down its ordinance, and granted clemency to the radicals.[2]

In July 1917 the Herrin ranches hired a hand named George Stewart, who had moved from Butte after 168 hard-rock copper miners were killed by poisonous gases, fire, and steam in a disaster at the Granite Mountain and Speculator Mines.[3] Within twenty-four hours he was complaining about the food, the hours, and the pay, in an attempt to recruit the other hands into the IWW. When the ranch's managers ordered him to cease, he reportedly threatened to burn Holly's crops. The sheriff was notified. Stewart was arrested and put to work for two months on a Lewis and Clark County chain gang while the authorities tried to figure out how they could deport him to his native Canada.[4]

One of the reasons Holly prospered at Wolf Creek was due the fact that his growing empire bordered the Missouri River, which was fed by numerous streams such as Falls Creek and Little Prickly Pear Creek that meandered through his fields, watering his flocks and herds and producing a vast carpet of grass that fed them. But the river that gave also took away. On the afternoon of April 14, 1908, silt-laden water began gushing from the bottom of the year-old Hauser Dam, a steel and concrete hydroelectric impoundment seventy-five feet high and a quarter mile long anchored to the limestone walls of Bear Tooth Canyon twenty miles upstream from Holly's compound. An employee of the United Missouri River Power Company, which owned the dam, spotted the spill, alerted by a peculiar gurgling sound, and hurried to the nearby powerhouse to warn the thirty workers tending the six turbines inside to run for their lives.[5]

Fifteen minutes later a breach thirty feet wide erupted with a thunderous crash. Six minutes after that, four workmen fleeing across the bridge on top of the dam barely escaped when a three-hundred-foot section in the middle of the structure tore loose. Hurling steel, concrete, and heavy timbers, a wall of water twenty-five feet high surged through the gap and roared into the canyon at ten miles an hour. A frantic phone call was made to the dam's general manager in Helena, who ordered telegrams sent and phone calls made to the towns downstream, warning them of the looming deluge. A Great Northern Railway locomotive roared out of the train yard in Helena bound for Great Falls. Horns blaring, it stopped at every station along the way and spread the news. Men on horseback galloped down the canyon alerting ranchers to move their animals to higher ground.

The wall of water smashed into the southwest corner of the powerhouse, tearing loose stone blocks and tumbling them downstream. The village of Hauser Lake, located on the left bank below the dam, was hit next by the maelstrom. The bunkhouses and boarding house, where many of the company's thirty power plant employees and their families lived, were smashed and swept away along with the commissary and a barn with horses tied inside. Another man who made it across the dam before it collapsed rushed to his house and got there just in time to usher his family to safety. They watched as the maelstrom carried their home down the canyon. At 7:00 p.m. the surge flooded Craig, ten miles downstream from Holly's compound. Within moments the town was completely submerged under twenty feet of water. Thanks to the early warnings, Craig's four hundred residents had fled to safety in the hills, where they spent the night waiting for the waters to recede. The only structure that emerged from the water was the top of a windmill. There was widespread panic among the fifteen thousand residents of Great Falls, sixty miles downstream from the Herrin compound. In an effort to save the Boston and Montana copper smelter on the left bank, a wing dam was hurriedly constructed to force the river away from the facility, and a section of the Black Eagle Dam built upstream from the Great Falls of the Missouri was blown up with dynamite.

Although the twenty-square-mile lake behind Hauser Dam had vanished downstream, when April 16 dawned it was clear that the smelter had never been in any danger. By the time the crest had reached Cascade, thirty miles downstream from the Herrin compound, the deep canyons in the mountains and the wide, meandering floodplain where the Missouri entered the flats had dissipated much of the water's energy. Despite breathless first reports of Craig's complete annihilation, structural damage to the school building, hotel, saloons, shops, and some twenty houses was minimal. However, most everything on the shelves of the Craig Mercantile was ruined, except for the canned goods. The Great Northern Railway depot had been swept off its foundation and deposited on the tracks, and a few frame structures were washed away. Along the flood's course, miles of railroad track were washed out, as well as telegraph and telephone lines. At one point, the river was described as being black with a parade of haystacks, shattered buildings, and livestock. At the six-hundred-acre Seven-Bar-Nine Ranch outside Craig, the Cooper family, including their seven-year-old son, Gary, was notified in time and cleared out before the floodwaters tore across a portion of their property.[6]

Miraculously, it was confirmed that only one person died, a workman whose boat was washed over the dam in the rush of water after the explosions.[7] At least one hundred fifty head of cattle were lost, along with uncounted numbers of horses and sheep. A hundred cows belonging to one of Holly's neighbors at the mouth of Wolf Creek, B. F. Stuckney, were swept away. At the John McGinnis ranch near Craig a beloved bull named General Donovon was drowned. Valued in today's currency at $65,000, he had been raised as a pet on an island in Lake Pend Oreille by a retired general named Warren, who named him after his best friend and taught the animal how to drink milk from a pail. Before he put the bull out to pasture the two had been constant companions.[8]

At least ten ranches along the river reported losing livestock. But the firm of H. J. Herrin and A. J. Galen was not one of them. Although their empire had stretched twenty miles down the left bank the Missouri, they had been compelled to sell 850 acres of low-lying riverfront in 1907 to the Capital City Power Transmission Company for seventy-seven dollars an acre.[9] They didn't have much choice. This land was destined to be flooded by Holter Lake, a reservoir eighteen miles long that would be created when Holter Dam was finally completed, after numerous delays, in 1918. As a result, their herds and flocks were already on high ground when Hauser broke.

Preliminary work on Holter Dam began in December 1907 when workers drilled to locate bedrock on either side of the river. Their construction base, called Camp Holter, was located on land a mile north of ranch headquarters on the left bank, on a parcel Herrin and Galen begrudgingly sold to the United Missouri River Power Company. When Hauser Dam collapsed, the workers fled to safety. But their cabins and equipment were washed away. The camp was quickly put back into operation after the waters receded, and crews returned to work. But not for long.

What happened next was the wind pushed clouds from the west and it started to rain. Thirty-three straight days of rain, from the first week of May until June 10, combined with melting snowpack to swell rivers and streams far above their banks, shut down train service, and cut off electric power and wire communications from one side of Montana to the other. A dozen people died in Eastern Montana flooding. Three feet of water filled the streets of Wolf Creek and Craig. The infrastructure damage in Lewis and Clark County was estimated at $2.75 million in 2019 dollars, a figure that didn't take into account damage to private property, such as the house that was washed away near Wolf Creek and carloads of flour and salt that were washed out of the mercantile.

As soon as the sun came out, the United Missouri River Power Company resumed the reconstruction of Hauser Dam and began construction on Holter Dam. As if the river was fighting for its freedom, the Missouri attacked Hauser Dam again on March 15, 1909. According to one newspaper, it washed out the structure's new coffer dam, flume, wooden framework, and unfinished concrete work, sending debris and a million board feet of lumber hurtling down the canyon.[10] However, two years later the six generators in Hauser's powerhouse began supplying energy to the city of Helena, but most of this electricity was used to power the copper smelters at Anaconda and Great Falls. Because of waning investor confidence and other financial problems, construction on Holter Dam was halted in late 1910, after only part of the concrete foundation had been poured, and wouldn't resume for six years.[11]

During this final phase of construction Camp Holter grew into a town called Holter, home to more than five hundred men and their families. Some 115 buildings were constructed, including bunkhouses and dormitories for unmarried men, cottages for married men and their families, a dining hall, a bathing house, storage sheds, garages, a hospital, photography studio, and a school, which boasted fifteen pupils on opening day in 1917. Despite advice to management that not much in the way of produce would grow here, huge local gardens soon supplied Holter with a constant supply of beans and potatoes.[12] A spur from the main line of the Great Northern railroad at Wolf Creek was laid four miles to the new town. A sewage system was installed, running water was piped into the buildings, and they were electrified. Although most of the structures were tents or shacks intended for short-term use, seven of them were renovated to provide permanent housing for the dam's operators.[13]

It took another two years to finally complete the dam's construction. The electricity Holter began generating in 1918 was used to power the locomotives of two railroad lines—the Butte, Anaconda and Pacific Railway, which the Anaconda Company used to haul copper ore from the Berkeley pit in Butte to its smelter in Anaconda; and the Milwaukee Road, which didn't convert to diesel locomotives until 1974. Holter also electrified what was then called the Holly Herrin Ranch. As a consequence, Holly began to operate what was hailed as of the most up-to-date sheep-shearing operations in the county.[14] Removing the wool from an animal, which had taken a skilled worker using hand blades ten or fifteen minutes, now took the same man only two or three minutes using electric shears.

Electrification at the Herrin ranch arrived just as the demand for American wool reached an all-time high. It was not only clothing shoppers who were driving this lust, it was war. After England began fighting against Germany in 1914, it placed an embargo on the sale of merino wool to the United States, fearing that the New England mills would sell this high-quality fabric to Germany and its allies (until the U.S. declared war on the Central Powers on April 6, 1917, America was officially a neutral power). The resulting shortages of raw material threatened to throw thousands of millworkers out of work. Holly and other Montana stockmen began increasing the sizes of their flocks to meet the demand, which soared after the United States entered the war. For the more than two million men in uniform mustered by the U.S., the standard uniform was made of wool—everything from khaki-colored shirts and great coats to socks, and from the jodhpur-inspired pants issued by the army to the strips of cloth called puttees, which the Doughboys wrapped around their lower legs for added support and protection. American sailors wore a blue wool uniform during the winter.

A week after America's entry into the war, an agreement was reached between the federal government and a committee representing stockmen in Montana and other western states to supply all the raw wool required for the war effort at a price set on April 2 at the wool market on Summer Street in Boston, and locked in place. Representing the Council of National Defense, which was established to coordinate resources for the war, financier Bernard Baruch told growers that in order to clothe American soldiers and sailors the government would require half of the 290-million-pound clip of raw wool expected to be produced in 1917. This figure included "territory" wool, which was grown west of the Mississippi River, and "fleece," which was grown east of the river. Territory wool in 1917 constituted two-thirds of the market. While many Montana growers were selling their clips for forty-seven cents a pound, in May 1917 Holly managed to sell his sixty-five-thousand-pound clip "in the grease" for fifty-two cents a pound, a figure that netted him almost $700,000 in today's currency. (Wool is naturally coated with a wax called lanolin, a fat secreted by the animal's sebaceous glands. Sheep grease, as it was known, makes the animal's coat water repellent. It is used by humans as a skin ointment. Once shorn, wool must be washed to remove dirt and vegetable matter and then scoured with detergent and rinsed with hot water to remove the lanolin before the fiber can be spun into thread and yarn. Holly's sixty-five-thousand-pound clip, once scoured, weighed about thirty thousand pounds.)[15]

His 1918 clip was even more lucrative. By the zenith of America's deployment in Europe, during spring 1918, the federal government had taken complete control of the wool industry. The changes directed by the wool division of the War Industries Board, which operated under the auspices of the Council of National Defense, benefitted growers by paying them a full 75 percent of the gross value of their product. Montana's twenty-five-million-pound clip in 1918 was bought for between fifty-five and sixty cents per pound, netting growers almost $14 million. The government had effectively put out of business most of the middlemen who had paid much less than that to growers in 1917, hucksters who capitalized on the sheepmen's lack of reliable and timely market information. Some of these war profiteers and speculators had made huge profits (one of these men made $7 million buying and selling wool, and never went near a sheep).[16] Dealers certified by the government were limited to a profit of only one and a half cents per pound on small clips and no more than 4 percent on large ones, commissions the government paid. Dealers took possession of the wool cars loaded with Montana wool in the Twin Cities instead of Boston, thus reducing transportation costs. From there it was sent to regional scouring mills and then to textile mills on the East Coast.

Lewis Penwell, a Helena attorney, politician, and wealthy sheep rancher appointed head of the national wool division, told the press that the War Industries Board had decided to commandeer every pound of wool produced in America for the war effort.[17] This critical commodity was used in the manufacture of uniforms, the fabrication of gaskets for engines, the weaving of felt blankets used in paper mills to dry the pulp, and the production of heavy clothing for workers involved in essential wartime industries. The government estimated that for each one of its two million soldiers and sailors, one hundred pounds of scoured wool was required over a twelve-month period to supply these industries.[18] That meant that to clothe and equip one man in uniform for a year required raw fleece from twenty sheep. The lag time between the shearing of an animal and the fabrication of its wool into a garment was six months to a year.

Penwell also announced that the government had ordered manufacturers to halt the sale of knitting yarns except to the Red Cross. "This has been made necessary by the profiteering in yarns," he told a reporter during an interview at the Montana Club, where he was staying during his stopover in Helena. "Manufacturers of $2 yarns have been permitted to market this stock in the usual way and by the time it was sold to women for knitting socks and sweaters for the soldiers it was selling for $4.50 to $5.00 per pound, one of the most flagrant pieces of profiteering we have witnessed during the war."[19]

From 1916 to 1918 the growing demand spawned a wool mania. In summer 1917 the American Red Cross issued an urgent call for 1.5 million each of knitted mitts, mufflers, sweaters, and pairs of socks. The need for socks was critical because soldiers spent weeks or months slogging around wet and frigid trenches wearing boots that leaked and provided no insulation. The result was frostbite and a chronic fungus infection called trench foot. In response, men, women, and children across the United States and Canada took up knitting wool yarn into socks, sweaters, vests, chest covers, head and neck coverings called "wool helmets," and fingerless wristlets designed so soldiers had easy access to triggers. Knitters also produced "stump socks" to cover amputated limbs. The Red Cross issued yarn and patterns, collected the finished goods, and shipped them to Europe. (Knitting was also used as a cover and a medium for spying—consider the little old lady sitting placidly in her rocking chair with her needles and yarn at a window in Belgium, watching the trains bearing German soldiers and armaments roll by, knitting her Morse-coded observations into a wool scarf, which she handed to a fellow spy, risking both their lives.)[20] Soon after America's entry into the war the Bradley Knitting Company of Delevan, Wisconsin, began organizing "sheep clubs" for boys thirteen to seventeen to encourage the production of wool.[21] The idea caught on, and by Christmas 1917 sheep clubs for both boys and girls had sprung up all over the country. Banks and businesses donated money to supply the clubs with ewes. Propaganda posters published by the Department of Agriculture urged Americans to join sheep clubs. The Comforts Committee of the U.S. Navy League summoned patriotic citizens to "knit a bit."[22]

Americans began mobbing the Red Cross for yarn and fabricating garments at a frantic pace. Boys clubs in Missoula sprang up to contribute wool socks to the war effort. Firemen in Great Falls spent their many idle hours knitting. "Yes, some of the boys were slightly inclined to smile when we got our yarn and knitting needles," one fireman told a reporter. "But most of them are getting over that now. They are beginning to realize that a man can be a man and a darned good one and still knit."[23] Butte firemen attacked knitting with the same zeal they attacked a burning building. Operating four knitting machines, four men working in shifts turned out four pairs of socks every forty minutes, 142 pair of socks in twenty-four hours.[24] However, a Missoula pastor told his congregation that "some may think they can bring their knitting to church. Let me tell you that there will be no knitting in this church."[25]

Near the end of the war, wool mania had created what some observers claimed was a wool famine. "No Wool Left for Your Suit," shouted a 1918 headline in a Montana newspaper. The article warned that because wool imports from Australia, New Zealand, and other sheep-growing countries had dried up, there would be no wool from Montana or any other state made into clothing for civilians for the next year and a half, "until a sufficient amount of tonnage is put upon the sea to care for both the government war requirement and for the usual needs of civilian life for woolen clothing."[26] The fact or fiction of the famine had been debated at a U.S. Senate committee hearing. Some witnesses charged the management policies of the Council of National Defense for a shortage of one million yards of cloth, citing manufacturers who reported that they couldn't get enough wool cloth to keep their workers employed full time. Many looms, it was argued, had been idle for three months. However, a dealer testified that the wool "scare" had been fabricated by manufacturers who wanted to sell the government more "shoddy," which is a lower quality fabric composed of virgin wool mixed with shredded recycled wool and sometimes other fibers, such as cotton.[27]

FIG. 5. Thomas Harland Herrin, 1913. Courtesy of the Molly Burke Herrin Estate.

FIG. 6. Marie Clinkenbeard Herrin, 1913. Courtesy of the Molly Burke Herrin Estate.

Wool shortage or not, the war was a bonanza for Holly's ranches. While he was making a fortune doing business with the government, his sole heir, Thomas Harland Herrin, had been excused from serving in the armed forces because he claimed an exemption based on his dependent wife and child. In 1913 he had married Marie Clinkenbeard, the strikingly beautiful seventeen-year-old daughter of a Great Falls photographer.[28] The first of their five sons, Harland Sanford, was three years old when his father was issued a draft card in summer 1917. Thomas's appeal for exemption was not impeded by the fact that Holly's business associate and lifelong friend, Albert Galen, was head of the Selective Service Board for the First Congressional District.

Holly's income continued to grow, providing him a stream of capital to invest in real estate. As the drought that began in 1917 worsened, he began shopping for irrigated land in the Helena Valley. In July 1919 he bought the M. H. Gerry ranch north of Lake Helena for $36,000, a property that included two hundred acres of watered alfalfa. In winter 1920 he moved 4,500 head of sheep and 500 head of cattle to this ranch, where he fed them the hay he had grown there that summer.

For Holly, it seemed as if life couldn't get much better. Except for one thing: once you've built an empire you have to figure out a way to defend it. So he began building walls—those you could see, and those you couldn't.

10

The Water Below and the Air Above

Along the Missouri during the last days of summer 1924 the streams swarmed with fish and the air with ducks. On some of these mornings a denizen of Wolf Creek named William Sutherland stowed his shotgun and fishing gear into his rowboat and ordered his retrievers on board. Drifting down Little Prickly Pear Creek into the Missouri below Holter Dam, it didn't take him long to fill his creel with trout and stuff his game bag with teal and canvasbacks fetched by his dogs. For Sutherland, living off the land was easy.

At least it was until the second day of October. That's when Holly Herrin filed a lawsuit against him in Lewis and Clark County District Court. Although Sutherland would be tangled in legal problems for the next two years, he had not broken any game laws. He had dutifully bought a hunting and fishing license. He was hunting ducks in season, which began on September 16. He did not violate the rule about using a shotgun more powerful than a 10-guage. He fished with a pole held in his hands (it was illegal to use nets, explosives, or multiple set lines). He did not take more than the twenty ducks and forty fish per day the regulations allowed.[1]

What got him into hot water was Holly's belief that these fish and waterfowl were not Sutherland's to take because they belonged to Holly, and that in stealing this bounty between August 3 and September 18 he had trespassed on Holly's property and damaged it. In a litany of grievances, Holly presented the Honorable A. J. Horsky with eight allegations. On September 18 Sutherland rowed his boat down the Little Prickly Pear Creek to the Missouri, alternately catching fish, then shooting ducks floating on the water or flying above it. After mooring his boat above the highwater mark Sutherland trampled on native and planted grasses on Holly's Sentinel Rock farm, broke down a section of five-foot barbed wire fence posted with no hunting-no trespassing signs, then destroyed some of Holly's hay and grain. Holly contended that because he owned the land on both banks of the Little Prickly Pear, he also owned everything in the stream, everything below it, and everything above. His assertion was backed by an 1895 Montana law, which is still on the books, that grants landowners possession of not just the land, but everything above and below it, the so-called heaven-to-hell doctrine.[2]

He also contended that Sutherland waded up and down Falls Creek on Holly's "home ranch" above Holter Dam—the site of his house, barn, and outbuildings—destroying hay and willows. He accused Sutherland of discharging a shotgun over his dwellings and cattle on the home ranch. Finally, Holly accused Sutherland of taking "a large number" of fish from a pond and killing wild ducks "which had been hatched in water courses" on Herrin's land, and which Holly had personally fed and protected by killing predators. Holly demanded that Sutherland pay him between $2.50 and $25 for each infraction, for a total of $107.50.[3] However, it wasn't this paltry sum Herrin sought in his suit, it was the precedent. Seeing himself as a hero of the landed class, Holly eventually dropped his demands for compensation in order to safeguard the purity of his cause.

In his defense, Sutherland argued that the old English common law barring hunters from trespassing on private property doesn't apply in Montana. Hunters can go wherever they please, he told the court. But Judge Horsky was having none of it. He ruled in Holly's favor on all eight counts of the lawsuit and awarded him one dollar. Sutherland hired a Great Falls attorney named Gerald Frary and appealed to the Montana Supreme Court. Holly was represented by E. G. Toomey, a prominent

Helena attorney who was chief counsel for the Montana Railroad and Public Service Commission but, like most lawyers in the West during the 1920s, took on all kinds of cases.[4]

Filed during summer 1925, *Herrin v. Sutherland* was seen as "one of the most important questions to be presented to the state supreme court in many months and one of the most novel in years."[5] In fact, the issue of the rights of land owners versus those of hunters and fishermen (and later recreationists) would evolve over the coming decades, but had never been codified into Montana law and had never been adjudicated. The conflict was inevitable. Although still sparsely settled in 1924, Montana's population had quadrupled that year from 142,924 in 1889, the year of its admittance as a state. "Who owns the fish and game?" the Associated Press asked. "After fish have been planted by the state can they be claimed by any one man? If all the people own the birds and trout, can farmers post their land and keep off hunters and anglers?"[6] One newspaper claimed that the printing and filing of the brief was paid for by the Montana Department of Fish and Game.[7]

In a unanimous decision handed down on November 24, 1925, the Montana Supreme Court upheld the lower court on all eight counts. The opinion was written by Chief Justice J. J. Callahan. "The owner of land through which a stream passes owns the bed of the stream if it is not a navigable stream [Falls Creek] and has the exclusive right to the fish in the stream which such fish are in the waters within his land. If the stream is navigable [Little Prickly Pear Creek] the owner of the land owns everything above the low water mark." The court further determined that anyone who enters a property owner's land without permission, or wades or floats on unnavigable water between the property owner's land, is a trespasser subject to prosecution. "It would seem clear that a man has no right to fish where he has no right to be," Callahan wrote. Finally, it concluded that the defendant was also trespassing when he fired over Holly's house, thus "interfering with the quiet, undisturbed, peaceful enjoyment of the plaintiff."[8]

Hunters and anglers were horrified. In 1925 Montana was still a place where many families depended on wild fish and game and whatever food they could raise in their gardens during the short growing season. Sportsmen campaigned the state game commission to appeal *Herrin v. Sutherland* to the Ninth Circuit Court of Appeals. One consequence of the ruling, they argued, was that the state government practice of planting fry in creeks on private land would have to cease.[9] But what the anglers were really concerned about was being denied access to their favorite trout streams.

Judge Calloway tried to reassure them. In an address to the Missoula Rod and Gun Club he explained that while it is true under Montana's laws, which are rooted in English common law, that the bed of a non-navigable stream belongs to the property owner, and walking along its banks or wading in its waters without his permission constitutes trespassing. However, even if the land is posted with no trespassing signs, this is not criminal trespass, but civil. To secure a remedy the property owner must hire an attorney and file a lawsuit, just as Herrin had done. On the other hand, a hunter who steps foot on private property without permission or fires a bullet that lands on private property he doesn't own is guilty of the misdemeanor of criminal trespass and is subject to fines and even imprisonment. The reason for the difference, he said, is simple. Montana's statutes address hunting, but not fishing.

However, Callahan added, "I do not think it is lawful for a landowner to prohibit a fisherman or hunter from getting across his lands to fish in public waters or hunt upon public land, if the fisherman or hunter has no other way to reach the waters or the lands. In such case it is the duty of the sportsman to ask permission of the landowner to cross, to ask the landowner to designate the way he desires the sportsman to follow and then, if the land owner denies the privilege, the sportsman may cross anyhow, giving due consideration to the rights of the landowner and avoiding doing him any damage." Callahan told the group that landowners will usually be generous, and most sportsmen considerate. "Friction between gentlemen," he said, "is easily avoided."[10]

His faith in the power of good manners was optimistic. Although their acreage had been stolen from the tribes, many white landowners before and after *Herrin v. Sutherland* regarded their land as fiefdoms they must defend against hostile neighbors and landless peasants. In some cases, as William Sutherland demonstrated, this paranoia was justified. In 1894 a man named William Kelly announced his claim to land whose deed was owned by another man. This was a six-hundred-foot strip of gently sloping shoreline on the left bank of the Missouri River in Chouteau County between the high-water mark and the low-water mark. The deed holder was Charles S. Gibson, a mine owner, former sheep rancher, and nephew of Paris Gibson, a U.S. senator and entrepreneur credited by some as the founder of Great Falls, Montana. In an act of peculiar bravado, Kelly barred Gibson from setting foot on this strip, which he said Gibson could not own because it was situated in its entirety below the Missouri's high-water flood stage. Gibson sued to eject the intruder. The Chouteau County District Court determined that Kelly's defense of his claim lacked merit, and ruled for Gibson.

Kelly employed a prominent Great Falls lawyer named Ransom Cooper to file an appeal. In January 1895 Cooper argued before the Montana Supreme Court that under English common law private property could only extend to the high-water mark of a navigable stream because the streambed was public property owned by the state. He cited numerous U.S. Supreme Court decisions that supported this argument. He reminded the jurists that Montana had adopted English common law as the basis of its legal system.[11]

However, a month later the Montana court held that although "the public [has] certain rights of navigation and fishery upon the river and upon the strip in question" Gibson indeed owned everything down to the low-water mark. Reversing the normal order of legal events, in which laws are passed and then challenged in court, the justices rationalized their ruling by citing the fact that different states had enacted both low-water and high-water as land title boundaries, the low-water mark for ownership would soon be in force in Montana as a result of statutes passed by the 1895 state legislature.[12] Although the ruling ejected the trespasser from Kelly's land, the much more far-reaching effect of the Supreme Court's decision lay in its lack of reasoning. It was unclear how it and the legislature could concede to riparian landowners what otherwise, under English common law, is public property.[13]

Herrin v. Sutherland did nothing to settle the issue. While seven of the eight actions cited in Holly's complaint involved clear acts of trespassing, the ruling involving one of them, Sutherland's wading of Falls Creek, was confusing. Did the Court hold that Sutherland was simply a trespasser because he trampled vegetation, or did the court hold that he trespassed by wading and fishing in a non-navigable stream?[14] The lack of clarity about who owns Montana's streams, their navigability, and who has access to them would confound lawmakers and law enforcers for another six decades. That is, until the issue was forced by a prominent and cantankerous member of the landowning class that was a major player in the brief history of nonindigenous people in Montana. This was Dennis Michael Curran—the nephew of Brian O'Connell, Mary O'Connell Herrin's youngest brother. In the late 1970s Curran announced to the world that he owned the Dearborn River.[15]

Holly Herrin's sure and swift reaction to Sutherland's trespass was informed by his experience a few years earlier with another outside force attempting to interfere with his "enjoyment." In that case, the interloper wasn't some lone sportsman. It was the federal government.

11

In the Grease

The fourteen-month period from August 1917 to November 1918 marked the first time the U.S. government attempted to control the production and prices of commodities. Before stabilization measures were put in place, speculators and profiteers had jacked up prices by exploiting increased demand generated by American prosperity, relatively high wages, and the war in Europe. Commodity prices were rising at an unnatural rate, and producers were unable to count on a reliable supply chain. "In normal times a rising price carries with it its own defeat," a 1921 report from the War Industries Board observed. "Purchasers will buy so long as they can make a profit. . . . But war is economically the greatest and the most scandalous of spendthrifts. No economic profit comes from the expenditure of an instrument of war and no economic profit is considered in connection with its purchase. The demand is absolute; the price is no deterrent."[1]

The annual consumption of raw wool in the United States increased from 450 million pounds in 1913 to 750 million pounds in 1918. Holly and other American growers were annually producing less than 40 percent of this total. The rest of it was imported, much of it from Australia and New Zealand. But in 1916 that supply dried up. Great Britain had contracted to buy every pound of wool produced by these future commonwealth partners for the duration of the war, and imposed an embargo to guarantee that it went nowhere else. However, in late 1917 the Crown bowed to American pressure and allowed some of the raw wool from Down Under to be shipped to the United States. Concerns about supplies became more acute as German submarines continued to disrupt Allied shipping (some 5,000 Allied ships were sunk, sending 1.4 million tons of cargo to the ocean floor). Speculators began hoarding woolen cloth. As a consequence of fears about future shortages, prices paid to growers rose 65 percent during the first half of 1917. But speculation and inflation in the market ended abruptly when the federal government took complete control of all raw wool in April 1918 and fixed the prices to growers at their July 30, 1917, levels, determined by those paid that day on the Boston wool exchange. Private traders competing with the government for wool produced in South America and South Africa were denied licenses, thus giving a syndicate sanctioned by the War Department complete control of purchases from those markets. The government also bought the entire U.S. supply of lanolin, at sixteen cents a pound.

The war ended before the War Industries Board predicted it would. As a result, the federal government found itself in possession of 313 million pounds of raw wool it no longer needed or wanted. Because no virgin wool had been available for civilian use since early summer 1918, cloth manufacturers had been using so much shoddy that the government was compelled to fix prices for that material, as well, in order to protect consumers. And it appointed a rag administrator, A. L. Gifford, to oversee the cost and distribution of this recycled fiber. It was finally decided that in order to avoid flooding the market with its huge stockpile of virgin wool and undercutting flockmasters like Holly, the government would auction off its surplus from time to time after the 1919 domestic clip had been sold. It instructed auctioneers to refuse any bid lower than the basement price it had established.

Even so, the postwar wool market was wobbly. First, there was a brief, seven-month recession in the global economy that began during the final days of the war. This was followed by a much more serious economic slow-down that dragged on from January 1920 until July 1921. Wholesale prices fell almost 37 percent, the most precipitous drop since the Revolutionary War. There was a decline in the gross national product, and an increase in unemployment as the economy strained to find jobs for returning servicemen. The Dow-Jones Industrial Average reached a peak of 119.6 on November 3, 1919, two months before the recession began. The market bottomed out on August 24, 1921, at 63.9, a decline of 47 percent.

But Holly had been lucky—or prescient. In May—two months before the mini-recession hit—he sold his entire 1919 clip for fifty-six cents a pound, a price in keeping with those of the previous two years. However, by the first days of summer in 1920, the wool market collapsed. Buyers in May had paid as much as sixty-five cents a pound for wool in the grease. On June 22 the price had dropped to twenty-one cents, and most buyers were not interested in purchasing Holly's clip or anyone else's, even at that level. He decided to warehouse his wool in Boston rather than sell it. Even at thirty-one cents a pound, which was offered from time to time in 1920, it cost him more than that to produce his wool. Some analysts blamed the falling demand for clothing on high retail costs and poor quality. Some growers blamed the federal government for first promising not to flood the economy with its huge stocks of wool, then turning around and doing just that. In fact, from January 1919 to October 1920, the war department dumped more than six hundred thousand pounds of wool on the market, charging buyers a whopping sixty-six cents a pound. Most of this surplus was foreign wool stockpiled in anticipation of a much longer war requiring a mammoth inventory of uniforms, blankets, and underwear for four million American soldiers and sailors.[2]

Some stockmen reduced the size of their flocks by selling their sheep for mutton. Others simply went out of business. Prices paid to the growers of other farm commodities plummeted, as Europe rebuilt its economies and closed its markets to American goods. In mid-1920 wheat sold for two dollars and fifty cents a bushel. By the end of 1921 that price had fallen to one dollar and nine cents.[3] In 1919 the potato crop yielded farmers eight dollars and thirty-five cents a hundredweight, dropping a year later to as low as eighty-five cents, a ruinous deflation of 90 percent (growers blamed exorbitant freight rates imposed in 1919, compelling them to withhold their crop, which then saturated the market a year later when shipping became cheaper).[4] Wool yarn plummeted from three dollars and twenty-five cents a pound in 1919 to one dollar and eighty-five cents. The price of pharmaceutical cocaine dropped from fifteen dollars to five dollars an ounce.

Adding to Holly's financial challenges in 1919 was the fact that the Franklin Model 9-B Touring Car he was keeping for winter visits to Helena in the Central Garage downtown was destroyed, along with thirty other cars, when a fire broke out. He replaced it with a brand-new Cadillac, which wouldn't be delivered to Helena until 1920 because of the shortage of new vehicles following the end of the war.[5] There were widespread cries from farmers and stockmen pleading with the government to impose higher tariffs and even embargos on foreign commodities, in order to prevent them from entering the American economy. Most everyone who remained in the wool market was waiting until after the November elections to see if these demands would be met.[6]

Holly, however, waited for no man. Even after he threw himself into the wool business in 1907, he continued to raise cattle and other commodities, wary of becoming dependent on only one stream of income. After the roundup in 1918 he shipped nine carloads of cattle, along with two cars of sheep, to slaughterhouses in Chicago. In October 1920 he was the first customer to use the new stockyards built by the Great Northern Railroad on the siding at Wolf Creek, where he loaded five carloads of sheep and ten carloads of cattle on a train bound for Chicago. He then boarded the train himself, looking forward to closing the sale in person and taking in the sights of the big city. Earlier that year he hired a crew to put up fifteen miles of fence around portions of his land. In September 1921 he sold five carloads of potatoes grown on his farm at Sentinel Rock. That year he also sold 54,000 pounds of wool that he had warehoused in Boston the year before for thirty-three cents a pound, netting him almost $18,000 ($450,000 in today's currency). Throughout the war and the Roaring Twenties, he hired threshing crews to harvest his extensive wheat fields every September. In February 1921 he even sold blocks of pristine ice cut from Holter Lake to the hotel in Wolf Creek. He had become such a prominent figure in the ranch business that in spring 1922 he was called to testify as an expert witness in a trial to determine whether two Brady, Montana, flockmasters had entered into a business partnership or not.[7] In 1922 he served as one of three dozen paid members of the board of directors of the Montana Life Insurance Company, which was founded eleven years earlier to compete with the four big national insurance companies, promoting itself by claiming that because of its local municipal security investments it was keeping Montana money in Montana.[8]

Meanwhile, he networked by volunteering and joining clubs (at the time it was called making connections). He served as an election judge and a member of the Wolf Creek school board. He became a Shriner. And an Elk. And a member of the Woodmen of the World.[9] In the years after he was initiated in a secret ceremony by "walking across the burning sands," he gathered for fun and fellowship with his fellow Shriners at the Algeria Shrine Temple. Now the Helena Civic Center, this is an enormous Moorish Revival building with an arched façade and a minaret designed by Link and Haire, Helena architects who were inspired by the great mosques of the Muslim world.[10] In 1926 he was elected "watchman" of the Woodmen's First Montana Camp (the Helena chapter). In 1928 he was elected "advisor" and was also selected as a delegate to the state convention in Bozeman. Some Woodmen "camps" initiated new members by forcing them to "ride the goat." This was a mechanical goat, much like the mechanical bulls in cowboy bars, that finally bucked off the initiate, then fired blanks at him emitted from its butt.

Courthouse lawyers must have smiled whenever they heard the name H. J. Herrin. Throughout the war and into the 1920s he continued to hire lawyers to file lawsuits, although none of the cases were as famous as *Herrin v. Sutherland* or *Herrin v. Sieben.* And other parties continued to sue him. In 1917 the federal government asked for damages in its claim that Herrin had cut nine thousand board feet of timber of government land and sold it. In March 1921 he sued the Great Northern Railroad for $2,990 in damages resulting from "needless delay" in shipping six cars of his cattle to market in Chicago. (This was the second occurrence of

Herrin v. Great Northern. In 1910 he alleged that because the company had failed to install proper cattle guards, one of its trains killed several Herrin cows that had wandered onto the tracks near Wolf Creek.) In 1922 he was sued by a neighboring rancher, John C. Fletcher, who wanted $1,000 and a permanent injunction to prevent Holly from ever running his sheep on Fletcher's land again. A week later Fletcher was charged with building an illegal fence across a public road on his ranch along Lyons Creek, next to Holly's land. He was arrested and posted a $200 bond.[11]

After the Republican landslide in November a protective tariff measure was passed by both the House and the Senate. But before he left office in March 1921, Woodrow Wilson, a Democrat, vetoed the bill. Democrats were not opposed to tariffs, as long as they were set low enough to generate some revenue without antagonizing America's trading partners. But Republicans wanted to build a wall around America with duties raised high enough to keep cheap foreign commodities out of the U.S. market entirely. They were especially concerned about the flood of wheat entering the United States from Canada. After Warren G. Harding took office, the Emergency Tariff Act was revived, passed again by both Houses, and signed into law by the president in May 1921. It imposed a fifty-cent-per-bushel tax on foreign wheat. Like wool, wheat had entered the United States duty-free since 1913, years when the federal government was controlled by Democrats. The new emergency tariff taxed raw wool at fifteen cents a pound, washed wool at thirty cents, and scoured wool at forty-five cents. Since most raw Montana wool was selling for a mere fifteen to twenty cents a pound in 1921, the tariff amounted to an actual embargo. By June virtually no foreign wool entered the U.S. market (although part of this stoppage was due to the fact that importers had rushed to fill their warehouses before the new tariffs went into effect).

In 1922 the Fordney-McCumber Tariff was passed to levy permanent duties on foreign commodities. Although the act lowered the tariff on scoured wool to thirty-one cents a pound, high tariffs were kept in place on many other commodities. In retaliation, America's European trading partners raised their own tariffs, effectively barring many U.S. products from their markets. France jacked up automobile duties from 45 percent to 100 percent, Spain raised its taxes on American goods by 40 percent, and Germany and Italy increased their tariffs on wheat, America's most lucrative export. According to the American Farm Bureau, between 1922 and 1927 farmers lost more than $300 million annually as a result. From 1922 to 1926 farm bankruptcies in Montana, the Dakotas, and Wyoming increased more than 70 percent, the highest rate for any section of the nation.[12] But these figures didn't include significant numbers of farmers who simply turned their assets over to their creditors and walked away rather than suffering the humiliation of court proceedings. Because farmers couldn't repay their loans, and couldn't buy much of anything, between 1921 and 1925 half of the state's 428 banks closed.[13]

Henry Ford blamed the crisis on the farmer. "The record number of farm bankruptcies and mortgage foreclosures may be taken as an indication of the bad state of farming, or again, it may be taken as an indication that money has been unwisely borrowed. A farmer does not plow with money." He argued that farmers were clinging to inefficient methods of operation such as using plow horses when they could be using Ford tractors (which, of course, most farmers would have to borrow money to buy). An avowed anti-Semite and an early admirer of Adolf Hitler, Ford was an advocate of "industrial farming." He scolded the family farmers for their expectation of making money from what amounted to a part-time job. "The real problem of farming is to find something in addition to farming for the farmer to earn a living at."[14]

The last thing in the world Holly needed was a job. Throughout the 1920s he continued to make money hand over fist as a farmer and a stockman. In May 1922 he pooled his raw wool with that of a flockmaster from Malta, Montana, named Ben Phillips. They sold their combined clip of 244 thousand pounds to the American Woolen Company for forty-one cents a pound, netting them more than $100,000 (almost $1.5 million in today's currency). The company asked the stockmen to keep details of this lucrative deal to themselves, which they did. But a newspaper extracted the information from "an authoritative source."[15]

The American Woolen Company was the largest wool cloth manufacturer in the United States, producing 21 percent of America's output at sixty New England mills powered by water and steam. Using his father-in-law's wealth, owner William M. Wood had cobbled together eight financially distressed mills in the late 1800s into what he called "The Woolen Trust" and updated them with technological improvements that reduced the need for skilled labor. Like Henry Ford, Wood was an efficiency fanatic and hated unions, especially after 1912.

In winter of that year, workers at his four mills in Lawrence, Massachusetts, went out on strike, demanding higher wages. Most of these employees were unskilled immigrant women from forty nations, and children under the age of fourteen. When the textile unions refused to organize them—and attempted to convince them to return to work—the International Workers of the World stepped in. The "Bread and Roses Strike" lasted two months (the name was taken from a poem: "Hearts starve as well as bodies; give us bread, but give us roses!"). Unarmed workers on picket lines were confronted by militiamen brandishing bayonets. After workers began sending their hungry children to live with affluent supporters in other cities—a brilliant public relations tactic that earned the strikers widespread sympathy—police responded by clubbing woman and children at the Lawrence train station. Two months into the strike Wood caved in and met all the workers' demands. Wages were increased as much as 20 percent. Alarmed, the other textile companies followed suit.[16]

For years Holly was able to closely follow the affairs of American Woolen, William Wood, and the wool industry, thanks to extensive coverage published in Montana's newspapers, which were the sole source of information in the state until the beginning of regular radio news broadcasts in the late 1920s. In 1919 he read about the development of yet another strike against the Wool Trust in Lawrence. Again, unskilled, immigrant loom operators walked out after their hours and pay were cut. The "54-48 Strike" lasted five months. The IWW, which had lost favor because of its opposition to the war, was replaced by organizers from the more conservative American Federation of Labor. But the outcome was the same. Wood was forced to the bargaining table, where he agreed to pay for fifty-four hours of work to employees who were allowed by a new law to work no more than forty-eight hours a week.

On May 27, 1920, Holly's attention was riveted by the news that William Wood and American Woolen had been indicted by a federal grand jury in New York City for profiteering. The indictment cited fourteen violations of the Lever Act, which was passed in 1917 to facilitate the government's price-fixing programs and to control the production of critical commodities, such as wool. It was amended to include a prohibition against excessive profit taking. The Department of Justice alleged that American Woolen's profits were 35 percent above its costs. Wood claimed they were only 12.5 percent higher. He was taken into custody and compelled to post bail of $25,000 by a federal judge before being released into the custody of his lawyer. A federal court ruled against Wood and the Wool Trust. But the decision was overturned by the Supreme Court on the grounds that the Lever Act addressed itself to wearing apparel, and woolen cloth was not yet clothing.

In retaliation Wood shut down his mills, throwing forty thousand people out of work in New England, fifteen thousand of those in Lawrence. When asked why, he blamed the closures on "railroad congestion and other things." (This was a reference to the lingering effects of the federal government's nationalization of the railroads during the war, resulting in tracks and rolling stock that were not properly maintained during the flood of goods the United States rushed to ships bound for Europe.) Later he claimed that orders for cloth had dropped off because of the financial cloud hovering over American Woolen following the indictment. The unions, the newspapers, and the mayor of Lawrence did not buy his stories. "Between the wool grower and the wool consumer stands Mr. William M. Wood," an editorial in the *Helena Independent* claimed. "He strikes against both. He closes his factories, and wool prices to the producer go down, woolen cloth prices to the consumer stay up, and his workingmen and women starve. . . . William M. Wood is the worst of strikers—a striker against the happiness of the American people."[17]

In 1924, Wood retired from American Woolen after suffering a stroke. He and his wife moved to Florida, where in 1926, he put a revolver in his mouth and pulled the trigger.[18]

12

Under the Swaying Palms

As the number of ruined farmers and stockmen rose steadily in Montana after World War I, Holly Herrin continued to prosper. Although the demand for beef in 1925 had fallen, due to imports from Argentina and advice from some doctors that red meat was bad for you, demand for lamb and mutton had increased. And the prices Holly got for his wool from 1925 to 1930 stayed solidly in the range between thirty and forty cents per pound.[1]

Although lacking much formal education, Holly was a hayseed by occupation only. He spent many nights in Helena hobnobbing at the Placer Hotel, sometimes accompanied by Mary Ellen. Completed in 1913, the seven-story Placer was one of the best hotels in the state. It boasted a ballroom, a café, a grill, a barbershop, and a jeweler. For many years it was the unofficial headquarters for lawmakers serving in the legislature, which met every other winter. When he wasn't buttonholing a fellow shaker-and-mover in the first-floor lobby, Holly liked to park himself in a rocking chair with a cigar and a newspaper on the second-floor mezzanine in order to observe the scene below. Besides keeping track of who was talking to whom, he noted the regular visits of the Come Along Girls, a trio of attractive young women who included the Placer on their rounds of Helena's hotels and dance halls. They were not prostitutes, however; they were hawkers informing gentlemen about the fabulous quality of the liquor being served in their speakeasy on the third-floor ballroom of the Conrad Mansion on Madison Avenue.[2]

Holly had no need for their liquor. He kept a personal supply of whiskey back at the ranch, accumulated before passage of the Volstead Act, which forbade the distillation, transportation, and sale of liquor but didn't criminalize Holly for drinking it. And a curious loophole in the law allowed him to keep and drink liquor he bought before Prohibition (this implied that customers kept their receipts, although the authorities never demanded to see them, accepting their word because it was easier than hassling them). Holly likely packed a bottle in his luggage whenever he drove the thirty-five miles for a stay in Helena. And like many members of the Montana Club, he kept a supply of booze in a locker at the subterranean rathskeller in the club's elegant building on Sixth Avenue.[3]

While Holly was enjoying the good life during the Roaring Twenties, some of his employees were not having as much fun. On the morning of June 26, 1925, a Herrin ranch sheepherder named Van Guy Steere left Wolf Creek in his Dodge truck with a load of salt he'd bought for Holly's sheep, and drove to a cabin where an acquaintance named Mike Loffler lived. Steere, who had been drinking moonshine, started an argument. Hoping to rid himself of this belligerent drunk, Loffler suggested they drive into Lincoln. When they got there, Steere demanded that they settle their disagreement by shooting it out. Loffler replied that he had nothing to fight about and nothing with which to shoot it out. He got out of Steere's truck and began walking toward Lampkin's Hotel, a big log building that was the centerpiece of a sort of resort that also featured picnic grounds and cabins rented for the summer by people from Great Falls and Helena. A large Sunday crowd was gathered on the lawns. Steere began firing a .30-.30 hunting rifle at Loffler as he walked toward the hotel. Directly behind Loffler in the line of fire was a mother and father with three children seated in a car. As Steere began firing again, this time into the air, L. J. Lambkin, the hotel's proprietor, emerged with a rifle of his own, took cover behind a tree, and ordered Steere to drop the .30-.30, which he did. Lambkin removed the bullet clip from the weapon, handed the rifle back to Steere and ordered him to leave Lincoln and never come back.

Steere yelled obscenities and announced that he was going to Helena. As he peeled away in his truck he sprayed gravel behind him. Barreling along the narrow Stemple Pass Road he forced a number of drivers into the ditches. Finally, Steere plowed head-on into a car carrying four men. Although the men suffered only minor cuts and scratches, their car was totaled. Steere harassed them with his rifle for an hour. When Sheriff Jim Barnes and his deputy arrived, they hog-tied Steere and drove him to the county jail in Helena, where he was charged with two counts of first-degree assault. Steere was a World War I veteran and was said to be a heroin addict. County attorney George Padbury announced that because of Steere's rampage, any miscreant who uses his vehicle as a weapon will be charged with assault; the first time in the county that the automobile was added to a long list of deadly weapons. "Henceforth," he said, "prosecutions will be started against all reckless drivers who collide with other persons."[4]

Another of Holly's sheepherders, L. W. Hince, lost several fingers on both hands after a wall collapsed on him during the 1906 earthquake in San Francisco. After he moved to Montana nothing unfortunate happened to him for two decades, until he was caught out on the open range during a December storm and suffered frostbite to his hands.[5]

On September 15, 1926, Holly found himself suddenly understaffed when two of his hired hands failed to show up for work. The next day he was informed that they would never show up. Fred Kremer, thirty-four, and John Crockett, seventy, were heading to the ranch after picking up some of Crockett's clothes at his residence in Winston, seventeen miles southeast of Helena. Then they stopped to give a ride to William French, thirty-five, a hand who worked at the Jim McMasters ranch near Winston. Kremer was at the wheel of an older model Studebaker he had recently purchased. A cautious driver who wasn't entirely comfortable with the big car, being more accustomed to driving a smaller Model T, he had affixed license plates to it only the day before. On a straight stretch of gravel road on a clear, dry afternoon he suddenly slumped against the steering wheel. The Studebaker veered sharply, its left-side tires dropping over the two-foot bank while its right-side tires stayed on the road. It traveled that way for fifty feet, accelerating to a high speed, before careening back into the center of the road. It turned over twice, landing on its wheels, and ejected all three men. They died instantly. There were no eye-witnesses to the accident.

The first motorists on the scene were horrified by the obliterated automobile and the scattered, mangled bodies. Although a bottle of moonshine was discovered near the wreckage, Kremer was a teetotaler, and it didn't appear that the other two men had been drinking because the bottle was stoppered and full. The authorities speculated that Kremer, who had survived the horrors of fighting with the 362nd Infantry in the Argonne Forest in 1918, had suffered a massive heart attack. When he slumped forward, the weight of his body pushed the gas pedal to the floor, giving the Studebaker enough speed to send it rolling. This was long before the era of mandatory seat belts. In fact, Kremer had a history of dizzy spells and heart problems brought on, it was thought, by getting kicked in the chest by a horse when he was a cowboy in Wyoming.[6]

In 1930 a fifty-five-year-old immigrant from Austria named Theodore Baron was tending to one of five flocks of Holly's sheep grazing on open range in the mountainous Lander's Fork area north of Lincoln. The head tender at the camp, Jim Burton, reported that Baron had been acting "queerly" for several days. The other men at the camp were quietly talking about how Baron seemed to be unraveling. Finally, Burton got word to Holly, asking him to collect Baron, take him back to Helena, and replace him with another herder. While Burton waited for a new man he searched Baron's tent, looking for a weapon, while the older man was out with the sheep, but didn't find one. The next morning Baron ate breakfast, tidied up his tent, and took the sheep out at dawn. Burton followed him. A mile from the camp he caught up with the Austrian. Baron had the muzzle of a .30-.30 rifle pressed against his cheek. Burton called out, but Baron said he didn't want to talk to anybody. When he pulled the trigger, the bullet blew off the top of his head.[7]

Despite his occasional problems with the help, Holly not only weathered the economic storms that had plagued Montana agriculture since World War I, but his assets continued to grow. But so did his indebtedness. In 1926, in order to shield his personal finances from any lawsuits, he incorporated his business interests as a legal entity called the Wolf Creek Live Stock Company. He appointed himself president and general manager and established a board of directors that included himself and Mary Ellen. However, after the stock market crashed in October 1929 he seemed to lose his heart for the game. Before the full effects of the Great Depression plunged America into double-digit unemployment, widespread bank failures, and food riots, he decided to sell out and head for the coast. In September 1930 he and Mary Ellen signed over their entire operation to the livestock company's three other major stockholders—his old ranch partner, Albert Galen, who was serving as a justice of the Montana Supreme Court; a lawyer named C. A. Spaulding; and a bank executive named Leon Sylvester Hazard, who served as the cashier for the Montana Trust and Savings Bank. The dollar figure of the transaction was not disclosed. Then he and Mary Ellen drove to Los Angeles to spend the winter.

That's the official version of the story, published in the *Helena Independent*. Family lore, however, paints a different picture. In this version of events, after 1926 Holly found it increasingly necessary to capitalize his burgeoning business interests by borrowing heavily, using his land and livestock as collateral. When the beef and wool markets wobbled after the stock market crash and wholesale commodity prices dropped by a third, he was unable to make his interest and principal payments. As a consequence, the Montana Trust and Savings Bank threatened to foreclose. In order to avoid a lengthy court battle, however, the bank's officers offered to buy out the Herrins. During the course of these negotiations in early 1930, Holly returned to the ranch from a meeting in Helena and was shocked to find Mary Ellen in bed with his banker. He grabbed a pistol and ordered the man from his house.

Circumstantial evidence suggests that this story or parts of it might be true. For example, in 1930 Holly was sixty-seven years old—nineteen years older than Mary Ellen. And, in fact, before it was merged with two other banks, the Montana Trust and Savings Bank secured ownership of the ranch from the Wolf Creek Live Stock Company (which went out of business in 1942 after all of its remaining assets were lost to foreclosure). The new Montana Trust and Savings Bank of Montana was unable to sell the ranch until 1935, when an industrialist named Irvin Rieke bought it and famously renamed it the Oxbow Ranch (see appendix A). Although Holly and Mary Ellen left Montana together that autumn, in April he drove back from Los Angeles without her. "I enjoyed the stay in Southern California," he told the *Helena Independent.* "But having read of the fine weather Montana has enjoyed all winter, I could see no use in prolonging my stay, so I filled up the gas tank and the oil cups on the car and drove home. Mrs. Herrin remained over for a few weeks with relatives and will be along later."

In fact, he and Mary Ellen were estranged. Trying to keep up appearances, it would take them six years to get around to officially ending the marriage. In 1936 Holly filed for divorce in Broadwater County District Court, claiming that she deserted him. She counterclaimed that in 1930 he abandoned her in California. She was awarded a decree of separate maintenance, and Holly was ordered to pay her a monthly alimony payment of $35, plus court costs and $100 in attorney fees. Holly appealed. Like many of his quarrels, the case went to the Montana Supreme Court, which ruled in his favor, reversing the lower court's decree and ordering a new trial. In July 1937 a divorce was granted to the couple by Montana's Ninth Judicial District Court in Conrad.[8]

In 1938 Holly married for the third time, to Cora Bess Thornton, a forty-eight-year-old spinster schoolteacher who lived with her widowed mother in an expensive house on University Avenue in San Diego. She would outlive him by almost four decades. Although he had said some years earlier that "I guess that when a person has lived in [Montana] for as long as I have he never feels at home anywhere else," in 1946 he died at their winter home in San Diego. This was a 1925 Spanish Colonial Revival house near Balboa Park in the Burlingame development, which was noted (and still is) for its quaint, elegant homes, palm trees, and rose-colored sidewalks. One of the last surviving veterans of the open range, gunplay in the streets, and the dangerous challenges of ranching under the Big Sky, he spent his last days on earth dying in bed from diabetes and other "infirmities of old age."[9] His legacy is an enormous ranch still in operation and a collection of far-reaching lawsuits. But he also left behind the continuation of his bloodline. This was his only child, Thomas Herrin.

13

For the Love of the Game

It was a game his team had to win. On the line was the league's 1912 pennant. Twenty years old, with dreams of playing professional baseball, Tom Herrin was a good athlete who had excelled in track and field in high school. In one memorable baseball game, he had pitched his Helena high school sophomores to a 19–8 win over the seniors.[1] The year before that he had played right field for a Holter Dam team that beat a team from the now-nonexistent village of Stearns, 6–3, before a crowd of five hundred that bet a whopping $500 on the outcome.[2] Baseball wasn't just the most dominant sport in America, for most athletes it was the only sport. Football was a college game. The new sport of basketball, invented in 1891, was also largely a college game slowly catching on in high schools, and it was also hosted back East by the YMCA. In 1912 the state college in Missoula fielded a basketball team that played a handful of games. Although Montanans loved prize fighting and horse racing, playing baseball was what most boys yearned to do.

On this final day of the season, a cool and overcast Sunday in September, Herrin's team, sponsored by a billiard hall/cigar store called the Smoke House, was scheduled to play back-to-back games against two different teams. If the "Smokies" won both games they would take home Helena's City League pennant, a triumph that would bring its amateur stars to the attention of the town's professional, Minor League team, the

Senators. Their opponent in the first game was a team of soldiers from the army base at nearby Fort Harrison. The Fort was 22-6 on the season and the Smokies 20-6. A win in both games would give Herrin's team a record of 22-6, pushing them ahead of the Fort, which would end up 22-7.

The contest started with a Smokies disaster. McConnell, their starting pitcher, was yanked with one out in the second inning after giving up ten runs, most of those the result of fielding errors. Tom Herrin was sent to the mound in relief. He managed to survive the inning without giving up another run. But in the third inning the army hammered the Smoke House again. By the end of the fifth, the score was Fort Harrison 16, Smoke House 0. Although the Smokies managed to plate four runs in the last two frames, Herrin gave up another six runs in the eighth inning before limping off the field. He had surrendered eleven hits and five walks, hitting one batter and throwing three wild pitches. However, he did manage to strike out seven batters, steal two bases, score a run, and drive in a run with a double. The next game pitted the Smokies against Holter Hardware (dubbed the "iron jugglers" by the sportswriters). Despite the fact that Powers, the Smoke House pitcher, struck out twenty-five batters, thus setting "the world's record for strike-outs," according to the *Helena Independent*, the Smokies lost that game, as well, 7–2.

Tom sat on the bench and stewed.[3] But he wasn't upset about the fact that his butter-fingered team had fumbled away the championship. That's because Herrin was a mercenary. Two months earlier he had pitched *against* the Smokies and *for* the Federals, a City League team sponsored by postal workers (dubbed the "mail hurlers"). That contest ended 4–4, a tie made possible by agreement between the teams to limit the game to seven innings. Herrin gave up only two earned runs, struck out nine, walked three, belted a double, and stole two bases. A day earlier he had pitched for the Federals against Fort Harrison, the second game of the day. Herrin got shellacked in an 11–0 shutout, marred by eleven errors committed by the Federals. Sharing the pitching duties with a usually reliable hurler named Keyes, Herrin struck out three, walked one, and hit a batter.

The day's competition was delayed twice. First, one of the four teams on the bill—the Bankers—failed to show up. Dubbed the "money-changers" by the sportswriters, the Bankers had in fact disbanded without telling anyone. After a conference, the managers decided that the Federals would entertain the paying fans by playing a double header. The second delay involved both players and fans. The umpire, a man named Olsen, had been enduring a tirade of verbal abuse from Pittson, the Federals' shortstop, throughout the first game against Holter Hardware. When Pittson challenged Olsen to a fight, the umpire ran to the Federals' bench and punched their second baseman, Fluhr, in the jaw. Pittson jumped in to defend his teammate, and a melee erupted that was finally quelled after the bleachers emptied and the crowd broke up the fight. Play resumed after copious apologies.[4]

In 1913 Tom pitched in the City League for two different teams, Senate Hardware and the Carroll Club, an athletic club that housed a bowling alley, handball courts, and a gymnasium (in 1915 the club would buy the Helena Baseball Field, where the City League played its games). Against a team called the Rough Necks he pitched a one-hit, one-walk gem for Senate Hardware, striking out eight and picking up a 3–1 win. He also pitched for an All-Star team made up of players from the City League, as they took on town teams from Toston, Bozeman, and Townsend. Herrin got the win in relief against Townsend in a ninth-inning, come-from-behind effort watched by several hundred paying fans.

In October 1913 he sealed his future as a strictly amateur player by marrying Marie Clinkenbeard. The meager and sporadic pay he might have earned playing for a Minor League club such as the Helena Senators was not enough to support a man *and* his wife.[5] At the rookie level of professional baseball, athletes played for the love of the game and the chance to advance to a higher level, where it was possible that one of the Major League clubs would buy your contract. Herrin finished the 1914 season batting .333, fielding .857, and steadily improving as a pitcher, racking up strikeouts while reducing his walks and wild pitches. But the chance to play for the Helena Senators evaporated when the club went out of business at the end of 1914 following fifteen seasons of mostly losing campaigns.[6] Professional baseball would not return to Helena until the Helena Phillies took the field in 1978 (later becoming the Helena Brewers, when it became affiliated with the Milwaukee Brewers).

After the wedding he moved out of the house he was sharing at 315 Edwards Avenue with his mother, her seventy-seven-year-old uncle and his seventy-nine-year-old sister.[7] He and Marie moved into a house on Ming Street a block away. While his marriage to Marie ruled out a life of professional baseball, it ushered in a life of fine dining, because she was a famously gifted cook. In 1914 her cake placed sixth out of 109 entries in a contest sponsored by Calumet Baking Powder, winning her a copper tray.[8] During these first years of marriage, Tom's sole source of income was a small business that sold coal. This was primarily mined at Bearcreek, an extensive underground complex south of Billings near the Wyoming border.[9] Herrin and his partner, F. J. Purser, bought loads of it, wholesale from coal trains that stopped in Helena, transferred it into horse-drawn wagons, and delivered it to homes and business for between five and six dollars a ton retail. The wagons were built with beds that were jacked up at an angle, allowing the coal to slide down a chute and into a customer's cellar. Coal burned for radiant heat or used to produce steam piped into radiators was classified by size, ranging from "nuts" to "eggs" to "lumps." The competition among fuel dealers was fierce. They advertised heavily and went door-to-door pitching their wares, keeping people warm but also fouling the cold air with the stink of toxic smoke. A month after his marriage, Tom bought out his partner, and began operating the business on his own.

In 1915 he was back on the mound for Senate Hardware and anyone else that would have him. Five- and six-inning "twilight" games were played after work on Wednesdays and Fridays and nine-inning contests were slated for Sundays. In June he pitched in relief for the East Helena town club against an All-Star City League team, striking out the side in his one inning of work. The East Helena club brought along their own band to entertain the 150 fans who showed up for a Sunday afternoon at the ballpark.[10] The 1916 season started with a game pitting City League All-Stars against the Colored Giants from Butte, "a dusky aggregation of baseball tossers," according to the *Helena Independent.* Tom was not on the mound, however, because he and Marie had bought a ranch on the left bank of the Missouri between Winston and the river twenty miles south of Helena (this land would be flooded in the early 1950s after the construction of the Canyon Ferry Dam). Mary Teresa helped the young couple financially with this purchase, using money she got in the divorce settlement from Holly and from the sale of 165 acres west of Holter Lake. This was grazing land for which she had filed a homestead claim in 1899; the Department of the Interior finally recognized her claim after throwing out a challenge by Roscoe Baxter, who argued that he, not Mary Teresa, had first filed for a patent on these four parcels. She was officially awarded ownership in 1907.

During the war years, organized baseball in Montana collapsed. Tom Herrin was one of the few City League ballplayers who did not serve in the armed forces. By summer 1919 most of the soldiers sent to war from Helena were back in civilian clothes. "The boys are returning rapidly," the *Helena Independent* noted in the winter of 1919. "In three months the season will be in full swing and the majority of them will be home again. They have had some splendid training in baseball as well as hurling hand grenades."

However, ten of them would never return. For Helena in general and Tom Herrin in particular, the most sorrowful of these losses was the death of Harold H. Joyce. His parents' only child, in 1914 Joyce was one of seven graduates of the high school run by Mount St. Charles College (what is now Carroll College). He won medals for his achievements in track and field and was awarded a letter in basketball. During the graduation ceremony he sang the farewell song with another member of the orchestra. Two years earlier he had sung several numbers in a lavish presentation of *The Doll Shop*, a musical staged at the Helena Theatre with a cast of 150 children, including Marie Clinkenbeard, who played two parts: the narrator of the prologue and the broken doll.[11] In 1915 Joyce acted in a play about college life called *Half Back Sandy*. He sang several songs, including a tune titled "Along Came Ruth." In 1916 he played a part in a comedy called *The Whirl o' th' Town* staged at the Masonic Temple. In college he excelled on the diamond, fielding several positions. Playing as well for the Federals in that raucous, fistfight-marred double-header, he was Tom Herrin's batterymate in both games.

Joyce briefly attended Gozaga College before graduating from Mount St. Charles College. In 1916 he enlisted as a private in the machine gun company of the Second Montana Regiment, an army reserve unit, and was quickly promoted to sergeant major and then commissioned a second lieutenant. The unit was sent to the Mexican border to join General John Pershing's forces chasing Pancho Villa, a hero of the Mexican Revolution who attacked a border town in New Mexico. After Pershing was summoned to prepare for war in Europe, Joyce was mustered out of the reserves. But after America's declaration of war on Germany in April 1917, his unit, now the 163rd Infantry, was mobilized into the regular army and he was commissioned a first lieutenant. He was ordered to recruit other soldiers. Among his first successes were thirteen high school boys from Great Falls, whom he escorted to Helena for induction.[12] The 163rd was sent to North Carolina for training and then shipped to France from Long Island in December 1917. Joyce took more military training in France, performing so well that he and two other Montana officers were transferred to the 128th Wisconsin Infantry and joined frontline fighting northeast of Paris. Two months later, on August 30, 1918, he was killed in battle at the town of Juvigny.[13]

The reaction in Helena was grief and anger. The *Helena Independent* ranted about socialists, anarchists, Wobblies, pacifists, slackers, and federal officials antagonistic to Montana's 1918 sedition law. "Peace . . . can only come now when the comrades of Harold Joyce can march along a great white way to Berlin and every damn Hun is flat on his back with his legs in the air."[14]

In winter 1919 Tom Herrin sold his Winston ranch to the A. B. Cook Stock Company. Then he and his mother bought the D. A. G. Floweree place on Prickly Pear Creek. This was 340 acres of prime, flat land with a high water table less than five miles from the dome of the Montana State Capitol building. Although it wasn't the massive real estate empire Holly had amassed, it was the beginning of Tom Herrin's successful career as a farmer and a stockman in his own right. And significantly, for the next two generations of Herrins, the Floweree place would become the core of the ranch where Keebo and his sisters were raised.

14

No Longer the Lazy Crop

By June 1920 Tom and Marie Herrin had brought three children into the world; first, Harland, followed quickly by John Winton and then Gordon. Even with a house full of kids and a farm and stock operation demanding most of his time, Tom found the energy to step back on the mound for the first game of the new baseball season. The contest pitted the Helena city team against a team from Butte sponsored by Montana Power, the utility created by the Anaconda Mining Company in 1912 to distribute electricity generated by several Missouri River dams near Great Falls. Although Tom was pitching with a sore arm, he managed to get through the first two innings without giving up a run. But the Butte team hit him hard in the third, fifth, and eighth innings, and his teammates committed nine errors. This was partly due to heavy rain the night before, which left the ballpark a rutted mess. In the end Butte handed Herrin the loss, 13–8.[1]

Although Tom was not pleased with his performance, nor that of his team, he was happy about the rain. Montana had entered its third straight year of the historic drought that was ruining farms, triggering bankruptcies and bank failures, and driving people away in such numbers that it was the only state that lost population during the Roaring Twenties. In 1919 a mere seven and a half inches of precipitation fell on the Helena Valley, less than two-thirds of its already meager annual average. (Holly's ranches had fared even worse, receiving less than five inches for the entire year.)[2]

The recent deluge meant Tom would not have to work so hard irrigating his hay, oats, and commercial potato crop. The foundation of his water rights was Prickly Pear Creek, a sizable stream that meandered through the Floweree place on its way from Bullock Hill in the Helena National Forest to Lake Helena, an arm of the much larger body of water backed up behind Hauser Dam. The work of getting the water in the creek to his crops was repetitive, back-breaking, and boring. It centered around the use of a movable dam made of rubberized canvas attached to a pole. Tom grabbed one end of the pole, his hired hand grabbed the other, and together they dragged the dam from one point to another along one of the many irrigation ditches that radiated from the creek. When the dam was in place they weighted the skirt with shovel loads of mud, and the flowing water was forced over the banks of the ditch and fanned out into the fields. Then they moved to the next ditch, where another canvas dam was waiting to be moved. Although a cumbersome and time-consuming process, flooding potato plants is a better method than spraying them because the water reaches the roots more efficiently. Plus, some fungal diseases that attack potatoes thrive in the warm, moist conditions that can be created by overhead sprinklers in hot weather.

This kind of American agriculture—now rarely practiced—was the opposite of raising the "lazy crop," what some Englishmen derisively called the Irish method of growing potatoes in "lazy beds" before the Great Famine of the 1840s. Using the lazy-bed method, a poor tenant family dug a shallow trench on their rented land with a spade or a stick, tossed in the eyes of their seed potatoes, covered them with turf after they sprouted, and returned three months later to harvest the crop. There was often no need for fertilizer because many varieties of potatoes grow in any kind of soil. And because it was Ireland, where it rains a misty rain most every day during the growing season—accumulating thirty-five inches a year in County Waterford, for example—there was no need for irrigation.

One of the reasons for the devastation in 1840s Ireland caused by *Phytophthora infestans* (the mold that turns potatoes into reeking bags of black rot) was the fact that only one variety of potato was planted. This was the Irish lumper, a white, knobby tuber that grows well even in soil with poor nutrients. After the Great Famine it disappeared from cultivation. Tom Herrin and other growers in the Helena Valley planted at least five varieties of potatoes. The Bliss Triumph was a red spud with white flesh that was best prepared by boiling it with the skin on. The Netted Gem was what is now called the Russet Burbank. The Hammond, which was not known by that name outside the Helena Valley, was a baking potato. Early Six Weeks was a small white potato best served mashed.

Early in 1920 Tom and his mother went shopping again. This time they bought the farm next to the Floweree place. This was 272 acres of similarly flat, fertile, irrigated land that had been owned by T. A. Grimes, the partner of Holly's nemesis, Henry Sieben. The Grimes place had been bought in September 1919 by Hugh Rogan and flipped to Tom for a small, quick profit. Because Rogan had paid the staggering sum of $30,000 for the Grimes place, people breathlessly called it "hundred-dollar land." By way of comparison, winning bidders at a 1919 auction in Valley County paid only fourteen dollars and sixty-two cents an acre on average for some 8,400 acres of state-owned land.[3] But most of this was best suited for grazing, not farming, as the doomed Honyockers had been discovering. And some of it wasn't even very useful as range land.

Born in Ireland in 1856, Hugh Rogan was called the "Potato King" of the Helena Valley. He had been raising this cash crop along the Prickly Pear since 1898, and got a boost from the market during the war because under the right conditions, a spud can be kept uncooked for many months, making it the perfect survival food at a time when other foodstuffs were running short. By 1920 he was shipping carloads of table spuds and seed potatoes all over the country. Locals calling his four-digit telephone number were buying hundred-pound burlap bags of Hammonds for two dollars and fifty cents each, which Rogan delivered to them. Each bag contained a hundred or so big, white baking potatoes. He also raised a variety called the "Sacramento," a crop he had nurtured from a single seed potato he personally cajoled from none other than Luther Burbank.[4] In October of 1920 Rogan shipped 61,000 pounds of potatoes to an out-of-state wholesaler. If Rogan was the king, Tom Herrin would soon become the prince, profiting from the highest wholesale prices ever paid up until that time in America. By 1922 he was growing 175 bags of Netted Gems per acre, with several hundred acres in production. Potatoes had become big business, in fact, America's number one food crop. Tom may not have been living the rough and tumble life of the open range cattleman that Holly had lived, but his farms were making him rich. And although he didn't share Hugh Rogan's veneration for their homely crop, which wags called "Murphies" in a reference to the Irish love-hate relationship with the spud, Tom threw his considerable energy into promoting it, and himself, at the same time.

One effective marketing ploy he employed was entering his product in contests. In 1922 Tom's spuds were awarded third among fifty commercial competitors at the Northwest Exhibition in Spokane, which drew entries from all over the West, and fifth among eighty-one entries in the certified seed category (these were sold to other growers). The following year he won fourth in the Netted Gem class at the Pacific Northwest Potato Conference. His spuds would continue to win awards through the Roaring Twenties, including two firsts at the 1926 Billings fair. His relentless advertising of these awards increased demand, especially for his certified seed potatoes. In 1924 he parlayed his growing notoriety into his election as the president of the Lewis and Clark County Farm Bureau, which had been organized in 1917 as the result of conversations held during summer picnics attended by farm families. One of the Farm Bureau's first acts was financing the killing of squirrels, gophers, and prairie dogs accused of destroying crops. Then the bureau turned its attention to the organization of potato clubs for farmers' children.[5] Tom would serve as head of the organization for six years, until the Depression eviscerated the farm economy and interest in the bureau waned.

In 1927 he was elected vice president of the Montana State Farm Bureau, which was financed in part by the U.S. Department of Agriculture in an effort to make the occupation of farming more profitable. In 1928 he was elected president of the Montana Potato Marketing Association. Under Tom's management the organization lobbied officials to lower freight rates and sent agents into Louisiana and Texas to market Montana's seed potatoes, which resulted in a successful effort to secure contracts before the next year's crop was in the ground. The pursuit and administration of elected and appointed offices suited Tom's personality. Like Holly, he was outgoing and gregarious and was not averse to the sound of his own voice. A staunch Republican like his father, he had his eye on higher political offices and an understanding that one path to the state capitol building, and possibly to Washington DC, started with doing good work—or at least noteworthy work—in local organizations.

Although the name Thomas Herrin was becoming known among farmers and stockmen, he didn't gain more widespread notoriety until the events following his appointment to the Montana Fair Board. On September 11, 1925, he was accused of violating the state law forbidding "the recording and registering of bets and wagers upon the result of a contest of speed of animals." The Montana attorney general, A. L. Foot, alleged that Herrin, along with the other members of the board, plus some twenty-four unnamed "Does" and "Roes," used pari-mutuel gambling machines to accept bets and pay off the winners of horse races staged at Helena's famous one-mile track, during the Montana State Fair. In fact, a form of wagering was indeed sanctioned by Herrin and the board during the six days of horse racing at the fair. This was called the "Florida System": To bet on a horse a patron bought a two dollar "share" of the animal's "ownership." A "receipt" for this purchase was issued. Receipts were pooled, and the pool was divided among the owners if their horse won. For example, a long-shot named Operator came from behind in the third race on September 11 and paid his owners $145 for each of their $2 shares.

Although the Florida System was pari-mutuel gambling by another name, a test case of its legality had already been decided when a Lewis and Clark district judge ruled that the payouts from a day at the track the previous July did not violate the law. Attorney General Foot chose to ignore this ruling. In an outrageous and widely derided act, he demanded that Governor John Erickson call out the Montana Militia to shut down the last day of the fair by blocking the gates to the fairgrounds.[6] Erickson refused. Foot's case against the fair board marched on, compelling board chairman Lewis Penwell to acknowledge the technical misdemeanor arrests of himself, Herrin, and the other defendants by posting a $500 bond on their behalf. Foot, a Republican, was accused of using his power to punish Lewis and Clark County for voting against the GOP gubernatorial incumbent, Joseph Dixon, who was thrown out of office in the 1924 election. Foot was also accused of lying in bed with civic boosters in Billings and Great Falls, who wanted the state fair moved to their town. Critics also pointed out that baseball pools collecting money on the outcome of Major League games were operating in every large town in Montana, and Foot had done nothing to shut them down. After almost a year of litigation in the lower courts, Foot's attempt to prosecute the fair board came to a head before the Montana Supreme Court. In April 1926 the justices observed, first, that Montana does not ban horse racing. Then, it ruled unanimously that mutual horse owners sharing a pool does not violate the letter of the law.[7]

The ruling encouraged the fair board—with Tom Herrin elected as its vice president—to begin organizing for the 1926 exposition. Although the legislature had refused to appropriate any money in 1915 after supporting it for years, the 1925 fair was a roaring success, attracting double the attendance of the 1924 fair, largely because of horse racing. (Of course, people don't attend races simply to see animals run, they want to experience the thrill of betting. Like prohibitions against alcohol and religion, a government that outlaws gambling simply makes it more attractive.) The 1925 fair was financed by a Lewis and Clark County mill levy and loans from Minnesota banks. The levy was collected again for the 1926 fair, and contributions for additional financing were secured from the railroads and Helena businesses. The 1926 fair was attended by the largest crowds in a decade, on one day pulling in twelve thousand people to look at sheep and pigs and vegetables, listen to bands, wander around the carnival, and gamble on horse racing, which featured a field of nine thoroughbreds competing in a one-mile race.

The highlight of the 1927 fair was a visit by Col. Charles Lindbergh. Flying the *Spirit of St. Louis*, the cotton-skinned monoplane he had piloted nonstop from New York to Paris the previous May, "Lucky Lindy" was midway through an airborne tour of all forty-eight states, including Helena and twenty-two other capitals. Twenty-five thousand people were packed into the grandstands and the infield waiting to see the hero and hear his voice. Finally, at 1:50 p.m. a silver plane appeared in the sky south of the city. There was a collective gasp and a deafening cheer that echoed off Mount Helena. Lindbergh circled above the fairgrounds so the enormous crowd could see the famous craft. Women fainted. Children screamed. Then he maneuvered it into the wind and landed on the municipal golf course. He finally made his entrance at the track in a big green convertible shared with dignitaries, surrounded by a parade of Boy Scouts, Camp Fire Girls, the 163rd Regimental Band, two lines of ex-servicemen and carloads of officials, including Tom Herrin. Following Lindbergh's remarks about the importance of commercial aviation, he visited wounded soldiers at Fort Harrison and was honored that evening at a banquet served to 1,200 guests at the Masonic Temple.[8] Overshadowed by the spectacle of Lindbergh's visit was a troupe of thirty Flathead Indians and their show horses, which had just recently performed at Madison Square Garden in New York. They entertained the crowd with what the newspapers called "Indian relay races, buck races and squaw races."[9] Tom Herrin would serve on the board until the fair was abandoned in 1932 when, during the darkest days of the Depression, there was not enough money from any source to finance what was regarded as a luxury. Great Falls boosters would eventually get their wish when the North Montana State Fair morphed into the state's new state-wide fair.

Like most farmers in winter 1924, Tom kept busy repairing his equipment so it would be ready when it was time to plant. And although he was also heavily involved in the affairs of the Farm Bureau and his growing family, he and Marie found time to rehearse and perform in a three-act play called *The Goat*. This was a locally written farce set in a Great Falls apartment on the morning following a blizzard. Marie played the female lead and Tom a supporting role whose booming laugh "made a big hit with the audience," according to one review. The play was performed at the Marlow Theater, a massive brick edifice built in 1918 with seating for 750 on the main floor and an additional 650 seats on the two levels of the balcony. It featured stairless ramps to the second-floor mezzanine, which provided a smoking lounge for men and a ladies' powder room with a maid and "writing compartments." Further ramps ascended to the balcony. Designed as a venue for live productions, the Marlow's stage was sixty-five feet wide and thirty-five feet deep, large enough to accommodate the most lavish production of the time—*Ben Hur.* There were dressing rooms, a lobby with a hundred-person capacity, ushers and usherettes, two ticket windows, a pit large enough for a small orchestra, a proscenium arch above the stage, and a heavy asbestos curtain to shield patrons from the flames if fire broke out back stage.

Two vaudeville performances were featured on Thursday evenings. Some of the many other early attractions included a Broadway play called *The Gold Diggers* and a touring musical review, *The Vanities of 1923.* In addition, the Marlow showed the latest silent movies. The night after *The Goat* was performed to a large crowd, the Marlow offered *Chastity,* featuring Katherine MacDonald, dubbed "The American Beauty" by film pundits. The hundreds of notable personalities who appeared on the Marlow's stage included Will Rogers, Woodrow Wilson, Boris Karloff, Charlie Pride, Stan Laurel, Burl Ives, John F. Kennedy, and Myrna Loy, the actress who was born in Helena and made her theatrical debut dancing in an elementary school play staged at the Marlow in 1918. Kennedy got up on stage in 1960 to campaign for the support of the Montana Democratic Convention meeting at the theater. Although still in excellent condition, the Marlow was demolished in 1972 to make way for a parking lot.[10]

Throughout the Roaring Twenties Tom continued to play baseball, sometimes in front of paying spectators and sometimes nonpaying onlookers. By 1922 the old City League had been brought back to life with four teams, the Eagles, the Elks, East Helena, and a team supported by the neighborhood around Union Station and the railroad yards called the Sixth Ward. In July 1926 Herrin took the mound for the Sixth Warders against the Elks. Thirty years old, he pitched his team to a 6–4 complete-game victory, striking out twelve, driving in a run with a single, and scoring a run.

A year later he was on the mound for the Helena Merchants against the League Allstars. As lesser sportswriters like to say, the game was a seesaw battle. Herrin gave up two runs in the second inning but the Merchants scored a run in the third and the fourth to tie it. In the fourth the Stars rallied for three more runs but the Merchants came back with four runs of their own in the eighth to take the lead. The Stars tied it with a run in the bottom of the ninth. The Merchants took back the lead in the tenth. But in the bottom of the frame with two outs and the crowd on its feet, the Stars plated two runs to win. Herrin pitched the entire ten innings and drove in two runs with a pair of singles. He gave up nine hits, a walk and hit a batter, but he struck out eight.

On Independence Day in 1927, in a cow pasture in the Helena Valley near the old Warren School, where a peevish bull had previously ruined a Sunday School picnic by chasing away the children, Tom pitched again before a crowd of a hundred. Entering the game in relief for the married potato growers of the Prickly Pear against the area's bachelor farmers, he took the mound in the top of the ninth with the scored tied 13–13 and notched the win when his team scored a run with one out in the bottom of the frame. Three years later, after a sabbatical, he again took the ball, this time for a team called Intermountain-Y against another City League team called Orange Crush, which was sponsored by a bottling company.[11] The local paper described the event: "Tommy Herrin returned to the game and carried much of his old-time steam with him, striking out nine batters in the last three innings which he pitched after taking Robinson's place at the start of the fifth [in a seven-inning contest]. The 'boy' from the valley started out strong with a pair of strikeouts to give the crowd a thrill," but Herrin gave up five runs in his three innings of relief and his team was crushed by the Crush 14–2. The loss dropped Intermountain into last place in the four-team City League, which also included East Helena and the Kiwanis Club.

It turned out to be Herrin's last recorded game of hardball. He was thirty-eight years old. With the addition of Keith in 1924 and Wayne two years later, he now had five sons. Like many farm couples, Tom and Marie had succeeded in growing their own workforce. While that would safeguard their prosperity until the end of their lives, the Herrin boys would discover that the success of their parents, grandparents, and great-grandparents would not guarantee them the same result. The reality was that even an irrigated farm that would expand to a thousand fertile, sun-drenched acres was still not enough farm to go around.

15

How to Prosper When Times Are Dark

In 1929 Tom and Marie decided to diversify the farm with the addition of a dairy business. They bought a number of Holstein cows—the popular dairy breed developed in Holland—hired hands to milk them and drivers to deliver milk and cream to grocery stores on a strictly wholesale basis. This decision would turn out to be astute. As the Depression deepened and simple food such as milk and spuds were the only staples many families could afford, the Herrin Dairy and potato operation became a critical local supplier. The economics of dairying required that in order to make a profit, or at least tread water, the dairyman must grow his own forage and grain, which the Herrin's had in abundance thanks to the high water table and their canvas dam approach to irrigation. Large fields were cross-fenced with barbed wire so that grazing cows and their calves could be moved from pasture to pasture in order to let the grass recover. Some of the pastures were harvested for their hay, providing the Herrins with enough home-grown fodder to feed their herd throughout Helena's long winter.

The Herrins didn't suddenly jump into the dairy business. They had been keeping milk cows for several years to help feed their large family and their hired hands. The care and upkeep of these animals was generally routine. But at 6:21 p.m. on June 27, 1925, one of the hands, a Scandinavian immigrant named Jens, was milking a big Holstein in the barn when the ground began to violently shake. The epicenter of this 6.6 magnitude earthquake was located sixty miles south near the town of Three Forks. Reacting to the unstable ground beneath her feet, the cow decided to lay down before she fell down. Unfortunately for Jens, she laid down on top of him. After a struggle to free himself, he strode from the Herrin farm in a huff, abandoning his job. When the ground stopped shaking with the first of several aftershocks seven minutes later, Tom was compelled to finish the chore.[1]

Despite this incident, the life of a typical Herrin Dairy cow was tranquil and uneventful. Take that of Sunshine, for example, a gentle, big-boned, fifteen-hundred-pound gargantuan, colored in broad splotches of black and white. After spending a summer night outside in a field, she headed at first light toward the milking barn with the rest of the herd. Although most of the other cows were nursing, she was no longer feeding a calf. Her firstborn and second born had been castrated and sold for slaughter. Her third was now fully grown and serving as one of the Herrin bulls. And her only female offspring was also a productive member of the herd. Once Sunshine found her place in a long row of open stalls in the barn, she lowered her head through a wooden grate and began eating the grain that had been put there for her. Like all of the Herrin cows in the early years of the dairy, Sunshine was milked twice a day by hand, a laborious, thirty-minute chore. Every day during her lactation cycle, which usually lasted about three hundred days a year, she produced eight or nine gallons of milk. Like most cattle, Sunshine's idea of hygiene did not compel her to avoid laying in mud or her own manure. Therefore, her hooves and udder had to be cleaned with an iodine solution before she was milked. The first few squirts went not into the galvanized steel bucket used to collect her milk, but into a bowl for the barn cats or into the mouth of a lurking mouser in order to clear Sunshine's four nipples of contamination.

The warm milk was quickly strained into five-gallon steel cans to remove hair and other foreign material, then cooled immediately to a temperature a few degrees above freezing to inhibit the growth of bacteria. When the cream rose to the surface it was skimmed off and placed in separate steel cans. The Herrin Dairy collected as much as a quart of cream for every gallon of milk, and sold it separately. Although some Montana dairies homogenized and pasteurized their milk—such as the Ayrshire Dairy south of Great Falls—the Herrins sold only raw milk. Homogenization is the process of agitating milk to break down the fat globules that constitute cream and blending them into the balance of the liquid. Pasteurization is the process of heating milk in order to kill dangerous bacteria. During pasteurization milk was heated to 140 degrees Fahrenheit and the temperature was held there for twenty minutes. Because milk from some herds in the United States had been responsible for spreading tuberculosis, typhoid fever, infantile diarrhea and brucellosis—a disease that causes cows to abort—mandatory pasteurization eventually became the law in every state. However, during the Depression and into World War II, whether or not to pasteurize was up to the individual dairies. The Herrins chose not to. Their decision was based on the high cost of equipment and the labor it required, but also on the fact that the state sanitary board had declared the dairy's herd free of tuberculosis and brucellosis several years running.[2]

The Herrins earned their health certificate by carefully managing the herd. By 1933 the dairy owned ninety-nine cows, mostly Holsteins. Fifty-nine of these animals were calves (important dairy citizens because a young heifer will not lactate until she has given birth). The herd grazed freely under the open sky. The Herrins relied on their bulls to grow the herd's numbers and replace the geriatric cows that died after living out their life span of twelve to fifteen years. Outside animals were never added to the herd, thus promoting herd immunity to common bovine ailments.

By 1932 the herd was electronically milked with a machine that replaced the sore hands and tired fingers of the Herrin workforce and freed the family from the rigid twenty-four-seven schedule demanded by their Holsteins. The machine filled five-gallon canisters with warm, fresh milk that was immediately strained and cooled in the refrigerated milk house. After the cream was collected, another machine filled one-quart glass bottles with milk and half-pint bottles with cream. The bottles were sealed using caps stamped with the words "Herrin's Dairy." The bottles were delivered every morning to a dozen groceries, several cafés, St. Peter's Hospital, and the swanky Park Avenue Apartments. The deliverymen picked up used bottles and drove them back to the dairy, where they were cleaned in a bottle-washing machine and sanitized in an oven before being used again.

Herrin's Dairy aggressively competed against other milk suppliers by promoting itself with extensive newspaper advertising. "When you drink Herrin's milk," the ads promised, "you drink bottled sunshine." While touting the certification of its product by the Montana Livestock Sanitary Board, the ads painted the dairy as a modern factory. "This milk is electrically milked, immediately cooled, mechanically bottled and mechanically capped. This gives you a product that does not come into contact with human hands." Visitors were welcome to see this assembly line efficiency with their own eyes. In addition, the ads claimed: "Our Milk is Strictly Safe for Babies" (breastfeeding had steadily declined among American women since the 1890s, widely condemned as a disgusting habit practiced by the uneducated lower classes).[3] In what was a common publishing practice of the time (and still is) the *Helena Independent* thanked the Herrins for their advertising dollars by sending reporters to the dairy whenever new equipment was added. In 1938, for example, the paper announced that a "modern" Frigidaire cooler had been installed in the milk house by the Carlson Appliance Company. The aeration, straining, and rapid cooling of milk has been adopted "by the best modern dairies in the country," the paper gushed, "and as a result of this attention and care, an absolutely pure and safe product has been furnished to the market." The paper then quoted the owner of the company, Mr. Carlson, attributing the declining infant mortality rate in the United States to his industry's refrigeration equipment.[4]

Tom Herrin's ad blitz was fueled in part by the debate over pasteurization. One of his competitors, Meadow Gold Dairies, had installed expensive equipment to treat its milk, and touted this innovation in its advertising. "Take no chances with baby's milk—to be sure it's safe be sure it's pasteurized." An example of the advertising strategy that first frightens the consumer with a health scare, then promises a product that will prevent or cure the condition, Meadow Gold's ads listed the serious diseases that could be caused by raw milk, all of which, it claimed could be avoided with pasteurization. "All these germs can be made harmless and still the process alters very little, if any, the color, odor, and taste of the milk. The food value is not changed and digestibility is not made worse, but better." In the early debate over raw versus pasteurized milk, which continues to this day, it was never mentioned that you could also avoid contracting tuberculosis from raw milk by simply not drinking it.[5] But in the early decades of the twentieth century most adults consumed milk every day; even though some of them wondered why they had so much trouble digesting it.[6]

The dairy not only weathered the Depression but reaped the Herrins a sizable income, year after year. The family bought the most up-to-date farm equipment and the best trucks and cars, mostly Cadillacs. One fine summer day, Tom drove from the ranch downtown in his brand-new black Cadillac and parked in front of the Senate Hardware Store. After paying for his purchases, he walked back outside, climbed into the Cadillac and drove away. Twenty minutes later he realized that this vehicle was not his beautiful automobile. He immediately turned around. In fact, a man named Floyd Barnes had parked his identical black Cadillac near the Herrin vehicle and had gone off on his own set of errands. When Barnes returned, he slid behind the wheel of the Cadillac and saw that he had entered the wrong car. Both men, in fact, had left the keys in the ignition, which was the trusting custom of the time. Barnes contacted the police, who alerted the Highway Patrol to be on the lookout for the man's stolen vehicle. When Herrin returned to the scene of the crime, both men shared an embarrassed laugh.

One of these Herrin vehicles, however, was the agent of a tragedy. On a January night in 1936, twenty-year-old Winton Herrin, Tom's second oldest boy, was driving a dairy truck to town with a load of fresh milk. In the passenger seat was Earl Hill, twenty-four, a Herrin employee for the last year. Winton stopped the truck to check the tires because the steering wheel was hard to turn. Although the men determined that the tires seemed soft, they drove on. A few hundred yards later, near the one-room Warren School, the truck hit a patch of snow and loose gravel and crashed through the railing on a small bridge, overturning in a ditch. As soon as they climbed from the wreck, Earl Hill dropped dead. The impact had driven one of the rails through the windshield, crushing his chest.[7] Although the Highway Patrol and the coroner ruled that the crash was unavoidable, Hill's estate sued the Herrin Dairy. Eighteen months later the court dismissed the suit.

Shortly before the ruling, Winton drove with two friends to the big Independence Day rodeo in Lincoln. Afterward, they went skinny-dipping in the Blackfoot River a mile below town. Surprised by a party of young women, Winton dove into a deep hole. At the bottom of the hole, he hit his head on a rock. The impact broke his neck. Paralyzed from the neck down, he was washed downstream into a log jam, where his friends jumped in to save him from drowning. A month later, still conscious until gripped by a fever of 107 degrees, he died at St. Peter's Hospital in Helena.[8]

Throughout the Depression the Herrins continued to take leading roles in the civic life of the community. Marie was elected president of the Lewis and Clark County Home Demonstration Club, and president of the DeMolay Mothers Circle.[9] In 1936 Tom followed in his father's footsteps and declared his candidacy for the legislature. Filing for a seat in House District 92, he faced six other Republicans, three of whom would move on to run against the Democratic field in the general election in November, where they would win all three Lewis and Clark County seats. Herrin was not one of them. He finished fifth with only 11 percent of the votes cast (the winners included attorney E. G. Toomey, who had represented Holly Herrin in *Herrin v. Sutherland* a decade earlier, and Judge George Padbury, who presided over the more colorful criminal cases in Lewis and Clark County).

In 1940, figuring that practice makes perfect, Tom threw his hat in the ring again. This time he paid for a series of small newspaper ads that ran in the days preceding the July primary election. The photo in these ads portrayed a man who looked confident, or arrogant, and smiling, or smirking, depending on one's point of view. He looked, in fact, like many politicians. The mood at the Herrin ranch on the morning after the primary was festive. Tom was in third place with ten of forty-one precincts reporting (the top three GOP finishers would meet a trio of Democrats in the general election). But by the next day he had fallen out of the running, coming in fourth in a field of ten. This was a better showing than his 1936 attempt, but it convinced him that an elected post was not in the cards.

After Pearl Harbor, life at the Herrin ranch continued much as it had before the war, at least for a while. The youngest boys, Keith and Wayne, were not old enough in 1942 to qualify for service in the armed forces, but at ages sixteen and thirteen they were old enough to work in the fields and at the dairy. Although Harland and Gordon were issued draft cards, they were exempted from conscription for the duration of the war (the reader may recall that the 1940 Selective Service Act was sponsored by U.S. senator Edward Burke, George Burke's younger brother). Gordon was exempted because he worked on a farm that raised at least sixteen "animal units," according to a formula intended to separate significant protein producers from mere subsistence farmers. Harland was exempted because he was married. The fact that their father had been appointed to the five-member Lewis and Clark County draft board in the summer of 1942 did not reduce their chances of qualifying for deferments. When Keith turned eighteen he also qualified; a fact he would come to regret when his friends and contemporaries began returning home from the war.

As America ramped up its industrial might against fascism, the Herrins faced two shortages. The first was minor: because much of the nation's rubber production had been commandeered by the military, the dairy was forced to suspend Sunday milk deliveries in order to conserve the tires on its trucks. They joined twenty-one other Helena-area dairies and creameries in making the announcement. All of that competition underscored another growing problem: a labor shortage. As young men traded their civvies for uniforms, the Herrins were forced to perform much of the daily drudgery of running a dairy largely by themselves.

The loss of Winton was not just heartbreaking, he had been a critical member of the workforce and his loss was felt there as well. A rumor was circulated in 1942 that Tom was hiring Japanese workers to fill the void. He was compelled to buy newspaper ads dispelling this falsehood. In fact, most of the five hundred Japanese living in Montana in 1942 worked for the railroads; half of them were Japanese-Americans and half were Japanese-born aliens. By April 1942 a thousand Japanese were imprisoned at the internment camp at Fort Missoula—along with a thousand Italian seamen—but these were prominent businessmen and professionals who had been rounded up on the West Coast, separated from their families, and shipped to Montana without trial.[10]

Another domestic victim of the war was the Herrin Dairy. Tom Herrin said that due to the labor shortage he could no longer find enough reliable, competent help. He sold his milk routes to the Helena Creamery, and he auctioned off 110 head of purebred Holstein and Guernsey cows, calves, and bulls, along with 21 head of horses and the motorized equipment, trucks, and tractors he had used to operate a commercial dairy for fifteen years. To launch his new line of business he bought 80 head of purebred Hereford heifers as the foundation stock for what he was now calling the Herrin Hereford Ranch. (A cowboy artist named Shorty Shope designed a logo for the ranch featuring an antic cartoon cowboy sprinting behind a cloud of dust under the caption "Tearin' to Herrin's.") Four years later Tom bought a high-bred Hereford bull for $2,550 (the equivalent of $25,000 in 2020) that descended directly from a famous bull named Royal Aster. Raising beef cattle required far less labor than operating a dairy.

Despite the wild dip in prices Montana stockmen were sometimes forced to endure, business was fabulous. After years of wartime meat rationing, consumers' pent-up appetite for beef encouraged stockmen to multiply the size of their herds and small rural business owners to expand into cattle ranching. Tom was soon specializing in the breeding of champion Hereford bulls, the massive red-and-white cattle that originated in the West Midlands county of Herefordshire. In the postwar era, bulls were bred intensively for the fat-marbled steaks American consumers

FIG. 7. Tom, Marie, Keith, and Gordon Herrin, Herrin Hereford Ranch barnyard, 1956. Courtesy of the Molly Burke Herrin Estate.

demanded. These high-bred animals lived and foraged together in pastures segregated from the choice heifers that had not been consigned to the slaughterhouse; come breeding season they were turned out with the females. Not a bad life.

The highest price paid in America in 1950 for a yearling Hereford bull went to the Herrin ranch. The bull—Larry Domino 23rd—was sold to a Washington State rancher for $5,060. At that auction the ranch also sold forty-seven other young bulls and heifers for $45,200. By now the Herrins had built a covered sale ring complete with bleachers and an auctioneer's booth (a favorite place to play in coming years for Marcia and her siblings). During their annual sale, the Herrin men wore matching green-and-white-striped western shirts in order to point themselves out to buyers who had questions about the cattle. Tom Herrin soon arranged for the inclusion of the Herrin Hereford Ranch on a statewide tour of cattlemen from all over the West. In 1952 the ranch sold a champion bull named H. H. R. Advance B-52 for $10,000 to an Alberta stockman.

16

Greener Pastures

The work of calving, branding, castrating, doctoring, feeding, and pasture management on these seven hundred well-watered acres could now be handled by the family and a hired hand or two, who also helped tend to the oats, potatoes, and strawberries. This was despite the fact that by 1956 the number of Herrin sons living on the ranch had dwindled from five to two. The heartrending death of Winton was followed that autumn by the departure of his oldest brother. Harland Sanford Herrin had put the plow and the milk pail behind him when at the age of twenty-three he married Elizabeth Wardlaw, the daughter of a plasterer who had served with the Scottish Highlanders in the Second Boer War.

This was not, however, Harland's first marriage. In 1933, when he was eighteen, he ran off with a classmate named Fern Farnum to Livingston, Montana, where they found a county official willing to tie the knot for them. They were members of the same 4-H club and seniors at Helena High School, which a week before had staged the tenth annual Vigilante Day Parade. This spectacle, featuring a cast of nine hundred students, had been conceived in 1924 (and still occurs every year) as the principal's effort to channel youthful high spirits and sexual energy into something less destructive than the traditional "Junior-Senior Fight," an actual brawl carried out over the course of several spring days since the 1890s. The parade was seen as an educational opportunity intended to tell the story, through wagons and floats, of Helena's pioneer history. Students in blackface and brownface portrayed "Negroes," "squaws," and "bucks." There were stagecoaches, hanging trees, and whores. Fern and Harland found themselves as cast members on one of these floats. In the spring sunshine and the carnival atmosphere, one thing led to another. Their marriage, however, did not last. In August Thomas went to court and had it annulled, claiming that Harland had married without his knowledge or consent. An 1895 law still in force in 1933 decreed that any male under the age of twenty-one was considered a minor who needed the permission of his guardians in order to marry. In denying Fern Farnum any claim on property Harland might inherit as Tom's heir, she was also ordered to cease using the name Herrin.[1]

If Harland harbored bruised feelings about his ruined marriage, he kept them to himself. But a decade later, piloting a training plane, he dropped a bomb on his father's ranch. He had earned his pilot's license in the late 1930s, after discovering that his true calling was aviation. He developed into such an accomplished pilot that he was hired by the Morrison Flying Service at the Helena airport to teach other people how to fly. When the company landed a lucrative military contract after Pearl Harbor, his first students were soldiers from Fort Harrison, and later seamen sent to Montana to train as U.S. Navy pilots.

In January 1943 Harland and a couple of his students were passing the time inside a hangar when he had a fun idea. The soldiers agreed. The next day Tom Herrin received an anonymous phone call warning of an impending attack. Hearing the drone of airplanes, he went out on the porch of the farmhouse and turned his eyes to the sky. A small yellow biplane was flying toward the ranch from the south, accompanied by a much larger army aircraft. A small object appeared and grew larger as it plummeted to earth. Something exploded at Tom's feet with a resounding bang and a cloud of smoke. In fact, Harland's "bomb" was a sack of flour and a dynamite blasting cap. "What that kid needed," Tom told a newspaper, "was a few more trips to the woodshed."[2]

Despite Harland's lapses in judgment, the "kid" was the first Herrin to graduate from college. In June 1936 he was awarded a bachelor of arts degree in chemistry from Intermountain Union College in Helena. A big man on campus, he served as president of four organizations, and was elected to the student senate. He was also inducted into the "I" Club, which required initiates to hike a hundred miles, demonstrate proficiency in volleyball, basketball, baseball, and tennis and "survive an initiation."[3] After college he was hired to work as a laboratory assistant for the state livestock sanitary board, testing the blood of cattle for Bang's disease, which causes heifers to abort. In 1940 he was transferred to a division of the state board of health surveying the working conditions and occupational diseases inside Montana's five hundred industrial plants. Elizabeth Wardlaw was the first of three "Bettys" Harland would wed. The second Betty, whom he wed in 1945, was Elizabeth Burke "Biddy" Morrison—the widow of Ralph "Red" Morrison, Harland's employer and founder of the flying service, which Morrison operated until he was killed in a bomber crash in 1942 in Florida. After divorcing Morrison in 1954, Harland married Mary Elizabeth "Betty" Behring.

Harland was also the first member of his clan to serve in the armed forces. After the military determined that his services as a flight instructor were no longer necessary to the war effort—meaning he would lose his deferment—in April 1945 he enlisted as a private in the U.S. Army. Following the defeat of Germany and Japan, he was returned that November to civilian life. As the co-owner of the flying service his income multiplied. He volunteered his time to the Montana Pilots Association and the Civil Air Patrol, the civilian auxiliary of the U.S. Air Force. Meanwhile, he flew all over the continent on business trips and searched Montana's backcountry for missing hikers from the air.[4] In 1954 he moved to St. Louis, where he sold auto and aviation insurance, dying there in 1992.

The next son to flee the Herrin ranch was Wayne. Born in 1927, he was the youngest of the boys. By his twenties he seemed to be conforming to the kind of physical country life his father, grandfather, and great-grandfather had lived. He dutifully milked cows, weeded potatoes, harvested grain, castrated calves, and repaired tractors, a skill at which he was so adept he won a state-wide 4-H club contest in 1947 and was awarded a trip to the organization's national congress in Washington

DC, and a complimentary excursion on the way home, to Chicago. (A few years earlier he had won another 4-H trip, this one to Pennsylvania, for a sort of science fair exhibition in which he built and operated a miniature milk pasteurization plant.) In 1951 he married Louise Hansen, a young woman from a nearby ranch. Their wedding was a lavish double-ring ceremony at a Lutheran church with three hundred guests in attendance. Featured was a pink, four-tiered wedding cake topped with a miniature bride and groom, flower girls dressed in lavender gowns, a ringbearer in a white linen suit, an organist, and a soloist who sang "I Love You Truly," and "Always." The flower arrangements included white carnations, snapdragons, gladioli, camellias, lilies-of-the-valley, and dozens of red and pink roses.[5]

It would be fun to speculate that the floral exuberance of his wedding might have inspired Wayne's surprise career move four years later. Abandoning his wife and young son, he traveled to Portland, Oregon, where he joined his lover, a tall, dark-haired, good-looking man named Don Preston. In downtown Portland they opened a shop called Flowers Incorporated, which moved into the newly built Sheraton Hotel in 1960.

Meanwhile, Wayne had found his true calling: designing and building parade floats. During the 1960 Festival of Roses, he and Don Preston designed and supervised the building of a third of the thirty-nine floats in the annual parade, whose theme that year was "Prominent Cities of the World." The duo won the grand sweepstakes trophy for a float depicting Paris, which was commissioned by the Montgomery Ward Co., and they won the "world" trophy for a float depicting the city of Sapporo, Japan, which was built with ten thousand orchids flown in from Hawaii.[6] Two years later they again won the sweepstakes trophy for their depiction of the first elephant born at the Portland Zoo. They designed almost half of the floats in the 1964 parade, whose theme was "Between the Bookends." Their sweepstakes-winning creation, built for the U.S. National Bank, was "Return to Paradise." Derived from James Michener's 1951 short story collection, $51,000 worth of flowers were used in its creation. They also entered floats in the Torchlight Parade, the highlight of Seattle's summer Seafest.

Wayne's creative career was sparked during the early years of World War II when he was recruited by Keith—his high school older brother—to help him build attractions entered in the Vigilante Parade. In 1941 Keith's entry was the unanimous choice of the judges as the sweepstakes winner. He and his crew built a log cabin on the back of a flatbed truck, burned a corner of the structure, and pin-cushioned it with charred arrows. Wearing a cowboy hat, Keith writhed in pain on the ground outside the front door. The float was called "The Attack of the Flaming Arrow," and depicted "the Indian method of burning a settler's shack by shooting fiery arrows into it while the owner lies dying beside it."[7] In 1942 Keith reprised his theme of frontier violence with a float exploring the uses of torture. Winning first prize for "Pioneer" floats, it was called "They Wouldn't Talk." Wayne, however, did not get the chance to enter his own float in the Vigilante Parade because it was canceled from 1943 to 1946—his years at Helena High. Throughout his partnership with Preston, Wayne never lost the support of his family, who visited him on the West Coast from time to time, welcomed him and his partner on visits to the ranch, and ignored whatever scandalized shock his abandonment of his wife and son—not to mention his homosexuality—had generated in Helena.

After a string of winning seasons at the top of float-building's minor league, in 1969 Herrin and Preston broke into the big show. That is, they moved to Pasadena, California, and began designing and building floats for the world-famous Rose Bowl Parade. They won the coveted sweepstakes trophy in the 1971 parade for a float called "Georgia—Wonderland of Fun." Herrin and Preston covered the trunks of two trees with white iceberg chrysanthemums and white cattleya orchids, each blossom glued in place, and created the foliage with white mums with overlays of white roses and orchids. A pair of peacocks perched on branches were flowered with white roses, orchids, and gladioli. Three Southern belles sat in swings hanging from the branches. The parade grand marshal that year was evangelist Billy Graham, who attracted protesters from the women's liberation movement. They accused him of being a sexist. When asked about his opinion of women's liberation Graham deferred to his wife, Ruth, who replied, "I've always been liberated."[8]

On a blustery New Year's Day in 1973 more than a million spectators lined the five-and-a-half-mile route through the streets of Pasadena to watch the spectacle of marching bands, herds of horses and riders, and fifty-nine floats, featuring John Wayne as parade grand marshal and Pat Nixon waving from an open car. The theme of that year's parade was "Movie Memories." Herrin and Preston won awards for three of their eleven entries. These were "Mutiny on the Bounty," built for the province of Nova Scotia; "The Possible Dream," for the Virgin Islands, and "Ziegfeld Follies" for the Bank of America, which was highlighted by a spiral staircase sweeping around an arrangement of white cattleya orchids, and Ziegfeld Girls wearing headdresses a dozen feet in diameter.[9] Earlier that day a man was stabbed to death on the parade route, and police arrested a score of rock-throwing drunks.[10]

For the 1977 parade, whose theme was "The Good Life," Herrin-Preston Parade Floats Inc. pitched a number of design ideas to the city of Glendale, which winnowed the list to two. One was a scene of a happy family on a Sunday stroll. The other was a very large peacock. The city council debated and finally went with the peacock after a councilman named Carroll Parcher exclaimed that "Peacocks have been good to Glendale. We won our first sweepstakes in Pasadena in 1923 with a peacock. It's our city bird. Gentlemen, I say, let's go with the peacock." The council allocated $18,500 for the project. The float, christened "Life Is Beautiful," was completed fifteen minutes before the judging deadline, using the labor of 140 seniors at Hoover High who plucked rose and orchid petals from their stems for four days and glued them to the skeleton of the gigantic bird.[11] The peacock was a good choice; it was judged the most beautiful float in the parade and awarded the grand sweepstakes trophy, prompting Glendale's mayor to crow, "We definitely are proud as a peacock."[12]

Wayne and Don continued to build floats for a few more years. But by 1983 their long and successful run as both a business and romantic partnership came to an end. Herrin-Preston Parade Floats became Wayne Herrin Inc. They sold their modest three-bedroom house in Pasadena and went their separate ways. Wayne decided he could make more money landscaping and building homes. In 1993 he died of pneumonia in Phoenix.

FIG. 8. *Standing left to right:* George Burke, Catherine Burke, Marie Herrin, Tom Herrin. *Seated:* Molly Herrin, Marie's cocker spaniel "Goldie," Lillian Potee (Marie's mother), Keith Herrin, Christmas 1949. Courtesy of the Molly Burke Herrin Estate.

17

An Heir Is Born

When Keith Herrin married Molly Burke in 1949 he had rarely ventured outside Montana, the exception being his recent annual January visits to the National Western Stock Show in Denver. He had never gone to college, had always accepted the staid Republican politics of his father, and had never worked anywhere except his family's ranch. Molly had lived and traveled all over the United States, earned a college degree, adhered with an almost religious devotion to the New Deal politics of the Democratic Party, and earned her living in a man's profession. So, what did they have in common? Well, they were both tall, good-looking, and athletic. They had agreeable smiles. And they couldn't keep their hands off each other. Within five years of their wedding night, they bore four daughters; a fifth arrived in 1957. Local wags speculated that they must have decided to keep at it until they brought forth an heir.

Finally, in 1958, he arrived. That is, Keith Herrin Jr.—nicknamed Keebo—became at birth the designated recipient of his parents' portion of the ranch; the other half of it would fall to his cousin, the oldest son of Gordon Herrin. Gordon had married a petite telephone company clerk in 1940 named Alice Seiler, who occasionally sang in clubs, and with her spawned six children of their own. While Gordon worked for his father, the couple had lived in town for a few years before buying their own hundred-acre place on the ranch's eastern border. The

Herrins were no different than most American farm families in terms of their ideas about inheritance, which holds that the oldest son—or in some cases sons—should be willed the farm. The daughters were almost always excluded—and still are—from the passage of agricultural property between the generations. As one study noted: "Farmers are farmers' sons. Notable in our modern day, heralded by many as a gender-neutral society, it is farmers' sons, not farmers' daughters, who become farmers and take over ownership and management of the family farm."[1]

When Keebo was a year old, his parents were alarmed to discover a cloud in his right eye. The family doctor recommended they take him to see a specialist at Columbia-Presbyterian Hospital in New York City. They made an appointment and flew back East with him, the longest trip of his father's life. After examining the baby, a pediatric oncologist gave his parents the bad news: your son has a rare cancer called retinoblastoma, a tumor in his retina that we cannot treat. To prevent the cancer from spreading, the eye will have to be removed. (These days, treatments for the disease include radiation therapy, cryotherapy, laser therapy, and chemotherapeutic drugs administered into the artery feeding the retina.)

Keebo was fitted with a glass eye with an iris that matched the blue of his left eye. In all other ways he developed into a normal toddler and young boy. He played with his toy tractors and trucks and galloped around on his stick horse. When he was a little older he began riding real horses, at first hanging onto one of his sisters or clutching the back of her saddle, and later climbing into his own saddle on Cutie, his quarter-horse-pony mix. In the summer he tagged along mascot-like with the girls all day as they wandered around like a pack of wild monkeys in what was a childhood paradise of forts, barns, ponds, streams, gardens, pets, and farmyard animals. One of their daily stops was the sheep shed, where they fed the bum lambs from baby bottles.

The old two-story Herrin farmhouse, whose core was a log cabin built in 1880, had been divided into a sort of duplex, one half for Keebo, his sisters, and parents, and the other for his grandparents Tom and Marie. His uncle Gordon, aunt Alice, and their children lived in their own house on their own acreage. When the Herrin girls went off to the one-room Warren School a mile from the ranch, Keebo and Laura, older by a year, played with their cousins. Tom and Marie regularly bundled up Keebo and took him on overnight fishing trips to Canyon Ferry Lake in their camper (conflating the words, Keebo called his grandfather "Campah"). After Wayne moved to Portland with Don Preston, his abandoned wife and son moved into town, and Keebo's grandparents moved into their vacant one-bedroom cottage, turning over the big ranch house to Keebo and his family.

Every night Molly gathered her brood in the living room, where they perched above her on the back of a couch as she read to them from books such as *Black Beauty* and *Old Yeller*, the dog whose fate elicited from both mother and children wailing sobs. Most Sundays were devoted to hamburgers and fries. That is, they either piled into their 1953 Chevy station wagon and ordered take-out from the Zip-In'n-Out on the Great Falls road, or they assembled in the living room, where Molly went from child to child, wrote their orders on a pad, and gave them to Keith, who flipped buns and burgers and added condiments, which Molly delivered to the "customers" carhop style. The same station wagon ferried the family to the Sunset drive-in theater for second-run features such as *The Parent Trap*. Molly would occasionally ride her horse there with a neighbor to watch the more adult fare for free from a hill outside the fence.

When Keebo was five years old his family noticed that he was using the sounds of their voices to help him find his way from one place to another. Then the cloudy demon that had robbed him of his left eye appeared in his right eye. Molly flew with him back to New York, leaving his father to tend to the girls and the ranch. Keith hired a live-in maid, an overweight woman with a room in the attic who soon suffered a heart attack and died. Catherine Burke stepped in to help, but her service to the family ended abruptly after she argued with Marcia one day and was compelled to hit her over the head with a frying pan, causing insult but not injury.

Molly checked into an apartment that New York-Presbyterian provided for the families of long-term patients, while the doctors tried one treatment after another. Although the experience was a wrenching ordeal, there were a few brighter moments. Besides the attractions of Manhattan, there were visits from her sister Mary and Mary's husband, a lawyer named Lou Flax. While Molly had chosen a country-mouse life, Mary had become a city mouse. She and Lou had met while serving as staff attorneys for the Atomic Energy Commission in Washington DC. Lou moved from that agency to the Federal Power Commission and then into the private sector, where he worked as a corporate law-yer representing clients such as Texaco, which he previously had been responsible for regulating. His family had insisted that Mary convert before the wedding, and she did—from agnostic, like her sister, to Jew. On one of their visits Lou and the Burke sisters found themselves one morning seated in a restaurant near Charlton Heston, who was feeding his toy poodles from his plate. (Having two lawyers in her family would be a critical part of Molly's arsenal when push came to shove in the upcoming unpleasantries between herself, her husband, and his brother.)

None of Keebo's treatments showed any effectiveness in reducing the size of the tumor or arresting its growth. Finally, the decision was made to remove his eye, leaving him blind. Again, he was fitted with a glass eye. Without complaint, he soon adjusted to the dark world that was now his home. The heightened sense of sound and smell that the sightless often develop allowed him to navigate around the ranch on foot and on his bicycle, although his wrecks were not uncommon. He attended the Warren School with his sisters, and competed on Cutie in horse events called O-Mok-Sees. These are similar to the patterned horse racing events called gymkhana that were developed by English imperialists in India. Staged in a dirt arena chalk-marked into lanes, pole bending is one of the timed events, as is the flag race and the keyhole race, in which the rider gallops full speed through the gap between a set of poles, spins the horse around and returns through this "key-hole" to the finish line. (O-Mok-See is a Blackfeet phrase describing a courage-building ceremony staged before warriors set out on a mounted expedition against the enemy. They galloped in circles around groups of drummers, working themselves into a frenzy, jumping from their horses occasionally to dance. It roughly translates as "riding big.") Keebo competed in these field days by guiding Cutie while big-sister Marcia, sitting behind him, offered instructions about when to turn. She held her hands in the air to demonstrate to the judges that Keebo, and not Marcia, was in control. When the girls were young, O-Mok-Sees became a family passion that continued, for three of them and their parents, long into their adult lives.[2]

In the mid-1950s Gordon and Keith, now incorporated as the Herrin Brothers Partnership, began experimenting with cattle and crops in a campaign to extract as much money from the two ranches as they could. There were now between them twelve kids to feed. They abandoned the registered Hereford operation and replaced it with a herd of commercial cattle; that is, instead of breeding high-quality bulls and heifers for sale as breeding stock to other ranchers, they decided to raise animals that were doomed to slaughter.

Because they had entered the beer business by raising malt barley, they decided to plant hops, as well. Used to flavor beer, hops is a vine— technically a *bine* that uses stiff stalks and stout hairs to help it climb. Its flowers are seed cones that contain balsam and a sticky yellow substance called *lupulin* that adds bitterness and notes of citrus to beer, offsetting the sweetness produced by malt. Although it grows quickly, even during Montana's relatively short growing season, it's not a crop you can raise by simply throwing a seed in the ground and walking away. It requires carefully prepared soil, nitrogen-rich fertilizer, a lot of water, and trellises. These are constructed in the hop yard by stringing wire between tall, angled poles to which are staked heavy twine that gives the bines a platform for climbing toward the sun. The bines are unruly, and must be trained to follow the paths of the twine. The first crop was a failure, and they didn't try another one.

More successful but ultimately a failure was their sugar beet operation. The eighty acres they devoted to beets had been what locals called the "old Peter Penny place." The Herrins had bought the land after the former occupants were forced to flee for their lives in 1942 when someone in their six-room ranch house botched the filling of a gasoline-fueled lantern, resulting in a fire that quickly became an inferno. People in downtown Helena, five miles away, could see the flames lighting up the night sky.[3]

In late April—a month before the last frost—seeds were planted in rows between ditches that drew water from the Helena Valley Irrigation Canal and Prickly Pear Creek. In much the same operation as their irrigation system for potatoes, the Herrins then flooded the fields by forcing the water out of the ditches with canvas dams. Unlike potatoes, sugar beets require tons of barnyard manure, which must be worked into the soil with a plow and a mulching disc before planting can begin. The ugly, beige-colored tubers must be thinned, and weeded. To perform these backbreaking tasks the Herrins hired a crew of seasonal Mexican farm workers. This workforce included whole families who lived in a large bunkhouse on the ranch while they worked, supervised by an English-speaking foreman. The Herrins supplied the food, which the Mexicans cooked outdoors, preparing tortillas the traditional way on a flat griddle over a wood fire in a brick stove. When they were finished working the Herrin place the families moved on to the next farm. In order to make some walk-around cash, Marcia Herrin and her sisters occasionally helped with the weeding. But once the plants matured, weeding was no longer necessary because their leafy tops overshadowed lesser plants.

In late September the beets were harvested. First, the tops were cut off and fed to the Herrin cattle. Then the tubers were pried from the ground using a tractor fitted with a digging implement that fed them onto an attached conveyor belt, which deposited them into a dump truck. The beets were shipped by rail to the American Sugar processing plant in Missoula. Operating twenty-four seven, the plant washed the beets and cut them into slices the size of french fries that were then soaked with hot water and compressed into pulp to extract the sugar "juice." Further refining produced crystalline sugar and molasses.

By 1962 the Herrin brothers were growing seventeen tons of beets per acre, netting the family an annual payment from the company of

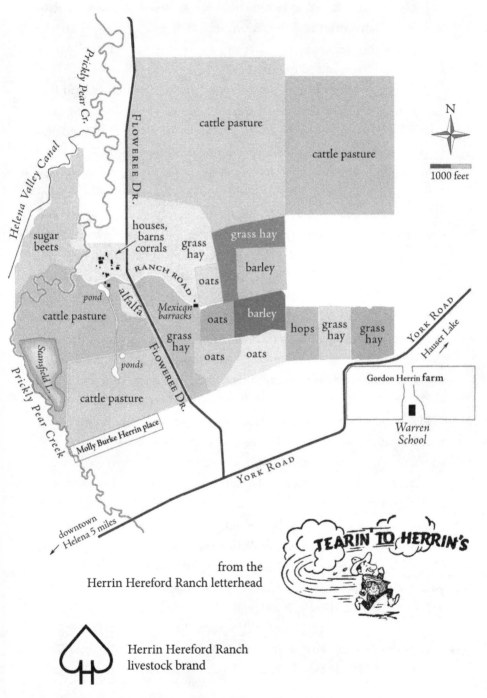

Herrin Hereford Ranch
Based on field surveys conducted January 1967

N

1000 feet

Prickly Pear Cr.

Helena Valley Canal

FLOWEREE DR.

cattle pasture

cattle pasture

sugar
beets

houses,
barns
corrals

grass
hay

grass hay

barley

RANCH ROAD

oats

pond

alfalfa

Mexican
barracks

oats

barley

hops

grass
hay

grass
hay

cattle pasture

grass
hay

oats

oats

YORK ROAD

Hauser Lake

ponds

Stansfield L.

cattle pasture

Gordon Herrin farm

Prickly Pear Creek

Molly Burke Herrin place

Warren
School

FLOWEREE DR.

YORK ROAD

downtown
Helena 5 miles

TEARIN' TO HERRIN'S

from the
Herrin Hereford Ranch letterhead

Herrin Hereford Ranch
livestock brand

MAP 3. Herrin Hereford Ranch, 1967. Created by author.

more than $13,000 (worth around $110,000 in 2020). Still, the margin of profit was so thin that after American Sugar closed its Missoula plant in 1966 to concentrate its production facilities in Billings, the cost to the Herrins of shipping their product to what boosters called the "Magic City" priced them out of the market.

The focus of the two ranches returned to cattle, potatoes, and hay. Meanwhile, the kids immersed themselves in O-Mok-Sees and their 4-H clubs. Their parents hired a pair of Mexican wranglers, Pablo and Geraldo Rivera, to break the family's young horses and ride herd on the cattle. On the Herrin place this involved moving them on horseback from pasture to pasture (the ubiquitous four-wheeler had not been invented), bringing in cows to be doctored and calves to be branded and castrated, and rounding up animals for shipment to slaughter. When they stayed at the ranch, the Riveras lived in what the family referred to as "the Mexican cabin." The brothers, however, were not treated like servants. Pablo competed in O-Mok-Sees as part of the family's team. Riding a bay mare named Scat, his favorite event was the quarter-mile race, which was staged against three other quarter horses on the one-mile oval track at the fairgrounds.[4] Their long journeys between Mexico and the ranch were made a good deal more fun after Tom and Marie sold them their 1956 two-door, yellow Cadillac Coup de Ville.

Marcia and her siblings had joined a 4-H club called Bobbins and Bales. Founded in 1902, 4-H ("Head, Heart, Hands and Health") was a program for rural kids that was intended to supplement elementary schooling with instruction in the latest farming, ranching, and homemaking practices. In many ways it was the agrarian equivalent of America's urban youth programs, the Boy Scouts and Girl Scouts. Sponsored by the United States Department of Agriculture and administered through land-grant colleges such as Montana State University in Bozeman, it was believed that adult farmers listened to new ideas about agriculture only if these were presented to them by their children.

In 1968, when he was in the fifth grade, Keebo threw himself into Bobbins and Bales. His projects included sheep breeding and lamb fattening. In May he bought a lamb from his sisters for ten dollars and named him Tom Slick after one of his favorite cartoon characters, a grinning, maniacal race-car driver who drove a vehicle called the Thunderbolt Grease-Slapper. Keebo loved the noise blaring from this TV show, and the vivid descriptions his sisters provided. About the lamb, Keebo wrote (typing the report himself with a typewriter whose keys he had memorized): "I couldn't catch him very easy. . . . He always ran away from me, but after a while he got better about that." Over the next six weeks Tom Slick grew bigger and fatter. But then, in August, the lamb got sick. Keebo stayed with him, giving him water, but the animal bloated (a painful condition caused by the build-up of gas in the rumen). "He had spells and kicked up," Keebo wrote. "About 2 hours later all of a sudden he tried to get up and then he died."

The following May Keebo bought another lamb from his sisters, again for ten dollars. He named it Nuttin (because it rhymed with mutton). Nuttin weighed seventy-nine pounds; eighty-four days later he weighed ninety pounds and was sold at the annual 4-H Fair for twenty-five dollars and twenty-nine cents. Factoring in the five dollars and eighty-six cents worth of oats and barley required to fatten the lamb, Keebo's profit was fifteen dollars and eighty-six cents. He wrote that when he took charge of the lamb, "luckily he was tame. Every time I worked with Nuttin he acted better." For Keebo, these 4-H experiences with sheep were intended to teach him lessons in farm economics, perseverance, and the harsh reality of raising and caring for animals that would one day be led to slaughter.[5]

But Keebo needed no reminders about the value of tenacity. Despite the fact that the cancer had spread into the bone of the orbit and his brain and compelled him to wear an eye patch because there was no longer room for his glass eye, and despite the fact that his father had abandoned him and his sisters, leaving his family destitute, he remained cheerful and optimistic. In his 4-H report covering 1969 he wrote: "I hope next year will be as fun as this year."

18

Dark Acres

The neighbors saw what they wanted to see and disregarded the rest. Keith and Molly Herrin and their kids, it seemed to them, could well have been the poster family for rural America. They were pretty, prosperous, hardworking, and civic-minded. The lives of the children were filled with endless summer days riding horses, herding cattle, swimming, playing badminton and roller-skating on their paved outdoor court, jumping on the trampoline their father built for them, and holding meetings of their secret Hawk Riders Club in one fort or another, guided by strict adherence to *Roberts Rules of Order*. They made money raising and selling sheep and calves and occasionally weeding the sugar beets for extra cash. One year Kitty raised and sold a grand champion Southdown lamb named Oscar for $350 and promptly used the money to buy downhill skis. They were surrounded by aunts and uncles and grandparents and cousins, including the three boys brought into the world by Mary and Lou Flax, who took the train out from Washington DC, to spend part of their summers at the ranch. In high school the phone at the Herrin house rang constantly with clamoring and debauched calls from boyfriends (monitored on the party line by their grandmother Marie, who reported perceived scandalous language to the girls' father). The Herrins were regularly mentioned in the *Independent Record* for their triumphs on horseback, their farming, stock raising and 4-H successes, and the girls' scholarships to college. Mary Herrin was featured in the *Western Horseman* magazine.[1]

In the winter the kids ice-skated on the stock pond, and sometimes Keith tethered six sleds together and pulled the kids across the snow-covered pastures with one of his horses, a rope tied to the saddle horn. Even during bad weather, they were responsible for feeding and caring for their 4-H animals. Keith often piled the kids behind the wheel of his huge hay truck and directed them to steer from pasture to pasture as he stood in the bed and heaved down hay to the cattle. The Herrins never once raised a hand to their children. Whenever one of the sisters reported that another sister had hit her, Molly told her to hit her back. Not that the parents never lost their tempers. When Kitty was six, her father asked her what she wanted for her birthday, and she told him she wanted a pistol.

"Why would you want that?" he asked.

"So I can kill Nazis."

Enraged, he tried to grab her, but she eluded him and fled into the bathroom, locking the door behind her. He pulled up a chair outside, determined to wait her out. But after a while she climbed through the window, went to the barn, and hung out there till he was asleep before returning to the room she shared with her sisters. (Although many fathers, after their experiences in World War II, might have shared Kitty's attitude about fascism, Keith had never served in the armed forces. His anger was based on his belief that this sort of extremism in a young girl could only have been planted there by Molly, whose liberal politics were the opposite of his. As an example of their differences, he once pointed to a white boy dancing with a black girl at a 4-H party and exclaimed, "That just isn't right." Molly, on the other hand, had been raised by a woman who would later contribute money to the Black Panther Party.)

In 1966, while also serving as a 4-H leader, Keith was elected president of the newly formed National Saddle Clubs Association, which he organized by recruiting members in twenty-four states and Puerto Rico.[2] And he served as chairman of the pre-rodeo entertainment committee, which put on opening warm-up events for the big crowds attending the

Last Chance Stampede. In one of these events, he barrel raced against a motorcyclist named Jim Black. Riding Lucky Streak, his chestnut mare, Herrin most always won.[3] Another event was the "Devil's Cowhide," a race in which each of several riders dragged at full speed a passenger spread-eagled and face-down on a cowhide, which was roped to the saddle horn of his horse, around a barrel at the opposite end of the rodeo arena and back to the starting line in a cloud of choking dust. Another odd event was the "Dinner Bell Handicap," in which nursing foals were separated from their mothers and penned on the racetrack while the mares were penned in the rodeo arena. Informal bets were laid on which frantic baby would be the first to reunite with its mother after the foals were released.[4]

Meanwhile, Molly served on the Warren school board and worked as the board's clerk. She also volunteered to be an election judge. Once a week she bundled up her kids and took them to the library, where they each checked out one book. The family was not religious, but Keith and Molly succumbed at Christmas and Easter to pressure from Marie Herrin and dutifully marched the kids to St. Paul's United Methodist Church. Because the family was chronically late, they were the object of everyone's attention as they made their way down the aisle to Tom and Marie's front-row pew, which the devout Marie "rented" with an annual tax-deductible tithe to the church.

What the community didn't see—or refused to see—was the inexorable slide of the ranch into insurmountable debt, and the disintegration of Keith and Molly's marriage. Because Molly filed the taxes for the ranch, she saw, beginning in 1960, that the operation wasn't bringing in enough money to support two big extended families. Part of this was the conflict between Gordon and Keith, who had different visions of how their thousand acres should be exploited. Gordon was a farmer at heart who wanted to experiment with different kinds of crops. Keith was a stockman whose passion was horses and cattle. While Gordon was planting sugar beets and barley, Keith was growing the herd until it reached five hundred pairs—that is, five hundred cows and their calves. But their eighty acres of sugar beets became worthless once the processing plant in Missoula closed. And the prices for beef cows fell 10 percent in 1960, wiping out the ranch's profit margin for the year. By 1965 prices were only 80 percent of what they were six years earlier. It would be a decade until they rose back to their 1959 level. Foreign imports and a glut of domestic beef on the market were blamed for plummeting prices. Compounding these financial setbacks was the inflation rate, which began ratcheting up in 1960 and spiraled by 1970 to six times the 1961 rate.

In 1964 Thomas, the Herrin patriarch, suffered a heart attack and was taken by ambulance from the ranch to St. Peter's Hospital in Helena. A month later he was dead. (Later that same year Molly's father, George Burke, died at the age of eighty-five, after first arthritis and then a stroke in 1952 disabled him. Molly's mother, Catherine Burke, cared for him until his death. Tough and wiry with a bone-crushing handshake, she lived to the age of ninety-three, when she decided to stop eating.)

In Tom Herrin's will he left 15 percent of his estate to each Harland and Wayne, and 35 percent each to Gordon and Keith. The boys, he noted, "have given all their time and labor to the ranch for many years and because of this I feel [they] have been unable to establish themselves in any other business." However, Tom also stipulated in his will that his sons would not get their shares until Marie died. For the next decade she would control the Herrin's wealth, which included highly liquid stocks and bonds found concealed after her husband's death under the desk blotter in his office. She added this small fortune to her own family money, which she doled out to Gordon and Keith whenever they needed big ticket items for the ranch, such as a new stock truck, a swather, and a hay bale stacker (which would later be instrumental in yet another financial calamity).

In 1965 the families were advised to incorporate in order to shield themselves personally from any legal or financial liabilities the ranch might incur. By then what became Herrin Ranch Inc. was borrowing heavily from the Production Credit Association to stay afloat. The PCA had been founded in 1933 to loan money to farmers and stockmen who put up the equity in their real estate as collateral. Owned by its borrowers, it operated much like a savings and loan, capitalized with money from commercial banks and repaying these loans with the principal and interest paid by borrowers like Herrin Ranch Inc. The money was intended as a line of credit used to buy the supplies, labor, and equipment these farmers and ranchers needed to turn a profit and repay the loans with interest. But the Herrins were using the money for day-to-day expenses as well, even though in this era before credit cards they also took advantage of the charge accounts offered by downtown merchants—clothes from the Globe and groceries from the Garden Spot, paid for twice a year after the crops and the cattle were sold.

In 1960 Gordon was elected president of the Lewis and Clark County Farm Bureau. The American Farm Bureau Federation was founded in 1919 "to make the business of farming more profitable and the community a better place to live," according to its mission statement. By 1960 the federation had become a politically conservative, rabidly anti-communist organization that extolled the virtues of capitalism and attacked most government attempts to control the economy. The Montana branch agitated for the United States to cease its financial support of the United Nations because the organization believed it was controlled by the Soviet Bloc. It demanded that the U.S. Postal Service and customs agents seize publications and books published behind the Iron Curtain. It called for the end of government control of agriculture and farm subsidies, applauding a delegate who said that although that would hurt farmers "we should practice what we preach." (This apparently brave position, however, was simply posturing, because the Montana Farm Bureau knew that commodity subsidies would never be eliminated for wheat as long as the cotton and tobacco states controlled the farm bill.) It urged the Board of Regents to fire any employee of the University of Montana who "further and aid socialism or communism." The response from the faculty council of Montana's six-unit university system was tepid. It is the "right and duty" of American citizens, including state employees, the council replied, "to voice honest differences of opinion on public issues."[5]

The bureau successfully lobbied the U.S. House to shelve the 1961 Wilderness Act passed by the Senate. In his arguments against the bill, the head of the Montana State Farm Bureau called it one of the worst pieces of legislation ever passed by the Senate because it would restrict grazing, mining, and timber cutting. However, he *would* support putting aside a small piece of Montana designated as wilderness if it could be a place "where the western Senators who voted for the wilderness bill could be exiled to the solitude they are so desirous of creating for us and our grandchildren." The bill was revived in 1964 and passed both House and Senate despite the bureau's objections. By a vote of 373–1 in the House, the law established protection from development for five great swaths of pristine land in Montana—the Bob Marshall Wilderness, the Gates of the Mountains, the Selway-Bitterroot, the Anaconda-Pintler, and the Cabinet Mountains.

Before he was replaced in 1962 with a new Farm Bureau president, Gordon used his pulpit to launch a series of public rants. He lambasted Medicaid and federal aid to education. Parroting the Farm Bureau Federation's official line, he called the federal government's Wheat Stabilization Program a "socialist" attempt to take over American agriculture and rob farmers of their "freedom." This program was a decade-old allotment system intended to address the glut of wheat on the market, which tended to depress prices. Farmers who volunteered for the program agreed to restrict the number of acres they planted to wheat in exchange for a guaranteed fixed price per bushel, paid by the government, which then stored the grain in silos at taxpayer expense.[6] The program included payments for acres that were not planted to wheat. "Our government was established on . . . principles of the Ten Commandments," he wrote to the *Independent Record*, apparently confusing the Old Testament with the U.S. Constitution. "the principle of a free people—free to raise what they want, where they want to raise it."[7]

A referendum put before wheat farmers in 1961 asked them to renew the program, which proposed smaller acreage allotments and higher payments. Eligible to vote were U.S. wheat farmers who harvested at least 13.5 acres. Although the referendum went down to defeat in Montana, thanks to Gordon and his Farm Bureau cronies, it was approved by an overwhelming majority nationally, compelling Montana farmers to abide by the vote. Gordon complained bitterly about the decision, claiming that "there is no difference between the Billy Sol Estes case and the wheat referendum," referring inexplicably to the fast-talking Texas con man who leveraged cotton allotments and fertilizer tanks into a vast, illegal fortune.[8]

In another tirade, Gordon accused what he called the "socialist" Federal Bureau of Reclamation of destroying land values in the Helena Valley and forcing the failure of "many" farmers. At issue was the cost of water produced by the Helena Valley Irrigation District. This was a bureau project constructed in the 1950s that siphons water from the Missouri River after it turns a pair of electricity-generating turbines in the Canyon Ferry Dam and pipes it into a canal twenty-five miles long that circles around the valley, feeding forty miles of irrigation ditches. Not only does the district supply water to farmers, it is a source of Helena's municipal water. Gordon claimed the district was forced on the 40 percent of valley farmers who voted against it by the 60 percent who did. A bureau spokesman pointed out that this is how democracy works, and that the figure cited by Gordon about the water's cost was more than twice the actual figure. He also refuted Gordon's claim that his sugar beets require nine acre-feet of water, pointing out that according to a Montana State College bulletin two to three acre-feet of water is sufficient to grow beets in the Helena Valley.[9]

Gordon was elected Farm Bureau president on the strength of his efforts to prevent Lewis and Clark County from using property taxes to pay for improvements of the runways at Helena's airport. Badly constructed in 1935, one of the runways was so spongy that on March 23, 1960, the left landing gear of a forty-passenger Convair jet taxiing prior to liftoff sank into it up to the axle.[10] Gordon and fellow members of the Farm Bureau's Helena Valley unit voted 2–1 to lobby voters with the message that airport improvements should be paid for by the users of the airport—airlines and passengers—not taxpayers. "We oppose subsidy to any industry, including agriculture, by any level of government," the county Farm Bureau said. "Government subsidies have inevitably led to loss of freedom by the industry concerned at a great price in taxpayer dollars. Air service industries cannot be catalogued as an exemption to the policy."[11] In its battle against the Helena Chamber of Commerce—the leading champion of runway improvements—the Farm Bureau was joined by the Northern Pacific and Great Northern Railways. In their ads urging taxpayers to vote no on the airport bond, the railroads argued: "It isn't right that you should have to pay for somebody else's seat on the airline. The cost should be charged to the man who rides on the airliner."[12] Five insurance company members of the chamber of commerce countered with an ad pointing out that in 1959 the railroads made $14 million from the sale of timber, oil, gas, minerals, and real estate rent from their vast land grant holdings across Montana—given to them by American taxpayers—yet objected to paying their "fair share" of city and county taxes.[13] In June voters approved the measure by a wide margin.

Gordon was on the losing side of yet another contentious airport bond issue six years later.[14] As president of a shadowy group called the Lewis and Clark Concerned Taxpayer Committee, he opposed using property taxes to lengthen and strengthen the runway that was built in 1960, arguing, again, that the airlines and passengers should pay for it. Without revealing his identity, he circulated anonymous "fact sheets" that included personal attacks on one of the board members and the man's wife, Sandy and Beth McPherson, accusing them of supporting the bond measure for personal financial gain. The allegations included an unsubstantiated allegation that sales of the Texaco brand of aviation fuel sold at the airport would line the board member's pocket because he was a part owner of the Texaco bulk fuel plant in Helena (in fact, the airlines paid Texaco's corporation headquarters for their fuel, not the bulk plant). The *Independent Record* published a lengthy editorial a week before the vote that ridiculed the "Concerned Taxpayers." Gordon was finally compelled to out himself as the organization's president.[15] He told a reporter that the only reason the airlines wanted a longer runway was to bring in bigger loads so they could make bigger profits.[16] It would be fun to speculate that Gordon's antipathy toward surrendering his property taxes to the airport was retaliation for his brother Harland's bombing of the Herrin Dairy in 1943. But his motive was likely much more ideological than emotional.[17]

While Gordon was tilting at windmills and blaming the government for his financial problems, he quarreled with his brother Keith about the operation of the ranch. Keith reacted by throwing himself into his cattle and horses. And he began a series of secretive adulterous liaisons with his neighbors' wives. One autumn day in 1962, Molly was driving the kids home from the Warren School in the family station wagon when she made a detour down a country lane and stopped in front of the rural mailbox belonging to a married couple who lived in a big stone house behind the gate. She rolled down the driver's side window and reached beside her on the seat for a pair of black high heels. She opened the mailbox door, shoved the shoes inside, and drove her bewildered children home.

19

Res Ipsa Loquitur

In August 1969, six months after he abandoned his family, Keith was granted a divorce. In the settlement Molly was awarded full custody of her six children, and he was required to pay her $450 a month in child support beginning July 1, 1969, plus $1,320 for various expenses, including the balance of one of the medical bills for Keebo's treatment at Presbyterian Hospital. A few days before he fled Montana, he sold 481 shares of Herrin Ranch Inc. to Gordon for $48,100, payable in twenty annual installments, taking $500 up front to finance his exodus. He signed over these payments to Molly, stipulating that if she were to die during the twenty-year term of the note or remarry within ten years, the payments would be placed in a trust for Keebo, under the stipulation that if the boy were to die before the final payment was made, the balance of the money would revert to his father.

In the understated language of the law, which is often accurate but not necessarily true, Molly and Keith split up because of "various and diverse and unhappy differences." In fact, years before the divorce Keith had become involved with another woman. This was Shirley Beaver Baertsch, who had been the wife of a telephone installer and racehorse owner named Forrest "Skeeter" Baertsch. The Baertsches had been members of the Helena Trail Riders, and in 1965 began boarding two ponies at the Herrin Ranch, where Keith and the girls had been training them for the three Baertsch children to compete on in O-Mok-Sees. The Baertsch family became frequent visitors to the ranch, and one thing led to another.

Two weeks before Keith left Helena, Gordon ordered him to divest himself of any claim to the corporation. And because Keith intended to marry Shirley Baertsch, he wanted a quick divorce from Molly, who refused to agree to any property settlement that didn't provide some sort of income for her and the children and a guarantee that she and the children would not be forced to leave the ranch. Keith agreed "to do whatever is within his power" to prevent Gordon from evicting them.

The February day Keith picked for his getaway did not go quite as planned. Although Molly and Keebo were away in Great Falls at the School for the Deaf and Blind, Laura, the youngest daughter, had come down with a cold and was spending the day at home, presumably in his care, instead of attending the Warren School with her siblings. He brought Laura's lunch into her bedroom and wheeled in the family's portable television on a TV tray to distract her. He had packed his guns, saddles, and clothing in a car parked out of sight in a shed on Gordon's place. When all was ready, he drove to the Helena airport and unloaded his belongings into a small airplane that belonged to a cattle buyer who had helped him land a job managing a ranch. Five hours later they touched down in Wheatland, Wyoming. Keith's new life had began.

On August 23, six days after he was granted a divorce, he married Shirley Baertsch in Wheatland. She had divorced Skeeter Baertsch on June 6. The district court had initially awarded custody of their two young boys to their father, and Shirley had been granted custody of their four-year-old daughter. But following two events in July, Skeeter asked the court to reconsider its ruling. First, police were called to a Helena home where Shirley was staying following her exodus from her husband. At trial she had testified that the cause of their divorce was not another man. However, Skeeter had gone to the home and discovered another man on the premises—Keith Herrin, who at the time was still married to Molly. (He was back in Montana ostensibly to take possession of a horse, which he failed to do because his daughters had hidden the gelding—once the Herrin herd sire—on a neighboring ranch.) A vituperative argument erupted at Shirley's home and the police asked Skeeter to leave, which he did.

A week later Shirley was exercising her visitation rights at Skeeter's Helena Valley home, where the boys had always lived. A disagreement with her older son, aged nine, turned violent when she attacked him with one of her high heels. The father intervened and slapped her with the back of his hand. Although she denied striking the little boy, photographs of his bruises were introduced into evidence, as was testimony from a neighbor about the injuries. The court ruled that the girl should be removed from Shirley's custody and given to Skeeter, and that her visitation rights be curtailed. Shirley appealed to the Montana Supreme Court, which upheld the lower court's decisions (see appendix 3).

Keith and Shirley stayed in Wyoming for only a few months before he took a job managing a large Angus ranch near Centralia, Missouri. After a short posting there, they moved back to Montana, where he managed the Newman Ranch near the largely abandoned town of Cohagen in remote Garfield County. In 1976 they returned to Helena, now jobless and looking for some way to make money.

After Keith left Helena in 1969, Molly faced the challenge of supporting a large family whose breadwinner had jumped ship. Over the coming months she could count only on the child support Keith was ordered to deposit with the court, plus Gordon's annual payment for Keith's shares in the ranch. Her income would amount to less than 80 percent of what was required to support a family of seven and their animals at a subsistence level. On top of that, Gordon demanded that if she were going to stay on the place she would have to pay him $125 a month rent for what had been her home of twenty years, where she had raised the children, kept house, and worked in several capacities for the ranch, keeping its books and filing its taxes. He also wanted pasture rent for the family's horses; they were allowed one horse each for free, but their other five horses would have to pony up ten dollars each.

But a matter more pressing than money was the accelerating decline of Keebo's health. In late 1969 the huge, fast-growing tumor in his brain and orbital socket began protruding from his skull. Suffering excruciating pain, he was put in his mother's bed and would stay there for three months, too weak to walk and, finally, too weak to eat. In March he lapsed into a coma and was taken to Shodair Children's Hospital in Helena. With Molly and Catherine Burke by his side, he died there on April 5, at the age of eleven. His older sisters were called into the principal's office at Helena High, where they were told the news.

Keebo's death triggered the clause in the property settlement that directed Gordon to henceforth make payments to Keith for his shares of the ranch. But Keith told his brother to continue paying these annual installments to Molly, at least until the girls were married and their husbands, presumably, would provide for them. None of them, of course, would ever have been named as an heir to the Herrin ranch, had Keith decided to stay. Meanwhile, Gordon's financial problems worsened to the point that he felt compelled to sell fifty acres of his smaller place to a developer who would put a 308-unit trailer court called Leisure Village on the land. Gordon's ranching neighbors were enraged. Not only was valuable agricultural land lost forever, they argued, but all these new people would demand roads, utilities, and schooling for their kids, expensive things that would raise property taxes. Gordon replied that the sale was a matter of economics—the land under Leisure Village wasn't very fertile, he said, and he could make more money concentrating his operation on the land he owned with better topsoil. When the neighbors warned the county about the septic problems Leisure Village might cause because of the high water table, Gordon sniffed: "Pollution. The first Indian had a pollution problem. But we have technology to handle our pollution problems. And technology will keep up with them."[1]

Because Gordon did not want to live next to a trailer court, as a consequence of the sale he ordered Molly and her children to move out of the main ranch house so he could move into it (his mother was still living in the smaller house, which had been Wayne's home before he ran off with Don Preston). Molly drafted a letter to Gordon, aided by the attorneys in the family—sister Mary and Lou Flax—who discerned from Molly's many letters to and from lawyers that he was not only charging *her* rent he was cooking the books to charge Keith rent, as well. Why he believed he could charge rent to *anyone* was based on his assertion that the Production Credit Association demanded these payments after the ranch fell even deeper into debt by taking out yet another PCA loan in 1970. Since she was no longer keeping the books for the ranch, Molly had no way of knowing if Gordon was telling the truth. After this subterfuge was pointed out to Gordon by a Helena attorney Molly had hired, Gordon relented and allowed her to stay in the house. But he increased the rent to $175 a month plus $10 pasturage for each of the family's dozen horses.

Molly didn't want to give Gordon another dime for her family's herd. Although she had taken a job assigning Dewey Decimal System numbers to books arriving at the Montana State Library in Helena, she was no longer receiving child support for Keebo, nor for three of her five daughters, who were now past eighteen and enrolled at the University of Montana. But she was not without other resources. In 1950 she and sister Mary had purchased two parcels of land on Prickly Pear Creek three-quarters of a mile upstream from the Herrin ranch. Included were thirty-three acres of grassy meadows and dense copses of cottonwood and sandbar willow. Back in 1954 Molly had removed Keith from the deed on her twenty acres, concerned that it would be jeopardized by any financial problems the ranch might encounter. She now moved the horses to this land, which she and sister Mary owned free and clear.

Like many American alarmists during the height of the Cold War, Gordon and his Farm Bureau cronies believed socialists and communists were infesting Montana. But he was developing another obsession, as well: invasive weeds. While alien ideologies and foreign plants come on regardless of prediction, for Gordon the solution to these threats was the same: elimination. In the matter of knapweed, leafy spurge, and dalmatian toadflax that meant flooding them with herbicides, such as 2-4-D, 2-4-5-T, and Tordon.

In the early 1960s, Lewis and Clark County established itself as a weed control district and appointed Gordon as its chairman in order to do battle against the thirteen species of weeds the county declared "noxious." He soon came under increasing criticism from environmentalists for what they claimed was the county's indiscriminate spraying along the 1,100 miles of rural roads. Herbicides have very little long-term effect against invasive weeds, they argued, but kill plants that provide food and cover for a myriad of small animals and insects, including pollinators such as bees. There were complaints from people living along these rural roads about gardens and fruit trees ruined by Gordon's herbicides. Especially toxic, critics claimed, was 2-4-5-T, which contained dioxin. This is the active ingredient in Agent Orange, used by the U.S. government in the late 1960s to defoliate large swaths of South Vietnam and Cambodia in order to deprive communist troops of their jungle sanctuaries.[2]

At 1975 meetings between the Weed Control Board and its critics, a weed control specialist from the Cooperative Extension Service in Bozeman advised against using the herbicide along roads, a practice that had been abandoned by some state and federal agencies. A representative from the Montana Department of Fish and Game registered his general opposition to the use of herbicides and to specific weed control strategies like Gordon's that rely exclusively on herbicides. But Gordon ignored their objections and announced that the spraying would continue. He told a retired forester who was one of the more vocal of these critics to shut up. It was Gordon's position that weeds were a far more serious environmental danger than herbicides and that he, Gordon, was the true environmentalist for waging war against "weed pollution."[3] Yet the county stopped using 2-4-5-T in 1976 because of complaints, and in 1979 the Environmental Protection Agency banned it after significant evidence came forward that it caused miscarriages and health problems among residents in one area of Oregon's coastal mountains sprayed from the air with the herbicide.[4]

While Gordon was battling weeds, fending off critics, and scouring Montana for subversives, in 1978, Keith and Shirley filed a lawsuit against Molly, demanding that the annual payments she was receiving from Gordon be given to them, instead. These fifteen payments, including principal and interest, would amount to more than $45,000. They argued that the property settlement stipulated that this money was intended to be deposited into a trust to pay for Keebo's care until he was twenty-one years old, but at his death the payments were supposed to revert to Keith. For a few years he had graciously assigned the money to Molly so she would have some financial support for their daughters. But now the girls were women. Judge Gordon Bennett ordered Gordon Herrin to deposit his 1978 payment with the court. He then awarded this payment and all of the others to Keith and Shirley.

Molly appealed to the Montana Supreme Court. She argued that the trust for Keebo that was devised by the property settlement had never existed because he died before it could be established. The court agreed. "Because no trust was established, it could not cease; there being no trust, there was no property and income to revert to [Keith]." Justice John Conway Harrison wrote the unanimous decision taking the payments away from Keith and Shirley and awarding them to Molly. "The ranch was the only substantial asset of their marriage; Molly had contributed to the marital unit and to the upkeep of the ranch property; she kept only her own personal property."[5]

Following the decision, Keith wrote to Molly: "All those years I worked, during high school and until we were married, for nothing was my inheritance. . . . I pray you'll accept the Lord in your heart so you'll have something important in life. Unless you come to the Lord it is going to be a great disappointment to the girls when you don't want to spend eternity with them in Heaven." He enclosed a flyer warning Molly that "Hell is waiting for you! Unless you repent of your sins." It offered a "beautiful two-color, illustrated, three-hundred-thirty-six-page book, *Soon-Coming World-Shaking Events: As Foretold by God Almighty.*" The price was only three dollars. It promised that "Russia will be destroyed!" and explored the question, "Will America survive?"

In April, Molly received a check from Keith for $2027.14, the payment from Gordon that the district court had awarded him before its ruling was reversed. Written in the memo line were the words: "Blood Money."

20

The Last Acre

Following the district court ruling in their favor, Keith and Shirley were given permission by Gordon to build a house on the Herrin ranch at a spot that was in sight of Molly's land on the Prickly Pear Creek. But because the perennial water table was so high the county refused to issue them a septic permit. They appealed, but then dropped the matter after the Montana Supreme Court ruled against them in the matter of Gordon's payments because Keith didn't have enough assets to qualify for a mortgage.[1]

In January 1983 Keith finally landed a full-time job when he was hired by the Lewis and Clark County Weed Control Board as supervisor of the Weed District. Rather than face charges of nepotism, Gordon resigned from the board during the search for a new supervisor, but was reappointed after his brother accepted the position.[2] Like most of Keith's jobs, this one didn't last long. In July the Montana Department of Agriculture ruled that he had violated state law when he authorized his crew to spray herbicides along Ten Mile Creek, which was the source of half of Helena's municipal water supply. The product's label clearly stated that it should never be used around water because it kills aquatic plants. Board members said that the herbicide incident was only one of several reasons why Herrin was fired. "It was the final straw," one of them told the newspaper.[3]

The state could have pressed criminal charges against Keith, but was satisfied when the board fired him and compelled two other members to resign. Keith denied the charges and claimed that the board canned him because they had been told by the county extension agent that each one of them could be sued as individuals if they didn't take action against Herrin. In a letter to the Agriculture Department, Keith accused the agency of dealing "a severe blow to agriculture and the environment with the way you handled a 30-square-foot infraction."[4]

Gordon had resigned from the board several months before his brother was fired because the members were exploring tactics other than herbicides to combat weeds. "Someday they'll be sorry," Gordon told the *Independent Record,* posing for a photograph with a large container of Tordon and an even larger container of Roundup, an herbicide that kills almost every plant it touches and is cited as the cause of cancers whose victims have settled a $10 billion lawsuit against the manufacturer.[5] "I don't believe in complete chemical control but you can't get rid of the chemicals until you get rid of the weeds." He said because the state had imposed a ninety-day ban on the county's use of herbicides: "Weed control has been set back ten years and it is the Department of Agriculture and the State of Montana that did it. If they don't stand beside the weed boards in the state, they are not for agriculture but against agriculture." He explained how he uses herbicides on his ranch. "I use Tordon around here . . . I spray Roundup right down to the water's edge, too."[6]

Gordon's financial problems grew worse when he was compelled to hire lawyers to defend him against a liability lawsuit. On October 3, 1974, he was driving his massive hay bale stacker from the York Road along a dirt shortcut called Helberg Drive to a paved street called Herrin Road. A family who lived nearby, in one of Leisure Village's many trailers, plowed their station wagon into the huge machine. Their two-year-old daughter, Tanya Kimes, suffered a concussion. In 1983, after her parents claimed the girl suffered from learning disabilities and diminished memory and also had developed a tendency to daydream and fall asleep at odd times, they sued Herrin in Lewis and Clark District Court for $750,000.

Herrin argued that the parents, Ella Mae and Michael Kimes—and not himself—were to blame for the child's brain disorders, if in fact they even existed. He cited the father's drinking, the family's poverty, and their fighting. Testimony for the defense centered on Ella Mae's arrest in 1977 for using a .22 Magnum pistol to shoot her husband in the arm and the face outside the family's trailer. Mr. Kimes was soon released from the hospital. Mrs. Kimes was released on her own recognizance, and the charges against her were eventually dropped.

Herrin claimed that he had been distracted by a logging truck to his right barreling down the York Road and had not looked to his left at the approaching station wagon. Even so, he argued, because his bale stacker entered Herrin Road at an intersection, he had the right-of-way and the Kimes vehicle should have yielded. The plaintiffs countered that under Montana law drivers are required "to keep a look out" at all times.

Addressing the cash settlement, Herrin's attorney argued that even if Tanya's problems actually existed and had been caused by the accident, they weren't worth $750,000. And even if the jury found his client negligent—the attorney argued using a bizarre twist of logic—it should still not award Tanya any money because that would signal to her that there was something wrong with her. "If you shower that kid with money," he said, "is her lot in life going to be improved?" The expert witnesses employed by both parties testified that poor home environment may cause symptoms such as Tanya's. However, the jury never considered whether she had any brain damage problems because they decided that Herrin wasn't negligent and therefore her parents had no basis for a claim.[7]

In 1985 the parents appealed to the Montana Supreme Court. In *Kimes v. Herrin* the high court reversed the lower court's ruling and sent it back down for another trial. The justices argued unanimously that the testimony regarding the Kimes' home environment should never have been allowed because it was highly prejudicial and because it did not link Tanya's disabilities to her parents' behavior. Further, they said, the junction where the accident occurred did not fit the legal description of an "intersection" and therefore it was Gordon Herrin and not Michael

Kimes who should have yielded. It appears that Herrin settled out of court for an undisclosed sum.[8]

The events of February 4, 1984, would seem to reinforce Herrin's arguments about the girl's home life. But because these events were not part of the district court trial they could not be part of the supreme court appeal. At 1 a.m. a Helena cop noticed a car parked near the Capitol Chevron service station downtown and went to the window to investigate. Ella Mae Kimes (now Ella Mae Hunt, following her recent divorce from Michael Kimes) suddenly appeared from around a corner and was detained on suspicion of burglary. She appeared to be drunk as a skunk. The owner was summoned. He told the officer that nothing seemed to be missing, and noted that the pickup inside belonged to Michael Kimes. Ella Mae was released. Michael Kimes' son and a friend named Steve Yurish happened to be driving by the service station and agreed to take Ella Mae back to the double-wide trailer she still shared with her ex-husband. When they got to the trailer, Michael Kimes was passed out in the bedroom, they said, too drunk to be awakened. They left Ella Mae there and went to their own homes. Thirty minutes later the trailer was totally engulfed in flames. Awakened by the heavy smoke, Michael Kimes ran from the trailer and found his ex-wife standing in the yard by a tree, her dog in her arms, calmly watching the fire, he claimed.

Ella Mae was charged with arson, attempted homicide, and burglary, after it was discovered that the coins in the service station cash register were missing (also, Michael's pickup had been vandalized). At her trial it was alleged that she started the fire by pouring cleaning fluid on a couch. In fact, she worked for a drycleaner, but claimed she was simply cleaning the couch, which she owned. Her lawyer countered that Michael Kimes was a heavy smoker who often left smoldering cigarettes on the furniture. Steve Yurish recanted his statement to police accusing Ella Mae of the crimes for which she stood accused after admitting that Michael Kimes had promised to give him a stock car if he lied to the cops. Michael Kimes' son was promised an automobile engine for a similar statement. The prosecution asked Yurish whether it was his testimony that he could be bought off in a criminal case. "Not really," Yurish answered. "But he [Kimes] did promise us stuff."[9]

At the conclusion of a week-long trial the jurors reported to the judge that they were deadlocked six-to-six. He admonished them to sleep on it. The next morning, in an unusual move, the jurors elected a new foreman, but they still could not budge their decision further than seven for conviction to five for acquittal. In October, Hunt was tried again on the same charges. After the prosecution rested its case the defense called on the judge for a "directed verdict," which almost always happens in criminal trials but is rarely granted. In this case the judge immediately dismissed the homicide and arson charges against Hunt, and the prosecution indicated it would not pursue the burglary charges. She was now free to go and pursue her appeal against Gordon Herrin to the Montana Supreme Court.

In 1989 Gordon accepted the inevitable, admitting his failure as a farmer. He sold the Herrin ranch and moved with Alice into a small house in Helena. He had apparently forgotten about the anger among his neighbors that the construction of Leisure Village had incited when he told the newspaper that he was opposed to the building of a Crittenton Home for unwed mothers and their babies on the block where he lived. "It's time to say no," he told the city commissioners, "to what the residents don't want."[10] The home was built despite the objections of Gordon and his neighbors.

The sale of the Herrin ranch terminated the passage of thousands of acres of land and many hundreds of thousands of dollars from one son to another, a legacy of farming and stock raising that stretched back four generations to Daniel Herrin's early successes in 1877. The family that bought the ranch partnered with Mary Flax, Molly's big sister, who expedited the transaction by paying cash for forty-four acres of Herrin pasture adjacent to Molly's land on the north, a protective buffer adding to a brushy, undevelopable thirteen-acre cordon sanitaire Mary had bought in 1984 next to Molly's land on the south. In one of the sublime ironies of the Herrins' long history as land barons, the last vestige of their empire reverted to the blood relations of the wife that Keith had deserted and whom Gordon had essentially evicted.

In 1994, after wasting away for several months, Gordon died of a pulmonary embolism. His wife, Alice, would outlive him by twenty years, playing bridge with her friends up to the last week of her life. She had never told Gordon that in every election since their marriage she had negated his vote by casting her ballot for the Democrat.

While working at the state library, Molly took classes in library science at Carroll College in order to qualify for a job as the head of book processing at the Lewis and Clark County Library. For an avid, lifelong reader, and someone who could have returned to newspapering if it weren't for the stress of deadlines and the difficult people who infest newsrooms, this was a near-perfect job that paid better than the state library and offered a more congenial environment. In 1976 her daughter Mary and Mary's husband (a building contractor in Kansas) built Molly a two-bedroom house and hauled it in sections to Montana, where they installed it on her land. In the yard she planted strawberries and apple trees. In 2017 she was inducted into the Helena Sports Hall of Fame as a member of the 1966 and 1968 Helena Trail Riders National Championship O-Mok-See high-point teams. She competed in barrel races until the age of eighty-two, when she was still winning money. She would work at the library until 2003.

Later in her life Molly took up jogging. One summer evening she found herself in downtown Helena after work at the library in possession of both of her Chevrolet Suburbans, one of which had been in the shop for repairs. Rather than ask a favor, she drove one Suburban down Last Chance Gulch a mile, and jogged back to get the other Suburban, which she then drove a mile beyond the first. And so on, until she had transported both vehicles the five miles to her place on the Prickly Pear Creek. Illuminated by her dawn-to-dusk light, she walked to her tack shed, dished grain into three rubber feed pans, and carried them to the corrals. Then she called in her horses from the pasture. After a few moments they appeared, walking single file, Mokie in the lead, as usual, followed by Little Sister and then Chiquita. In the house she warmed up a serving of the big casserole she made once a week. In bed after dinner, she watched Jay Leno's monologue, and fell asleep.

APPENDIX 1

The Oxbow Ranch

In August 1899, when he was thirty-three years old, Holly Herrin finally found his place in the world. It was a grassy basin two square miles in area, walled on the west by steep, wooded ridges and bordered on the east by the clear-running Missouri River. Although frigid and snowbound in the winter, hot and dry in the summer, this was land that grew anything that can grow in what is now called climate zone 4a, including commercial potatoes and beans, garden vegetables, grain, fruit, and berries. The deep, chestnut-colored loam laid down by the river since the Ice Age was well watered by creeks and fifteen inches of precipitation annually. Holly's cattle and sheep thrived on the fescue, mountain brome, blue grama, and other hardy grasses flourishing in such abundance that he could harvest all of his own winter forage—one of the keys to his extraordinary financial success.

Another factor that helped grow his fortune was the railroad. The main ranch house was only four miles southeast of the Central Montana Railway (and later, the Northern Pacific) siding in the village of Wolf Creek, its proximity making Holly's shipments of wool and cattle to market much cheaper than the sometimes arduous trek to rail lines endured by many Montana stockmen. Added to these advantages was the construction in 1929 of a landing field a few yards from the ranch's main house. Three-quarters of a mile long and marked by night beacons,

179

this was intended to offer air mail pilots flying between Helena and Great Falls an emergency runway.

By September 1930, when he sold his entire operation to his partners in the Wolf Creek Live Stock Company, Herrin's empire stretched from the Gates of the Mountains downstream along the left bank of the Missouri and along the lower Little Prickly Pear Creek for almost twenty miles to the village of Craig. It also included a ranch in the Helena Valley. In all, this mass of land encompassed more than twenty-five thousand acres, nearly thirty-five square miles. While this holding was modest compared to some other equally old spreads, such as the PN Ranch downstream in Fergus County (whose fifty thousand acres are now owned by the American Prairie Foundation), its relatively rich soil still supports considerably more cattle per acre than the PN. Plus, Herrin owned eight hundred acres of irrigated farmland that could grow crops a month longer than the kitchen garden at the PN.

In the early 1930s, Helena's two local banks managed to weather the first assaults of the Great Depression. Despite a weeklong nationwide bank "holiday" in 1933 intended to freeze transactions and prevent a run on the banks, dwindling deposits and panic withdrawals of savings forced many Montana financial institutions to foreclose on delinquent debtors, including the Wolf Creek Live Stock Company.

In 1935 Montana Trust and Savings Bank of Montana finally found a buyer for the Holly Herrin ranch. This was Irvin Rieke, whose father owned Rieke Metal Products, a plant in Auburn, Indiana, that fabricated flanges, plugs, and seals for steel oil drums used in the petroleum and chemical industries. Rieke had grown up on the family's Montana ranch in the Missouri Breaks northwest of Winifred, and had yearned to return to the Treasure State ever since the family sold the ranch in 1930 and moved to Chicago, where his father, Theodore, founded the company. Irvin and his brother, Glenn, inherited the business in 1939 after Theodore died of a heart attack at the age of sixty.[1]

One of Rieke's first acts was to change the name of Holly's empire. He decided to call it the Oxbow Ranch, after the great twist in the Missouri a few miles upstream from the original ranch buildings. Despite his nostalgia for Montana, over the next decade Rieke spent very little time at the Oxbow, his visits restricted to summer vacations. The Oxbow's farm and stock operations were handled by managers.

In winter 1941 the United Iron Workers responded to requests from some of Rieke's employees to help them organize a union. The Rieke brothers were not amused. They laid off thirty-one workers, citing misconduct, loitering, and "slack business conditions." Armed with clubs, members of the Congress of Industrial Organizations (CIO), the umbrella organization to which the iron workers union belonged, joined some of Rieke's furloughed workers to block the entrance of the plant. A fight broke out between the unionists and other Rieke workers. Police escorted the company treasurer through the entrance in their squad car, which the unionists attacked, breaking a window. Irvin Rieke showed up with a pistol and waved it around. The siege of the plant continued for days. The CIO set up tents outside the plants; cots were delivered to other employees holed up inside. A federal mediator was brought in. Guards armed with machine guns were stationed at the entrance. A week later the strike ended.[2]

Labor strife at the plant would continue for months. But after Pearl Harbor both the CIO and the American Federation of Labor (AFL) pledged that until the Axis powers were defeated there would be no more strikes. By 1944 Rieke's plant employed 375 workers, most of whom were women. Filling contracts for the War Department, the plant operated three shifts a day, seven days a week: one small cog in the wheel that rolled over the fascists.[3]

In 1946 Irvin Rieke retired a very wealthy man, and moved his wife and four children to Montana. Back in 1940, anticipating his retirement but postponing it because of his company's critical contribution to the war effort (plus the enormous profits he was poised to make), Rieke built a two-story, seven-bedroom house at the Oxbow, a gleaming white stucco edifice. Each of its bedrooms was paneled with different species of imported hardwoods—mahogany, black walnut, ironwood, and bird's-eye maple. Mounted animal heads and the pelt of a mountain lion adorned the walls. The head of a bison bull glared at guests from its mount above the stone fireplace.[4]

Over the years Rieke had built the Oxbow into what the *Independent Record* called a "dream ranch." In fact, this was no longer the working cattle and sheep operation that Holly had spent three decades developing, but a glorified hobby ranch and would-be game preserve. In 1946 Rieke sold the ranch's herd of 220 purebred Herefords. In their place he brought in a few genetically pure Yellowstone Park bison and a collection of Brahma bulls. He also made plans to add more animals to a band of wild bighorn sheep that roamed the higher reaches of the ranch, which he would confine with an eight-foot fence.

He outfitted a bus to serve as the family's home away from home while they wintered on the road in Mexico and the South. He bought a fifty-foot, twin-engine cabin cruiser named *Holma* from a retired admiral and had it sailed from the East Coast up the St. Lawrence Seaway and the Great Lakes to Detroit, where it was loaded onto a freight car and shipped west. When the train reached Cascade the crew discovered that the *Holma* was too wide to fit through the pair of rail tunnels between Cascade and Wolf Creek. The boat was loaded onto house-moving dollies. But when it arrived at the Hardy Bridge two miles below Holter Dam the crew determined that it was too tall to fit under the girders. Finally, it was decided to deflate the tires on the dollies. At last, the *Holma*—fifteen tons of mahogany and brass—was eased into its new port on Holter Lake.

Rieke sold the *Holma* in 1969 to a tunnel construction executive who intended to sail her to his home in Hawaii. However, on her way up Holter Lake from the Oxbow to the marina at the Gates of the Mountains she ran out of gas. The crew dropped anchor, rowed to shore in a dinghy and hiked to the marina to get help. When the yacht finally docked, it was lifted onto a flatbed truck by a fifty-ton highway construction crane, driven to Kalispell for repairs, then to Puget Sound, where she began her voyage across the Pacific to Molokai.[5]

In 1970 Rieke sold the Oxbow to a retired Denver eye surgeon named A. J. Kafka. Included in the deal was the herd of 650 cattle that Rieke had been compelled to maintain when he realized that a game preserve was not going to pay the costs of running a huge ranch. Seven years later Kafka grew tired of the enormous work the Oxbow required and sold it to Tim Babcock, who had served as Montana's Republican governor from 1962 to 1969.[6] Babcock dismissed rumors that he intended to subdivide the ranch by creating cabin sites along the west shore of the lake.[7] In fact, he would later trade 254 acres of prime lakefront property—nine-and-a-half miles of shoreline—to the Bureau of Land Management in exchange for more than 11,000 acres of dry and windy prairie in Garfield County plus 3 acres of very expensive commercial land on the edge of Helena. The land swap consolidated the northern portion of the Oxbow and facilitated the BLM's consolidation of its holdings along the lake south of the big twist, an area that would become the ten-thousand-acre Sleeping Giant Wilderness. (The Sleeping Giant is a rock formation north of Helena created in 1878 when a 5.9 magnitude earthquake toppled a pillar of stone.)

While the deal guaranteed that the west side of Holter Lake would remain accessible to the public and would provide a continuing sanctuary for wild birds and game, Babcock profited from the deal by selling his Garfield County acreage to Benny Binion.[8] Former owner of the Horseshoe Casino in Las Vegas, Binion had been a moonshiner in Texas during Prohibition and head of the Dallas mob during World War II. He was convicted of murder—twice. And he owned a black thoroughbred racehorse he named N———.[9]

In 1983 Babcock took out a $1.5 million mortgage on the Oxbow from Connecticut General Life Insurance, but by 1987 had failed to repay the principal or more than $553,000 in interest (which had been accumulating at $678 a day). The insurance company foreclosed in 1987, but the action was dismissed by a judge in 1988 after an agreement was reached for sale of the ranch to a three-way partnership that included Andre Melief, the president of Country Lands, a conservation-oriented Connecticut corporation. Melief and his partners intended to run the Oxbow as a guest ranch. The initial asking price was $5.5 million, but details of the final sale were not disclosed. After the sale Babcock and his wife retained several grazing leases in the area and continued to live on the ranch for several years. He died in 2015 at the age of ninety-five.[10]

In 1990 Melief and his partners sold the Oxbow to Chris and Nora Hohenlohe, who restored it as a working cattle ranch, raising a herd of registered Angus. In 1999 they bought the adjoining Sentinel Rock Ranch along the Little Prickly Pear Creek, one of Holly's original farms, which was sold off to someone other than Irvin Rieke during the 1930s after it was seized by the bank.

In 2016 the Oxbow was sold yet again, this time to a limited liability company called Reve Americain (The American Dream).[11] It continues to operate as a working cattle ranch twelve decades after the summer day when Holly Herrin first set foot on what would become his fiefdom.

APPENDIX 2

The Sons and Daughters of Montana Pioneers

The Society of Montana Pioneers was founded in Helena in 1884, five years after the territory became a state.[1] Its mission was to document the histories of the people who arrived in the first wave of settlers invading Indian Country.[2] Although the Montana Historical Society, founded in 1865, was already preserving this chronicle, some Pioneers did not much care for the society's scholarly approach to history. They wanted a social organization that held meetings and put on parties, picnics, and dances where they could drink, tell stories, and network. During its early years, presidents of the Pioneers included William A. Clark—the notorious Copper King who bought a U.S. Senate seat by bribing Montana legislators, and Wilbur Fisk Sanders, one of the original Alder Gulch vigilantes who lynched at least twenty alleged road agents in 1864. (In his book, *Immortal Hero, New York Times* op-ed writer Timothy Egan posits strong evidence that Sanders assassinated Thomas Francis Meagher, governor of the Montana Territory, who disappeared mysteriously in 1867 from a steamboat docked in Fort Benton. Sanders and Meagher were political opposites and rivals.)[3]

Membership in the Pioneers was open to anyone who had established residence in the territory on the day Abraham Lincoln signed its existence into law—May 26, 1864. Everyone, that is, except military personnel ordered to duty there, criminals like Henry Plummer, and

Indians (who have been living in what is now Montana for at least twelve thousand years). The challenge for an organization that had established such a narrow membership requirement was the fact that eventually all of the Pioneers would die and the organization would evaporate. To forestall the inevitable, they gradually expanded the qualifications for membership to include anyone who had established residence in the territory by December 31, 1868. In 1901 Sanders proposed that membership be even further expanded to include anyone who had lived in Montana for thirty-three years, and in 1903 he proposed 1879 as the deadline. Criminals and Indians were still not allowed. Sanders argued that the 1868 rule was an injustice to those settlers who came a few years later and contributed as much to the commonwealth as the old-timers. The Sanders schemes also barred criminals and Indians. Both of his proposals were soundly defeated.[4]

It was in this atmosphere of challenged and loosened rules that Daniel S. Herrin was admitted into the Pioneers. Herrin was not a member of the first iteration of the Society of Pioneers, and was not included in its 1899 book, *Society of Montana Pioneers-Constitution, Members, Officers with Portraits and Maps*, which published biographical sketches of its members. But by 1904—the year he died on a Chicago operating table—he was apparently deemed qualified for membership. This qualification was based on a collection of biographical information about the Pioneers stored in a vault at the Montana Historical Society offices in Helena. When the author opened Herrin's file he expected to find letters, legal papers, bills of sale, the sort of primary documents that transcend anecdote and the typically flawed newspaper reporting of the era. But inside were only two short clippings from 1904 announcing Herrin's death.

The first one, from the *Helena Independent* of August 2, claimed that "In 1866 Mr. Herrin came from Penobscot, Maine, and located near Clancy, where he conducted a hotel."

The second clipping, from an unidentified newspaper, said Herrin "came to Montana from Penobscot, Me., in 1870, locating in business near where Clancy is now situated, where he conducted a hotel for a number of years."

In the matter of Herrin's origin, neither report is accurate. It was Canaan, Maine, not Penobscot (some fifty miles southeast). That fact is substantiated by the 1870 U.S. Census, which lists the Herrins as residents, on June 21, of a farm seven miles north of Canaan, including Daniel S. Herrin, his wife, father, daughter, three sons, and a "domestic servant." And if one of these dates of his arrival in Montana were correct, then the other one could not be. However, neither date is correct. It is not plausible, given the 1870 day of the census, that Herrin was a resident of Montana in 1866, nor at any time before 1870. For this reason, he was not a legitimate member of the Pioneers.

Other accounts place the arrival of the Herrin family in Montana several years later. In a biographical sketch of Harland J. Herrin published in a book titled *Progressive Men of Montana*, it is noted that his father, Daniel S. Herrin, "was engaged in farming until 1877, when he came to Montana." An article from the July 3, 1879, *Helena Weekly-Herald* recounted a journey through "Southern Montana" by a printing and newspaper subscription salesman. "At Clancy," he wrote, "a first-class dinner was obtained at a house which has just been opened for the accommodation of the public. It is kept by Daniel S. Herrin, whose family has recently arrived from the East." On July 22, 1875, it was reported in the same newspaper that there were two hotels in Clancy, neither one operated by the Herrins, suggesting that Daniel opened his establishment sometime after that date.

In 1962 the day arrived when the Society of Montana Pioneers was compelled to dissolve itself—there were only eight members left, and most of them were doddering. But a junior organization created in 1892—the Sons and Daughters of Montana Pioneers—was still in existence and continues to meet once a year, albeit attended by declining numbers. The only requirement for membership is proof of direct descendance from a settler who took up residence in Montana on or before December 31, 1868.

Based on that single, inaccurate newspaper squib in the Historical Society vault, the Sons and Daughters admitted into membership several of Daniel S. Herrin's great grandchildren in 1996, and his grandson,

Keith Herrin. The applications, which were filled out, "investigated," and approved by certain officers of the organization, including Secretary Shirley (Beaver, Baertsch) Herrin, stated that in 1866 Herrin's family "came by steamboat up the Missouri River to Fort Benton, then to Helena by ox team." According to Ken Robison, historian at the Overholser Historical Research Center in Fort Benton, there are no records verifying these events. There is, however, a squib in the *Benton Record Weekly* of May 17, 1878, noting that Henry H. Herrin—Daniel's oldest son—arrived May 15 in Fort Benton on the steamboat *Benton*, with 115 other passengers, after sailing from Yankton in what is now South Dakota. He was nineteen years old. There is no mention of the reason he was traveling alone.

The 2019 president of the Sons and Daughters, Timothy Sowa, told the author that "The 1870 census showed Daniels [*sic*] name but not his signature," apparently discounting the only document in existence that proves Daniel Herrin's residence on the exact day he and his family were counted. To argue that this document is not valid because it was not signed is nonsense. According to the journal *Historical Methods*, the signatures of Americans enumerated by the census has never been sought nor required.[5]

The shabby and self-promotional scholarship of the Sons and Daughters of Montana Pioneers regarding Daniel S. Herrin raises a question about *all* of its members' ancestors. Perhaps the organization should stick to dinners, parties, and meetings and turn over its biographical research to the Montana Historical Society.

Note: The author is a member of the Sons and Daughters of Montana Pioneers by virtue of his great-grandfather, Thomas Moran, who was documented as party to the 1866 Great Sun River Stampede.

APPENDIX 3

Baertsch v. Baertsch

Supreme Court of Montana

Baertsch v. Baertsch

No. 11799.

Decided April 2, 1970.

Appeal from the District Court of Lewis and Clark County.

First Judicial District. Honorable John B. McClernan, Judge
presiding.

Mahan Strope, Helena, Philip W. Strope (argued), Helena, for
appellant.

Leo J. Kottas (argued), Helena, for respondent.

MR. CHIEF JUSTICE JAMES T. HARRISON delivered the Opinion of
the Court.

This is an appeal from an order modifying a decree of divorce from
Lewis and Clark county.

It appears from the record that plaintiff wife departed from the family home in February of 1969 and on February 27, 1969, instituted an
action for divorce and sought custody of their three children. Defendant husband answered also seeking divorce and custody of their three
children. Following a trial before the court a decree dated June 5, 1969,
filed June 6, 1969, was entered in the district court.

In the decree the court found both parties entitled to a decree of divorce, and both fit and proper persons to have the care, custody and control of the minor children. The court granted custody of the two boys, Steven Curtiss, aged 9, and Stacey Lee, aged 7, to the defendant father, and the custody of the daughter, Susan Jeanine, aged 4, to the plaintiff mother, all subject to certain visitation rights, and the father to pay $75 per month for support during the time the daughter resided with her mother.

On Aug. 7, 1969, the father filed an affidavit charging plaintiff with cruel treatment upon Steven; with plaintiff threatening that if she obtained custody of the boys she would remove them from the state; that she had told the children she was going to marry and they would have a new father; that the boys had informed defendant they did not want to live with plaintiff; that the little girl had asked defendant to keep her; and he has sought to have the custody of the daughter given to him. Plaintiff then executed an affidavit wherein she charged defendant with failure to live up to the divorce decree; that he had beaten her; that the child Steven was in need of psychiatric assistance and counseling; and that since she had remarried and had a fine home life she should be granted the care, custody and control of all the children.

The court on September 11, 1969, following a hearing, entered an order modifying the decree of divorce, finding that there was a change of conditions since the entry of the decree in that plaintiff was not a fit and proper person to have custody of the children and that it was in the best interests of the children, as well as their desire, that they be in the custody of their father and that they be together and not separated.

The court then decreed that plaintiff was not a fit and proper person to have the custody of the minor children, that their custody was awarded to the defendant with reasonable visitation rights to the plaintiff in Lewis and Clark county; that the daughter be returned by the plaintiff to the defendant; that the provisions for plaintiff to have all the children for one month during the summer of each year, to have custody of the daughter and that defendant pay $75 per month as child support be expunged and eliminated from the decree.

Plaintiff thereafter moved to amend or alter the order to grant a new trial which was denied. This appeal followed.

While plaintiff poses two issues they both resolve around the proposition of whether or not there was credible evidence to uphold the district court's finding of a material change in circumstances since the entry of the decree of divorce.

Little would be served by a complete recitation of the testimony presented at the hearing before the court on the petition. However, certain facts do stand out and we shall briefly comment thereon.

Plaintiff left the family home in February of 1969, and the record indicates that she was interested in another man. Upon the trial of the divorce case she testified that she was not interested in anyone else, but at the time of an altercation brought about by discovery of the other man on the premises where plaintiff was staying on June 18, defendant was very loud in his conduct and police officers were called and requested him to leave the premises. At that time Herrin, the other man, and present husband of plaintiff, was still married to his wife. He obtained a divorce on August 18, 1969, and married plaintiff on August 23, 1969 in Wheatland, Wyoming.

Herrin and his former wife had six children, five girls and one boy, the boy being blind. His wife was awarded custody of all six children.

Testimony of the defendant is to the effect that the children have many times expressed themselves as desiring to stay with him and not with their mother.

Plaintiff mother testified:

A. Stephen [*sic*] right now, he is, I think, a very deeply troubled little boy, because he has, well, been pulled in two directions for over two years, now, and he's, I feel, been taught to be bitter toward me, because his father is bitter toward me; and I just feel that he is very—especially in the last year, his attitude toward me—there is no 9-year-old child, that could ever treat their mother the way Stephen [*sic*] has treated me, with the hardness and the bitterness and the absolute cruelty, really, and he's been cruel to me physically and mentally, and I feel that he is suffering very deeply from his problems that came up from time to time, *I'm sorry to say, to have to admit, that I have had a part in creating the problems that there is in my son now; and I just hope to God, as he grows up and he gets older, he will come out of it.* [emphasis added by the court]

While plaintiff charged in her affidavit that Steven needed psychiatric assistance there is no medical testimony to that effect.

As to her youngest son she stated:

Q. Now, your second child, your son Stacey, how old is he?

A. Stacey is 7.

Q. And what kind of a child is he?

A. He is a very quiet, sensitive child, which is exactly how Stacey has been ever since he was born. He is a very loving little boy, and this has been quite a traumatic experience for him.

As to both she testified:

Q. Shirley, just before lunch, we were talking about your sons, Stephen [*sic*] and Stacey. And I was asking you what was your relationship—What's your relationship, now, between you and Stacey, or Steve? How do you characterize that in your own words?

A. My relationship with my sons; they're very—I mean, they are very drawn from me. Since her remarriage plaintiff has moved to a ranch approximately 20 miles in the country from a small town in Wyoming, the nearest school being five miles away. Defendant's home remains as it had been all during the lifetime of the children, in the Helena valley.

Perhaps the most compelling evidence before the court was described in these words by defendant in his testimony:

"Q. Now, sometime back in the summer, after the Decree of Divorce, did Mrs. Shirley Baertsch, now Herrin, come to your place to visit the children?

A. Yes sir.

Q. When was that?

A. July 25th, I believe it was.

Q. And did she come to your home?

A. Yes.

Q. Did anything happen while she was there at the home?

A. Yes, it did.

Q. What was it?

A. Well, her and our oldest son had a little disagreement, and it kept getting worse, and worse, and worse, until she asked me to spank him; and I said, 'Spank him yourself, it's your own son.' So she proceeded to do it, and she couldn't do it. But she finally lost her temper and took off a high-heeled shoe, and began beating him with the spike end of the high-heeled shoe.

Q. Did you try to stop her?

A. I did finally stop her.

Q. In trying to stop her, did she then try to attack you?

A. That's right, she did.

Q. What did she do?

A. What—

Q. What did she do to you?

A. She started kicking and scratching and raising a little devil, and I told her to settle down and behave to the little kids or leave. And she kept it up, and I says, 'You do it again and you're going to get it.' She kept hitting and fighting, so I slapped back—slapped her face with the back of my hand, once.

Q. Did you have other people come there and see the little boys—the marks on the little boy and on you?

A. Yes sir. I took him up to his grandmother's house, and Maxine Olson called her, and she came up; and Karen Hamilton and the kid's grandmother.

Q. And they all saw the little boy?

A. They all saw him 15 minutes after it happened.

Q. And did you have any pictures taken?

A. Yes, I did.

The picture of the boy clearly shows bruises on his skin. A neighbor lady testified that she came to the Baertsch home after the altercation with the boy's mother and she stated: 'On his back I think there was four round marks that looked like he had been struck with something.'

Plaintiff in her testimony stated that the boy needed disciplining, that he was kicking at and being very cruel to his little sister and that she tried to stop him and started to spank him and the boy started kicking her with his cowboy boots; that at that time defendant threw her down on the floor, sat on her and injured her. Her counsel handed her the photograph of her son and asked her if she thought she put those little heel marks on him. To which she replied:

A. No, I did not, because I didn't have the opportunity to hit the child, I was thrown from him before I did.

Q. How do you think those marks got on him?

A. Well, I don't know; *I didn't intend to hit the child.*" [emphasis added by the court]

Following an objection and ruling by the court, the plaintiff added: "The child didn't cry."

On cross-examination she testified:

Q. Did you have trouble with him?

A. Yes, I tried to discipline Stephen [*sic*], yes.

Q. And you tried to discipline him?

A. Yes.

Q. And you had trouble doing it?

A. Yes.

Q. Did you strike him?

A. In what manner do you mean?

Q. Did you strike him?

A. I tried to strike him. From these statements it would appear that the version of the defendant is more credible and furnished a basis for the findings of the district court.

The district judge saw the witnesses in this cause, he observed the parties on the witness stand, their demeanor while testifying, their attitude toward each other and their children, and it appeared to the court that a substantial change of circumstances had occurred.

We recently reviewed the law applicable to matters of this kind in *Simon v. Simon*, 154 Mont. 193, 461 P2d 851, 26 St.Rep. 706, and we see no need to repeat it here.

At the conclusion of the hearing the court expressed the view that it was confronted with a difficult situation; that while children normally stay with their mother, in this cause they did not want to go to their mother; that it was the court's belief that brothers and sisters should be raised together when no part of the marriage relationship could be salvaged.

While there were conflicts in the evidence it stands without question that the home of defendant is a good and proper one, that his care of the boys is good, they are clean and well-kept, and the school is nearby, and grandparents live in the vicinity; that it is the only home the boys have ever known and the same was true of the girl until she was removed therefrom by the plaintiff when she left.

The court felt the best interests of the children would be served if the boys were left in the care, custody and control of the father, and the care, custody and control of the daughter given to the father. We see no reason to disturb the court's judgment. Upon the record before this Court we cannot say that the district court abused its discretion in its disposition of this matter.

The order of the district court is affirmed.

MR. JUSTICES CASTLES, HASWELL, and JOHN C. HARRISON, concur.

NOTES

2. FIRST-GENERATION AMERICANS

1. Addison Erwin Sheldon, *Nebraska: The Land and the People* (Chicago: Lewis Publishing, 1931), 21.
2. James William Spain, *In Those Days: A Diplomat Remembers* (Kent OH: Kent State University Press, 1998), 49–50.
3. George Francis Burke's obituary, published in the January 16, 1964, issue of the *Independent Record*, claimed that he attended the University of Minnesota and then moved west in 1898 with the engineering department of the Great Northern Railway. The University of Minnesota has no record of any George Francis Burke enrolled in the school nor is there any documented basis for the statement that he was working in 1898 as an engineer. Obituaries at the time were written by reporters, not relatives, but the "facts" of George's life were given to the reporter by George's wife, Catherine, who tended to believe the stories her husband told her.
4. A poster published by the Chicago, Milwaukee, St. Paul and Pacific Railroad, also known as the Milwaukee Road, showed a heroic farmer, in what would become known as the socialist realism style of illustration, guiding a plow across the prairie behind two horses. The sod he turned was transformed into coins. Krys Holmes, *Montana: Stories of the Land* (Helena: Montana Historical Society, 2009), 257.
5. *Valley County News,* May 20, 1904, 1.
6. In August 1915 George and Jennie took a seventeen-day tour of Yellowstone and Glacier Parks. Logging 1,943 miles in their black, two-door Model T Runabout, which cost them $390, they crossed the Missouri on a ferry at Mondak and drove along the Yellowstone River to the park, then north to Glacier, before heading home across the Hi-Line. *Glasgow Courier*, August 27, 1915, 7. Located on the

border between the two states, Mondak thrived until Prohibition because it was the closest watering hole for residents of the dry state of North Dakota (in 1889 Montana entered the Union as a wet state, North Dakota as a dry one). Mondak is now a ghost town. Alice M. Sweetman, "Mondak: Planned City of Hope Astride Montana-Dakota Border," *Montana: The Magazine of Western History*, Autumn 1965, 12–27.

7. Eastern Montana's roads, including Glasgow's main drag on First Avenue South (then called Front Street), were mostly rutted dirt paths scraped from the prairie. In wet weather they were impassably clogged with the clinging gumbo that results when ashy, volcanic soil called bentonite absorbs moisture and expands. Northwestern Railway officials avoided these roads in rainy weather by outfitting three Model T's with flanged wheels so they could travel on the company's tracks. According to an item in the May 21, 1915, issue of the *Glasgow Courier*, "One advantage in this form of automobile riding is that muddy roads and blowouts are not part of the game and no attention has to be paid to the speed limit."

8. *Valley County News*, November 23, 1915, 1.

9. "Negro Who Killed Sheriff Lynched by Montana Mob," *Herald Democrat* (Leadville CO), April 1913, 5. "J. C. Collins, a negro, the slayer of Sheriff Thomas Courtney of Sheridan county was taken from the jail at 10 o'clock tonight and lynched. The mob hanged him up to a telephone pole and then set fire to his clothing in a futile effort to cremate his body, after they had riddled the swaying corpse with bullets."

10. "Democratic State Convention," *Valley County News*, May 24, 1912, 1. Both weeklies at the time, the *Glasgow Courier* and the *Valley County News* were Republican newspapers. As fervently biased as is Fox News today, they covered politics with a vociferous advocacy of the GOP. Although the Valley County sheriff, James Stephens, had been elected on the GOP ticket, and his deputy, George F. Burke, was a Democratic, the *Valley County News* accused both "crooked" men of attempting to manipulate county politics to advance their personal power. "The political conferences of the sheriff's office in Glasgow and the political conferences of the democratic party held at the Coleman house or at G. E. Hurd's office, were by one and the same bunch," the *Valley County News* reported. "Mr. Burke, claiming to be a leader among the democrats, is now holding an appointment in the sheriff's office under a man elected on the republican ticket for sheriff."

11. At the top of the Democratic Party platform in 1912 was tariff reform, which was needed, the party said, because high tariffs imposed by Republicans were the "principal cause of unequal distribution of wealth." Tariffs in 1912 accounted for 20 percent of the cost of imported items, such as clothing and household goods.

12. "Deputy Sheriff Burke Arrested," *Valley County News*, August 23, 1912, 1.

13. The miscreant, a man named Hart, was incensed that Game Warden Burke had arrested him and loudly proclaimed his innocence in court until changing his

plea to guilty after George presented the judge with several fresh beaver pelts he had confiscated from the accused. "Trapper Taken by Game Warden," *Glasgow Courier,* October 6, 1916, 1.

14. *Valley County News,* April 2, 1915, 2.

15. Designed by architects John Link and Charles Haire, of Helena and Billings, and completed in 1916, the Rundle Building is a three-story fireproof brick western commercial with detailed terra cotta tile work, raised brick arches, and coped, shaped parapet walls reminiscent of Spanish Mission Revival architecture. It originally housed a billiards room and a bowling alley and served not just as the headquarters for the Rundle Land & Abstract Company but was also home to several retail businesses and an exclusive men's club with its own library, buffet, card rooms, and lounges. Also known as the Glasgow Hotel, in 2006 it was listed on the National Register of Historic Places.

16. "Burke Gives Peace Bond," *Valley County News,* October 19, 1915, 1.

17. "Burke Is Fined $10 for Assault," *Valley County News,* October 29, 1915, 1.

18. "Lower Court Reversed," *Glasgow Courier,* May 19, 1916, 1.

19. Burke's Commercial Club brethren, the merchants of Glasgow, encouraged population growth in Valley County because more people—that is, white people—meant more customers. To that end they supported the goals of the organization formed by new homesteaders on the Reservation called the Fort Peck Settlers Association. Their hardships were outlined in a plea to Congress presented in 1915 by Sen. Henry L. Myers of Montana. In it, they complained about the terrible weather and the hard, compact soil they said required at least three years of cultivation before it could grow a crop. They noted that the cost of fencing, farm implements, farm labor, and livestock were "20 to 40 percent" higher than they were anywhere else. Finally, they said that the price of $3 to $7 per acre payable annually to the federal government for five years was more money than they could extract from any of these acres. Cong. Rec. 11,426 (July 22, 1916). The area's native people, the Sioux and Assiniboine, had been granted the best land on the reservation—in the Missouri River floodplain—in exchange for giving up poorer land to homesteaders. Keith B. Jensen, "Analysis of Homesteading in Roosevelt County, Montana" (master's thesis, University of Montana, 1986).

20. "Congressmen Here Monday," *Glasgow Courier,* July 16, 1915, 1.

21. A Honyocker was a Slavic-born immigrant who migrated to Montana from Minnesota, North Dakota, South Dakota, and Canada. Joseph Kinsey Howard, *Montana: High Wide and Handsome* (Lincoln NE: Bison Books, 1943), 180.

22. Another of Burke's causes as a member of the Glasgow Commercial Club was his lobbying for a bill in the 1915 Montana legislature to annex a strip of land along the main line of the Great Northern Railway that lay in neighboring Sheridan County. This territory originally had been part of Valley County when the state entered the Union in 1889, but was ceded to Sheridan County during a splitting

of counties in 1913. The move was urged by merchants in the Sheridan County town of Culbertson, who did not like traveling fifty miles north to the county seat at Plentywood to transact business with the government. The bill failed.

23. "Geo. F. Burke of Glasgow was a recent visitor at the big exhibit of southern California products maintained free to the public in the Los Angeles Chamber of Commerce. He also attended the lectures, moving pictures and concert that are part of the daily program. The exhibit is the largest of any in the country maintained by a commercial organization." Reported in the *Glasgow Courier*, January 12, 1917, 1.

24. "Burke Commissioned Second Lieutenant," *Glasgow Courier*, April 12, 1918, 1.

25. Fort Vancouver was established in 1812 on the right bank of the Columbia River by the Hudson's Bay Company to protect its interests and those of England in what at the time was the Oregon Territory, whose ownership was contested by the United States. Built along the lines of the motte-and-bailey castles of Medieval Europe, the installation featured a wooden stockade twenty feet high, a bastion armed with cannons, and a moat eight feet deep filled with water spanned by a bridge that was drawn inside at night. Company mercenaries protected employees from hostile Indians. The original Vancouver Barracks was built in 1849 on a rise twenty feet above the old Fort. In World War I it was the headquarters of the Spruce Production Division, an enormous U.S. Army unit that harvested and milled Sitka spruce for lumber. Because it was light and strong and didn't splinter when hit by bullets spruce was used to build the frames of Allied warplanes battling the German Air Force. Soldiers were sent into the woods to harvest timber because of a labor war between lumber companies and union lumberjacks, including those from the International Workers of the World—the Wobblies. For more, see Ward A. Tonsfeldt, *The U.S. Army Spruce Production Division at Vancouver Barracks, Washington, 1917–1919* (Vancouver WA: National Park Service, 2013).

26. The building, now called the Capulet Apartments, is still occupied by tenants.

27. In what would become a strange, coincidental pattern of natural and unnatural disasters that followed the trajectory of Burke's employment, a dynamite bomb stowed aboard a horse-drawn wagon exploded on Wall Street three months later, killing thirty-eight people. Although never proven, it was alleged by police authorities that anarchists were the perpetrators.

28. "Chickens Home to Roost," *Glasgow Courier*, October 29, 1920, 4.

29. Howard, *Montana*.

30. "Green Ink Roger in Plentywood," *Producers News*, January 2, 1920, 1. The Nonpartisan League (NPL), an organization of farmers founded in North Dakota in 1915 with socialist roots, sent a newspaper editor, Charles "Red Flag" Taylor, to Plentywood, Montana, to establish the *Producers News*. On April 19, 1918, the first issue rolled off the presses, and within two years the newspaper claimed a

circulation of twenty-five hundred in a county totaling twelve thousand residents. The *Producers News* promoted the NPL creed of regulated rail rates and state-run banks and grain elevators. Taylor has been credited with building a substantial political movement in Sheridan County during the 1920s—the county elected a communist sheriff, a full slate of NPL-endorsed county officials, and a state senator: Charles Taylor. Taylor's credo appeared under the masthead: "A Paper of the People, by the People, for the People." The rotund newspaper editor never missed a chance to skewer his opponents, referring to them regularly as "small town Kaisers, crop grabbers, and paytriotic [*sic*] profiteers." "About the *Producers News*. (Plentywood, Mont.) 1918–1937," Library of Congress, accessed July 18, 2018, https://chroniclingamerica.loc.gov/lccn/sn85053305/. Provided by the Montana Historical Society, Helena MT.

31. "A nonpartisan stance proved to be the League's most original tactic. Side-stepping deep-rooted political parties allowed the NPL to offer those without influence a chance to shape their society. As a candidate-endorsing political organization, the Nonpartisan League took advantage of the newly created direct primary to bypass entrenched politicians. They simply backed anyone who supported the League's program, regardless of party." By 1919 the NPL had gained complete control of the three branches of government in North Dakota. Although crafted by socialists, the league's program was intended to expand the opportunities of farmers to own private property and make a profit from their land. The legislature created a state-owned bank into which all of the government's money was deposited, and used the money to offer low-interest mortgages to farmers. State-owned grain elevators and mills were established, rail rates for shipping grain were lowered, new income and corporate taxes were levied, the tax on farm improvements was abolished, a workers' compensation program was funded, housing for farmers and workers was built, and hail insurance was made a requirement to save farmers from losing their farms to bad weather. Michael J. Lansing, *Insurgent Democracy* (Chicago: University of Chicago Press, 2016), x.

32. "Roger Burk [*sic*] Now in Charge of Promoter," *Glasgow Courier*, August 26, 1921, 3.

33. "Sidney Herald under Control of New Man," *Helena Independent Daily*, September 1, 1922.

34. "Roger Burke Well-Known Editor Killed Near Plentywood," *Billings Weekly Gazette*, October 9, 1924, 3.

35. Wildcatters from the Frantz Company traveled from their headquarters in Denver to remote Winnett, Montana, arriving in October 1919. They were soon marooned inside the Schmidt Hotel (the hotel in some accounts is spelled "Schmitt") for seven weeks after the first blizzard hit—of what is remembered as the Big Winter. The rattletrap drilling rigs employed at the time functioned by driving eight-inch-diameter steel pipe into the ground one twenty-foot section

after another, a tedious and back-breaking process called "spud drilling" that was powered by steam from a boiler burning cottonwood logs. The first well hit artesian water. Drilling deeper, the wildcatters hit oil. That spring, after moving their equipment to a new lease, they hit a true gusher that produced more than two-thousand barrels of crude a day. The reservoir they tapped into was deep and relatively close to the surface. The oil in it was "heavy"—that is, its high specific gravity relative to water made it more valuable than "light" crude—and it contained almost 50 percent gasoline. At first, because their lease didn't allow them to build tanks, they had no way to store the crude, so they directed its flow into coulees they had dammed. Because there was as yet no local market for it, they gave it away. Stockmen arrived to scoop it up to use as an insect-repellent dip for their cattle. Motormen drove across rutted roads to skim off the gasoline that rose to the surface so they could fill the gas tanks of their Model T's. Finally, a pipeline was laid from Cat Creek to Winnett, where a Chicago, Milwaukee & St. Paul rail spur had been built east from Lewistown. In 1921 a crude refinery was moved into Winnett from the oil fields. Although the Frantz Company found a market for their oil in the railroads that were using it to heat the boilers on their locomotives, it fetched only a $1 per barrel, compared to the $1.25 charged for a barrel of water. For more, see "Cat Creek Oil Field 42 Years Old This Month," *Lewistown Daily News*, February 2, 1962, and "Cat Creek's Well Was Small," *Lewistown Daily News*, March 4, 1962; see also Richard Dale Hennip, "History of the Crude Oil Industry in Montana" (master's thesis, University of Montana, 1973.)

36. One of these challenges was a lawsuit filed against George and Jennie in June 1921. In it, a man named Arthur Ades sought $650 (or more than $8,000 in today's money) and $75 in legal fees for a lot and a house he sold in 1915 to George's younger brother, Roger, and Roger's wife, Verna. They were accused of defaulting on what was either a second or third mortgage, which was cosigned by the older Burkes and George's real estate business, Burke Realty. Because Ades apparently couldn't find all of the Burkes he published the summons for foreclosure in the *Glasgow Courier* on June 24, 1921.

37. "Thomas Arthur for the Texas," *Butte (MT) Miner*, April 4, 1920, 37.

38. In winter 1921 Arthur would become embroiled in a bribery scandal resulting from what he did or did not say in a Billings tearoom to a group of businessmen. According to one side of the story he boasted that he had personally engineered vote trading in the recently adjourned session of the Montana legislature, ensuring the defeat of a proposal that would create a state tax commission; in exchange, it was alleged that he essentially bought votes that would reduce a proposed 3 percent tax on oil production to 1 percent. The just-elected Republican governor, Joseph M. Dixon, labeled Arthur the "chief of the oil lobby," and convened a special session in order to get what he called a "more adequate" oil revenue bill

passed, which the regular session had defeated. In fact, Montana was strapped for cash and needed to raise funds from a constituency that didn't much want to give any money to the state. A constitutional amendment to create a commission that would oversee increased property taxes was defeated at the polls in 1920, but later passed. Arthur denied saying anything about vote trading, and the matter faded away. "Governor under Fire as First Witness in Bribery Probe" and "The Special Session Now Underway," *Glasgow Courier*, March 11, 1921, 1.

39. "Geo. F. Burke Visits Old Glasgow Friends," *Glasgow Courier*, December 29, 1922, 1.

40. However, it became a lucrative source of natural gas, which during the early years of exploration in Montana was considered a by-product of oil wells and was burned off. By 2006 there were fifteen hundred producing gas wells in the Bowdoin field, and plans were in the works to double that number if market forces remained strong, which they have.

41. "Geo Burke Promoted; Charge Mutual Wells," *Opheim Observer*, January 29, 1923, 2. "Mr. Burke is well known in Northern Montana," the paper observed. "He was formerly in the real estate business in Glasgow. . . . His quick rise to a post of much responsibility is due to his ability and energy."

42. See, for example, Leonardo Da Vinci's portrait of Ginevra de' Benci.

3. THE MIGRANTS

1. An oil field near Corsicana was accidentally discovered in 1894 by water prospectors. It was the first commercially significant find in Texas. An even larger oil field, the Powell, was discovered in 1923 a few miles east of town. Dick Platt, "And So Spake the Little Woman . . . ," *Corsicana Daily Sun*, May 22, 2012, https://www.corsicanadailysun.com/opinion/and-so-spake-the-little-woman/article_76081a3f-5768-5e46-931a-b476166bd836.html.

2. See chapter 2, note 40.

3. Tim Grobaty, *Long Beach Chronicles: From Pioneers to the 1933 Earthquake* (Charleston SC: Arcadia Publishing, 2012).

4. "Dillon Pioneers: Giudici Family," *Dillon Tribune-Examiner*, September 3, 1980, 9.

5. In 1940 so much oil had been pumped out of Signal Hill that Long Beach began to sink. By the early 1950s "subsidence" was causing the city's elevation to drop by two feet a year. Streets cracked, pipes warped, and buildings became unsafe. Long Beach began injecting water into the oil reservoirs and the subsidence stopped. *OC Weekly*, April 22, 2015, 1.

6. Although Hudson took a chance introducing the Terraplane during the darkest days of the Depression the automobile caught on immediately. Its appeal was based on its pricing at the lower end of the market, and on its performance. The eight-cylinder models had the highest horsepower-to-weight ratio of any cars in the world, which made them the favored vehicles of gangsters such as

John Dillinger, who appreciated their acceleration and handling. Dillinger's 1933 Essex Terraplane is on display at the National Museum of Crime and Punishment in Pigeon Forge, Tennessee. It has two bullet holes in the front cowl.

7. One of the buildings surviving the quake without a scratch was the Blackstone Apartments. It was appraised by an insurance company following the quake and deemed to be "one of the best-constructed buildings they had ever inspected." Although the company declared that it was confident there would not be another quake in Helena in anyone's lifetime, the Halloween aftershock proved this prediction wrong. "Pearl Company has confidence in city—is writing quake insurance," *Helena Independent*, October 26, 1935.

8. A computer simulation performed for the Lewis and Clark County office of Disaster and Emergency Services estimated that a 6.3 magnitude earthquake today would result in property damage of over $500 million. Another concern is soil liquefaction, especially in the area north of the city in the Helena Valley where there are alluvial soils and a high water table. See "Liquefaction Susceptibility," Lewis and Clark County Disaster and Emergency Services. Archived from the original December 25, 2012.

9. Dennis S. Swibold, *Copper Chorus* (Helena: Montana Historical Society Press, 2006).

10. "Court Enjoins Railroad Body," *Billings Gazette*, February 1, 1935, 6.

11. For example, John Frank Stevens, who built the Great Northern Railroad and the Panama Canal, got his education not from college but from his experience working for the Minneapolis city engineer. For more, see Gary Sherman, "Conquering the Landscape," *History Magazine*, July 2008.

12. "J. J. Carrigan is Elected Head of Engineers Group," *Helena Independent*, October 10, 1936, 6.

13. "Archie Bray Dies," *Independent Record*, February 17, 1953, 1.

14. "Health Officer Says City Water of Good Quality," *Daily Missoulian*, March 2, 1935, 8.

15. "Mass Meeting in Protest," *Daily Missoulian*, August 26, 1933, 1.

16. "New Liquor Control Bill to Appear," *Independent-Record*, February 1, 1935, 30.

17. "Confession of T. Carey Found in Files in District Court," *Helena Independent*, February 16, 1935, 1.

18. "To the People of the State of Montana," *Western Progressive* (Helena, Montana), February 17, 1935, 1.

19. "Lawyers Battle in Carey Trial," *Helena Independent*, May 17, 1935, 1.

20. "Dismissal of Charge against Carey Asked," *Great Falls Tribune*, November 28, 1936, 3.

21. "Montana Power Lowers Its Rates," *Helena Independent*, November 9, 1935, 1.

22. "Wild Scene Ensues at State House," *Helena Independent*, January 19, 1936, 1.

23. "Jerry O'Connell's Statement," *Helena Independent*, January 22, 1936, 6.

24. "None Dare Call It Spying," *Daily Missoulian*, February 26, 2020, 7.

25. Edwin Amenta, *When Movements Matter* (Princeton NJ: Princeton University Press, 2008).

26. "Endorsements Enliven Races," *Montana Standard*, October 28, 1938, 10. In Helena, a number of O'Connell's supporters walked out of the Consistory Shrine, a Masonic Lodge housed in what had been the old Ming Opera Theater on Jackson Street.

27. Still popular despite the smear campaign that tarnished his reputation, Thomas E. Carey was elected treasurer for the state of Montana in 1940. In 1944 he was found dead in a Spokane hotel room, apparent victim of a heart attack. Jerry O'Connell was active in progressive political circles in Washington State in the 1940s, then returned to Montana to practice law as a criminal defense attorney in Great Falls. He died of a heart attack in 1956 at the age of forty-six. Francis Townsend died in Los Angeles at the age of ninety-three.

28. "Burke, Edward Raymond," Biographical Directory of the Unites States Congress, accessed July 6, 2018, http://bioguide.congress.gov/scripts/biodisplay.pl?index =B001089. He served as president of the Southern Coal Producers Association from 1942 to 1947, and then as Washington representative and general counsel for Hawaiian Statehood Commission until 1950.

29. After Edward's primary defeat, Democratic National Committee Chairman J. C. Quigley said, "Burke is finally getting into the political party that he has been supporting for six years." "He Defined the New Deal Best So Now He's a Staunch Republican," *Brooklyn Daily Eagle*, July 28, 1940, 33.

30. In May 1938 a contract was awarded to R. P. England for $347,189.82. Excavation for the earthen-fill dam began in July 1939 but was quickly halted when a quicksand pocket thirty feet deep was discovered. After moving to another site, the contractor fought a short construction season and difficulty finding materials, until 1942, when the company's equipment was requisitioned for World War II. Courtney Kramer, "A History of Bozeman's Water System Part III," August 1, 2013.

31. Two years before George arrived at Fort Lewis, Ike Eisenhower, who lived in officers' quarters with his family, had been promoted to colonel at a time when promotions for offices were hard-earned. Eisenhower was then named chief of staff of IX Corps, which was responsible for the defense of the entire Pacific coast. In 1941 he was ordered to Fort Sam Houston in Texas. Duane Colt Denfeld, "Fort Lewis, Part 2: 1927–2010," historylink.org, April 18, 2008.

32. Mary Burke appears in a class photograph on page twenty-three of the 1942 edition of *Klahowya*, the Clover Park yearbook. Molly appears on page twenty-seven.

4. THE HOME FRONT

1. On December 29, 1941, the USS *Tennessee* was the first to arrive at Navy Yard Puget Sound bearing simple instructions: mend the badly damaged aft section and

return the ship to service as quickly as possible. It steamed away an impressive fifty-three days later thanks to the engineers, shipwrights, machinists, painters, and others from around the country who were joining the shipyard's payroll at a rate of sixty to seventy people a day. Jessica Wambach Brown, "Time Travel: Navy Yard Puget Sound in Bremerton, Washington," accessed on January 1, 2018, www.historynet.com/time-trave-puget-sound-bremerton-washington.htm. (The *Tennessee* and *Maryland* were dubbed the "Pearl Harbor Ghosts" because the Japanese had declared that their bombs and torpedoes had sunk them.)

2. Frank Wetzel, *Victory Gardens Barrage Balloons: A Collective Memoir* (Bremerton WA: Perry Publishing, 1995). Much of the information about daily life in Bremerton during World War II is drawn from Perry's book and Molly Burke Herrin's memory.

3. "Wages in Department and Clothing Stores, Large Cities, Spring and Summer, 1943," Bulletin of the United States Bureau of Labor Statistics, no. 801 (Washington DC: U.S. Department of Labor, Bureau of Labor Statistics, 1944), 12. Also, "Wartime Employment, Production, and Conditions of Work in Shipyards," Bulletin of the United States Bureau of Labor Statistics, no. 824 (Washington DC: U.S. Department of Labor, Bureau of Labor Statistics, 1944), 18. The number of civilian workers at Bremerton in 1938 was 3,469; in 1944 this number had grown to 32,643. Michael Lindberg and Daniel Todd, *Anglo-American Shipbuilding in World War II: A Geographical Perspective* (Westport CT: Greenwood Publishing, 2004), 153.

4. Hundreds of Black families moved to Puget Sound in the 1940s to take jobs in the war industries. They might have left abject poverty behind, but they couldn't escape the de facto version of segregation practiced in the north. In 1943, when he was ten years old, Quincy Jones came to Bremerton from Chicago after his father was hired to work in the navy yard. The family rented one of the eighty-five hundred small frame houses in the Bremerton Housing Development projects called Sinclair Park (also Sinclair Heights), on the west side of the city. This was a Blacks-only development; the other projects were built for white families, such as the Burkes. Every morning before he set out on his paper route Jones watched his father, Quincy Delight Jones Sr., trudge up the hill to the bus stop on his way to his carpentry job in the yard. Quincy Jr. fell in with the same sort of tough boys he had said goodbye to on the South Side, joining the new kids to steal fruit from farmers and live ammunition from the nearby army depot, including a battleship artillery shell. After the boys broke into the project's community center to steal lemon meringue pie from a freezer, he discovered something that would change his life. It was an old upright piano. See Quincy Jones, *Q: The Autobiography of Quincy Jones* (New York: Broadway Books, 2002), 26–35.

5. "Welcome to Bremerton Housing Authority," Bremerton Housing Authority, accessed August 18, 2018, www.bremertonhousing.org/index.php/about-bha/bha-history.

6. John Caldbick, "In-Depth History," Seattle Housing Authority, March 27, 2014, seattlehousing75.org/depth-history/. Abelia Court no longer exists. Rainier Vista became a slum, but was reinvented in 2009 as an area of housing for low-income, elderly, and disabled people.

7. Rockwell's *Rosie* was inspired by the section of Michelangelo's 1509 painting depicting the Prophet Isaiah, on the ceiling of the Sistine Chapel in the Vatican. Because Renaissance painters were prohibited from using nude female models, they used males instead. Also, see Gwen Sharp and Lisa Wade, "Sociological Images: Secrets of a Feminist Icon," accessed August 30, 2018, https://doi.org /10.1177/1536504211408972.

In 1942, Pittsburgh artist J. Howard Miller was hired by the Westinghouse Company's War Production Coordinating Committee to create a series of posters for the war effort. One of these posters became the famous "We Can Do It!" image—an image that in later years would also be called "Rosie the Riveter," though it was never given this title during the war. Miller is thought to have based his "We Can Do It! " poster on a United Press wire service photograph taken of a young female war worker, widely but erroneously reported as being a photo of Michigan war worker Geraldine Hoff. More recent evidence indicates that the formerly misidentified photo is actually of war worker Naomi Parker taken at Alameda Naval Air Station in California. The "We Can Do It!" poster was displayed only to Westinghouse employees in the Midwest during a two-week period in February 1943, then it disappeared for nearly four decades. During the war the name "Rosie" was not associated with the image, and the purpose of the poster was not to recruit women workers but rather as motivational propaganda aimed at workers of both sexes already employed at Westinghouse. It was only later, in the early 1980s, that the Miller poster was rediscovered and became famous, associated with feminism, and often mistakenly called "Rosie the Riveter."

8. Peter M. Bowers, *Fortress in the Sky: The Story of Boeing's B-17* (New York: Sentry Press, 1976).

9. The elaborately terracotta-covered building designed by the Henry Bittman firm has been known at times in the past as the Eagles Temple and as the Senator Hotel. The building was Aerie No. 1 of the Fraternal Order of Eagles, which was founded in Seattle.

10. "The Story of 5 Grand, the 5,000th B-17 Flying Fortress Built," accessed July 10, 2018, http://aviationtrivia.blogspot.com/2010/06/to-boost-morale-on-home-front -during.html#:~:text=14%20June%202010-,The%20Story%20of%20%225%20Grand %22%2C%20the%205%2C000th%20B,and%20named%20it%20%22YIPEE%22.

5. GIRL REPORTER

1. Each apartment featured a Murphy bed. In the years after the Park Avenue was built in 1923 frigid air was piped into the iceboxes of each apartment, eliminating

the need for visits from the iceman. See "Stores, Offices, Etc.," Helena as She Was, accessed August 27, 2018, http://www.helenahistory.org/Park_Avenue_Apartments.htm.

2. "The First Helena High School," Helena as She Was, accessed August 27, 2018, http://www.helenahistory.org/helena_high_school.htm.

3. For more about what was the typical journalism school's curriculum see Michael Lewis, "J-school Ate My Brain," *The New Republic*, July 1993, 5.

4. At issue was not in loco parentis, the concept of school administrators serving as surrogate parents for students. Pantzer responded to Marcia's demands by pointing out that the women's dorms had been financed with bonds that had to be repaid. If it didn't collect rent from women it would have to repay the principal and interest by taking money from other programs. Pantzer was besieged from all sides by the cultural upheavals of the era. The Student Facilities Council voted to allow women who had completed six quarters be granted the option to move off campus. Missoula Women's Liberation also endorsed the change. While the group's members identified themselves publicly with fictitious first names, Marcia Herrin used her full name. Herrin told a reporter that "coeds are asking for the same freedom of experience and moral choices as that presently had by young telephone operators and stenographers who live in apartments." Finally, Montana State University in Bozeman had already granted women who were juniors and seniors the option of living off campus. For more about the matter see various issues of the student daily, the *Montana Kaimin*, from October to December 1970.

5. Kirkpatrick, who was forty when she visited Missoula, had worked before the war as a reporter in England and published a newspaper called the *Whitehall News*, whose strident opposition to appeasing Hitler and Mussolini influenced Prime Minister Winston Churchill's decision to fight the fascists rather than negotiate with them. During the war she worked for the *Chicago Daily News*. When she applied for the job the publisher said, "We don't have women on the staff," to which Kirkpatrick replied "I can't change my sex. But you can change your policy." She entered liberated Paris with the French Free Army.

6. "Dear Molly, A careful look at last quarter's Honor Roll convinces me that you are not in school merely to meet interesting people or prolong your youth. Your name listed among the first-rate students is proof of an active interest in classes and studying. The J-school staff joins me in saying, 'Congratulations—keep up the good work!'" (April 21, 1946, letter to Molly Burke from James L. C. Ford.)

"Dear Molly, I know you were down at Murphy's Corner last quarter when you should have been studying because your grades were lousy! Anyone who can't find something better to do with his time than collecting monotonous rows of B's and A's one after another on a record sheet has better give up and go home. If you keep on that way you will have all the staff of the journalism school having to go out to the Merc or some other joint and buy new suits, because we'll be busting out buttons!" (January 26, 1948, letter from James L. C. Ford.)

7. "Fires occur regularly in the dry Big Belt Mountains of west-central Montana, averaging one significant fire every 13–25 years. In 1949, however, several years had passed without a fire. Consequently, a dense stand of Douglas fir and juniper sixty to a hundred years old covered the north-facing slope in Mann Gulch. The drier, south-facing slope had patches of similarly aged Ponderosa pine extending from the gulch bottom to the ridge line separating Mann and Rescue Gulches. This part of the Gates of the Mountains had been designated a "Wild Area" (a wilderness-like designation at the time) by Congress and no livestock grazing had recently occurred here, resulting in a two-to-three-foot high carpet of grass which covered the rocky, unstable slopes." Mann Gulch Wildfire Historic District, National Register of Historic Places Registration Form, National Park Service, May 19, 1999.

8. Molly C. Burke, "Tale of Horror and Sudden Death Related by Surviving 'Jumpers,'" *Montana Standard*, August 7, 1949, 14.

9. "Molly Burke Marries in Informal Rites at Presbyterian Church," *Independent Record*, October 16, 1949, 13.

6. LIGHTING OUT FOR THE TERRITORY

1. Henry's father, Marcia Herrin's great-great grandfather, was Daniel Herrin, born in Maine in 1739. Henry's wife, Rachel Starbird, died in Canaan in 1863.

2. Like many farmers in Canaan and the surrounding area of south-central Maine the Herrins finally got fed up trying to coax a living from the rocky, ungiving soil and moved west to better ground. Many of them started new lives in the Midwest, and a few of them lit out for the territories. As a consequence, from 1860 to 1940 Canaan declined by half in population, from fourteen hundred residents to seven hundred, according to the U.S. Census.

3. "On The Wing," *Helena (MT) Weekly-Herald*, July 3, 1879, 2. A traveler relates that "At Clancy a first-rate dinner was obtained at a house which had just been opened for the accommodation of the public. It is kept by Daniel S. Herren [*sic*], whose family has recently arrived from the East. A commodious barn, well filled with oats and hay for the benefit of horses, is kept in connection with the house. Being only fifteen miles from Helena, persons getting a late start from town will find this a convenient point to stop for the night."

4. The roadhouse no longer exists. But the following account of alleged larceny under its roof does. "EDITOR HERALD: Your readers will remember the published account of a theft of some money and a pair of sleeve-buttons by an individual bearing the flowery name of Posey, extracted from the pocket of Mr. Fisher of Clancy. Posey was arrested and tried, but he had secreted the articles, and as nothing could be proved positively, he was allowed to escape punishment. He

has since made his boast that they were not sharp enough to catch him. Last Wednesday a gentleman from Helena, Mr. Stevens, stopped at the hotel in Clancy kept by D. S. Herrin, and put up for the night. He was acquainted with the family, and knowing them to be strictly honest, on retiring he threw his pants with his money in the pocket, across the foot of the bed. The room was double-bedded, and after he had retired, Posey came in and took possession of the other bed, although he had been directed to another room with a single bed. In the morning Posey arose much earlier than usual and left for Jefferson City, and when Mr. Stevens came to pay his bill his money was gone. Posey has been ordered to give Clancy a wide birth [sic] in the future, and people will do well to lookout for the light-fingered gent. CITIZEN." *Helena (MT) Weekly-Herald*, February 12, 1880, 7.

5. The Homestead Act of 1862 stipulated that any adult citizen, or intended citizen, who had never raised a weapon against the U.S. government could claim 160 acres of surveyed government land. Claimants were required to "improve" the land by cultivating it and building a dwelling on it. After five years on the land the original filer was entitled to a deed to the property, free and clear, except for a small registration fee. Women were eligible. The process had to be completed within seven years. The Free Soil Party of 1848–52, and Abraham Lincoln's Republican Party demanded that the new lands opening up in the west be made available to independent farmers, rather than wealthy planters who would develop it by exploiting slaves, thus forcing yeomen farmers onto marginal lands. Southern Democrats had continually defeated previous homestead law proposals because they feared that free land would attract European immigrants and poor Southern whites to the West who were opposed to slavery. After the South seceded and their delegates fled Congress in 1861, the Republicans prevailed.

6. The Timber Culture Act of 1873 allowed homesteaders to get another 160 acres of land if they planted trees on 40 acres of this land (this requirement was reduced in 1878 to only 10 acres). The intent of the law was to seed the Great Plains with forests, which at the time were believed to cause rainfall. Plus, on the treeless steppes east of the Rocky Mountains, homesteaders needed firewood, windbreaks, hedges, and fencing material. (As a self-taught botanist named Jonathan Baldwin Turner discovered during the 1840s, the best species for these purposes was *Maclura pomifera*, the Osage orange; see Bill Vaughn, *Hawthorn* [New Haven CT: Yale University Press, 2015], 75–77.) Family members gave claims to other family members, which allowed them to continue using the land for years without formal ownership or taxes. Land speculators filed claims and sold the land when the proofing period was over. Nationally, only about 30 percent of Timber Culture Act claims were successfully completed. Because of such fraudulent claims the act was a failure and was repealed in 1891. The

Timber Culture claims of several Montanans were challenged. For more, see Katherine R. Goetz, "Timber Culture Act, 1873," last modified November 16, 2017, www.mnopedia.org/thing/timber-culture-act-1873.

7. Benjamin Herrin gained a sort of notoriety in 1877 after a benign tumor described as the size of an "ordinary" apple was removed from his left side. As the Helena surgeon worked, Herrin read a newspaper. The tumor, likely a soft-tissue lipoma, was placed before him on a table. He had felt no pain, the surgeon said, because the tumor had been numbed till it turned "white" with a frozen snowball treated with salt. The account of this surgery was published in several newspapers across the county. *St. Louis Post-Dispatch*, January 20, 1877.

8. Although the strike in nearby Lincoln Gulch had played out by 1873, gold and silver were still being extracted from the workings in nearby Keep Cool, Stonewall, Saur Kraut [*sic*] and Liverpool Gulches, in addition to the headwaters of Big Humbug Creek. "From Big Blackfoot Valley, Some Interesting Items from That Part of the County," *New North-West*, Deer Lodge, Montana, July 24, 1885, 3.

9. "Notice for Final Proof," *New North-West*, Deer Lodge, Montana, May 25, 1888, 4. For more details about the Herrin deeds, see "General Land Office Records," Bureau of Land Management, accessed May 31, 2021, https://glorecords.blm.gov/results/default.aspx?searchCriteria=type=patent|st=MT|cty=049|ln=Herrin|sp=true|sw=true|sadv=false.

10. Land records published on the online Montana Cadastral portal show that there is a cabin on the property that was built in 1871, probably by a gold miner squatting on the land.

11. "Notice for Final Proof," *New North-West*, Deer Lodge, Montana, May 25, 1888, 4.

12. "To Whom It May Concern," *Helena (MT) Weekly-Herald* May 3, 1888, 7.

13. "Harland J. Herrin," *Progressive Men of the State of Montana*, n.d., A. W. Bowen & Co., Chicago, 1575–76.

14. "Harland J. Herrin."

15. In 1889 Winstrom claimed in a sworn affidavit submitted to the local Justice of the Peace that Democratic Party functionaries from Helena had offered him fifty dollars for his services to work in one of Maryville's two precincts for their ticket in the upcoming election. In addition, they promised him twenty-five dollars walk-around cash. "Mr. Winstrom would not take their money," the *Helena Weekly-Herald* declared, "and has no hesitancy in telling about the attempt to bribe him." The newspaper speculated that others may have sold their votes but were keeping their mouths shut. "Democratic Boodle," *Helena (MT) Weekly-Herald*, October 3, 1898, 8.

Winstrom's affidavit demonstrates the highly politicized atmosphere in 1889 in the brand-new state of Montana. Many of the fortune seekers who swarmed into the territory following the Civil War were former Confederate soldiers politically aligned with the Democratic Party. See Ken Robison, *Confederates in Montana Territory* (Charleston SC: History Press, 2014). In 1889 Montanans got their first chance to vote in a national election, and overwhelmingly supported Republican candidates, the antislavery party of Abraham Lincoln. Both of the state's new senators were Republicans, as was its first representative. In the two Marysville precincts voters elected both Democrats and Republicans to the offices of constable and justice of the peace, but supported the Republic candidate for Lewis and Clarke County senator. (If there was in fact vote buying by the Democrats it's not clear what effect it had on the outcome.) In that first Federal election Lewis and Clarke County (spelled at the time with an *e*) would emerge as a Republican stronghold.

16. In 1900 the population of Montana was only 243,000 and most of its 77,000 square-mile expanse was unfenced. Ten years later the population had soared to 376,000 as young farmers and stockmen poured into the state to take advantage of the Homestead Act to try their hand at growing oats and raising cattle and sheep, which were increasingly turned out into the open range after the passage of the Homestead Act of 1900; that, and the 1902 Reclamation Act, encouraged young families to try their hand at raising cattle and, increasingly, sheep.

17. Albert J. Galen was born on a ranch near Three Forks, Montana, and spent his childhood riding horses and roping cattle. He graduated from Notre Dame University in 1896, and from the University of Michigan law department the next year. As a Montana lawyer, one of his early notable cases was winning a 1903 court order to cease and desist against unions in Butte, Montana, which were trying to organize messenger boys employed by his client, Western Union Telegraph. At the time, the telegraph was the most important means of communication in Montana's largest city, a vital network that was disrupted after a mob of striking messenger boys swarmed Western Union's offices, forcing the company to close. "Western Union Closes Its Doors," *Weekly Missoulian*, April 28, 1903, 3.

In 1904, when he was only twenty-eight years old, he won election as Montana attorney general, an office he held until 1913. In 1917 Galen was fined $500 for contempt of court arising from an alleged act of jury tampering. District Attorney Burton K. Wheeler, who would serve as Montana's Democratic senator from 1923 to 1946, charged that during a mail fraud trial Galen had met a juror in a bar and plied the man with "liquid refreshments." In a Helena alley, Galen confronted one of the witnesses against him, resulting in a fist fight. "Galen and Kelly Fined for Contempt," *Daily Missoulian*, June 14, 1917, 9; "More Fisticuffs Pulled Off in the Capitol City," *Anaconda Standard*, February 9, 1917, 2.

Galen served as the chairman of the Selective Service Board for Montana's First Congressional District in World War I, quitting abruptly to voluntarily join the armed forces. He was promoted to lieutenant colonel, named judge advocate of the American Expeditionary Forces in Siberia, and awarded the Distinguished Service Medal when the war ended. In 1921 he was elected associate justice of the Montana Supreme Court, a position he held until 1933. In 1930 he ran as the Republican candidate for U.S. Senate, losing by a wide margin to Montana's popular incumbent, Thomas J. Walsh, who led the Senate investigation of the Teapot Dome scandal, which resulted in the imprisonment of the secretary of the interior for corruption.

One summer evening in 1936 Galen borrowed a power boat from his son, James, who owned a ranch on the land beside the Missouri River that his father and Holly Herrin owned at the turn of the century. He headed across what had become Holter Lake toward his summer cottage on the opposite side at a place called Oxbow Point. But the only thing of Galen's that came ashore was his hat. Presumed drowned, a search for his body began. He was found in ten feet of water two weeks later. "Report Finding Body of Galen in Holter Lake," *Billings Gazette*, May 30, 1936, 1.

7. WILD AND WOOLY

1. "Shot Up the Town," *Semi-Weekly Billings Gazette*, December 30, 1904, 7.
2. "Champion of Wolf Creek," *Helena Independent*, October 23, 1901, 5.
3. "Both Charged with Arson," *Anaconda Standard*, January 12, 1902, 2.
4. "Guilty of Arson," *Daily Missoulian*, May 16, 1902, 5.
5. "Special to the *Daily Tribune*," *Great Falls Tribune*, May 18, 1902, 5.
6. "Suit for Damages," *Daily Missoulian*, February 26, 1903, 4.
7. "Basis for a New Trial," *Anaconda Standard*, August 19, 1902, 12.
8. "Jurors Are Charged with Misconduct," *Butte Miner* August 19, 1902, 9.
9. "New Trial for a Convict," *Anaconda Standard*, December 25, 1902, 14.
10. "Green's Second Trial on Charge of Arson," *Anaconda Standard*, May 8, 1903, 2.
11. "Green Acquitted on Arson Charge," *Anaconda Standard*, May 22, 1903, 3.
12. Nitsche was described in the 1900 U.S. Census as a white male born in Germany in 1854 who emigrated to the United States in 1880. He lived on property he owned at Township 15-17 North, Range 3-6 West in Lewis and Clarke County, Montana.
13. "Range War in the West," *New York Times*, January 8, 1901, 1.
14. An "information" is a formal criminal charge, one of the oldest common law pleadings. First appearing around the thirteenth century, it is nearly as old as the better-known term *indictment*, with which it has always coexisted. Although the information has been abolished in Great Britain it is still used in Canada and the United States. See Lester B. Orfield, *Criminal Procedure from Arrest to Appeal* (New York: New York University Press, 1947), 194–97.
15. For example, in Highwood a party of whitecappers was repelled by an armed man they threatened to tar and feather because he had married their leader's

divorced wife. "Whitecapping Case Dismissed," *Great Falls Tribune*, March 13, 1904, 12. And whitecappers terrorized a sheep herder and drove his flock off the open range. "May Call a Grand Jury to Investigate Attack by Cattlemen upon a Teton County Sheepherder," *Great Falls Tribune*, August 17, 1903, 8.

16. "Recognized Two of Alleged Whitecaps," *Anaconda Standard*, June 1, 1904, 3.

17. "New Trial Is Asked For," *Anaconda Standard*, June 12, 1904, 9.

18. "New Use of Fair Trial Law," *Anaconda Standard*, May 26, 1904, 13.

19. "Spray of the Falls," *Great Falls Tribune*, December 11, 1906, 6.

20. "H. J. Herrin Gets Divorce," *Helena Independent*, June 13, 1906, 2.

21. "Thomas O'Connell Dies," *Helena Independent*, December 12, 1905, 8. In 1905 life expectancy in the United States was forty-seven. O'Connell likely died of pneumonia, influenza, or tuberculosis.

8. A MAN OF MEANS

1. "Packers Claim That Profits Were Small," *Great Falls Tribune*, March 4, 1904, 3. Six years later, as the federal government readied itself to launch another investigation, the *Tribune* published an editorial attacking the 1904 report. "The government is going to prosecute the beef trust once more. Secretary Garfield made a nice mess of it the last time it was tried under the Roosevelt Administration. He went to the packers for his information. They showed him a nice set of books kept for public inspection, and they escaped on the immunity plea afterwards when prosecuted. They were so successful in defying Teddy Roosevelt and his administration that they have been made bold. Perhaps the government may have a better case against them this time. At any rate the government is on the right track so far as beef prices to the consumer is concerned. The beef trust fixed them as it also fixes prices to the beef producer, and in the spread between the two will be found the secret of the consumer's trouble." "After the Beef Trust Again," *Great Falls Tribune*, January 28, 1910, 4.

2. David Edwin Harrell Jr., Edwin S. Gaustad, John B. Boles, and Sally Foreman Griffith, *Unto a Good Land: A History of the American People, Volume 2: From 1865* (Grand Rapids MI: Wm B. Eerdmans Publishing, 2005), 577.

3. In 1786 Louis bought three hundred Merinos from this cousin, King Charles II of Spain, and bred them on his experimental farm at Rambouillet south of Paris. He didn't live to see the results of his experiments, however, because at the age of thirty-eight he was sent to the guillotine during the French Revolution. The Rambouillet is larger than the Merino, some rams weighing up to three hundred pounds. For carnivores who like mutton and lamb, the meat of the Rambouillet is favored over that of other breeds. Because they are gregarious, easily herded, hardy, and at ease grazing on wide expanses of open country, they were the perfect choice for Montana's early flockmasters. By 2019, 50 percent of the sheep in Montana were Rambouillets.

4. "Herder Forfeits Bail," *Helena Independent*, November 24, 1910, 8.

5. "Very Old Man Is Under Arrest," *Helena Independent*, November 28, 1910, 8.

6. In February 1912, Trodick sold for $1 this entire quarter section to the Wolf Creek Townsite Company, an entity created in 1911 to manage the land. McDonald, who had been leasing his saloon, continued in business at least long enough to get himself into trouble. On October 4, 1911, he refused to serve any more booze to a Japanese immigrant named Tose Takeuchi until the man paid his tab. Takeuchi tried to brain him with a brass spittoon. McDonald responded by grabbing his revolver and firing wildly at the "Jap" (as several newspapers labeled him). One of the bullets struck Takeuchi in the thigh and another one seriously injured a harness maker named Thomas Howard, a proverbial innocent bystander who was shot just below the heart. In his explanation for shooting Howard, who survived, McDonald claimed that the man was jumping around from place to place in the saloon during the melee and simply ran into McDonald's bullet. A jury acquitted McDonald of first-degree assault. Takeuchi and Howard sued McDonald. Takeuchi lost his suit and McDonald died of a heart attack at the age of forty-five, before Howard's case could be adjudicated. "Wolf Creek Saloon Man Acquitted," *Great Falls Tribune*, January 12, 1912, 6.

   Previous to the saloon shooting, McDonald had been involved in numerous altercations around Wolf Creek. In 1900 he was hauled into court to face charges of dynamiting fish in Little Prickly Pear Creek. In 1902 he was accused of poisoning a dog, whose owner then punched McDonald in the face, breaking his nose. In 1904 McDonald pulled a pistol during a fight with a neighboring saloon owner, whom McDonald had accused of burglarizing a Wolf Creek hotel. The gun exploded as McDonald was pulling back the hammer. "Martin Bray Is On Trial," *Helena Independent*, April 24, 1904, 8.

7. "Dearborn County Plan Is Beaten," *Helena Independent*, November 19, 1913, 3. The Dearborn County campaign wasn't Dan McKay's first rodeo. In 1912 his efforts resulted in the legislature carving three new counties—Blaine, Phillips, and Hill—from the northern portion of Chouteau County. Called everything from con man and huckster to "County Splitter" and "The silver-tongued orator of Milk River Valley," McKay was an immigrant from Scotland who owned a brickyard in Great Falls. He spent most of his working life, however, riding around on a big white horse and later a bigger black car, stopping wherever there was a gathering of farmers or townspeople to harangue them about the benefits of forming new counties. His sponsors were usually the men who owned prime city lots that would become the site of the new courthouse. McKay helped local county clubs organized the petition drives and draw new boundaries, which sometimes doglegged around the ranch of an uncooperative property owner. For each campaign he was paid $1,500. The money was less important to him, however, than the sound of his own voice and his growing fame. His career got

a boost in the 1915 passage of the Leighton Act, which allowed counties to split as they saw fit without permission from the legislature. Between 1913 and 1922, twenty-five new counties were born. McKay was the midwife to at least four and as many as nine of these out-of-wedlock births.

When drought and falling demand for commodities after World War I decimated the farm economy, many of these expensive little governments were forced to confiscate and then sell failed farms and ranches for a few cents on the dollar simply to keep themselves operating. Some of them became the *only* landowner in the county. But a century later McKay's scheme has delivered on at least one of his promises: property taxes are far lower in these backwaters than they are in the territory's nine original counties. The average owner of an average-sized house in Fallon County, for example, paid $643 in 2019. In Missoula County that figure was $2,176.

8. "Carter Controls Convention," *Weekly Missoulian*, September 9, 1904, 7.

9. "State Convention," *Billings Gazette*, September 7, 1904, 1.

10. A staunch, lifelong member of the GOP, Holly would pass on his political convictions to his son, Thomas, who would pass them on to *his* son, Keith. In a likewise manner the Burkes would pass on their fervent Democratic Party allegiance to their daughters. The political differences between Keith and Molly would become one of many causes of friction in their marriage.

11. "Party Machine Names Ticket," *Helena Semi-Weekly Independent*, September 18, 1908, 8. As an advocate for the Democratic Party the *Helena Independent* railed against the "Party Machine" that dictated the results of the GOP nominating convention. It also predicted that the one thousand Black voters living in Lewis and Clark County—and the other six thousand living at the time in Montana— would abandon the GOP in November. "These colored men have always been staunch supporters of the grand old party. They have always been the most reliable supporters which the party has had in this county. In the past, the republicans realizing this have never failed to give the colored vote adequate representation in the party councils. This year the party in a desire no doubt to present a "lily-white" exterior to the voters, have decided their colored brethren will not be allowed to brush shoulders with them, neither shall they take them by the hand, nor allow them to be recognized in their councils. In pursuance of this policy there were only one or two colored men in the convention and none of them were sent up as delegates to the state convention."

12. "Lewis and Clark: Senator and Four Out of Five Representatives Won by Democrats," *Butte Miner*, November 7, 1912, 9.

13. "Light Penalty Given Berzan," *Helena Independent*, May 4, 1921, 5.

14. "The Immigration Act of 1924 (The Johnson-Reed Act)," U.S. Department of State Office of the Historian, accessed September 6, 2019.

15. "Wolf Creek Taken by Incendiary Fire," *Helena Independent*, July 9, 1917, 1.

16. "Wool Sales," *Western News*, Stevensville, Montana, August 16, 1910 1.
17. "Herrin Tells of Trespass," *Helena Independent*, September 14, 1911, 8. E. A. Carlton was the attorney who defended Arthur L. Green in 1902 against charges that he set fires on Holly's ranch; Henry C. Smith was the district court judge who granted Green a new trial, following which Green was exonerated.
18. "Grazing of Sheep Makes War," *Daily Missoulian*, October 20, 1912, 7.
19. This is an entirely different stream than Prickly Pear Creek, which flows into the Missouri twenty miles south of the place where Little Prickly Pear Creek enters the river. See map 2. At some point in the state's history the namers of streams began to run out of names. For example, there is a rivulet in Powell County called Your Name Creek.
20. The prohibition against crossing corners rose out of the lack of an explicit policy. "There has never been a federal statute, no law enacted by the democratically elected representatives of the American people, that defines what property rights are, and are not, afforded at the corners. Who has use of, and who can pass, chess-bishop fashion, the imaginary point where four parcels meet? We've never decided for ourselves at a national level. Instead, the question has been left for regulators, judges, and enforcement agencies to answer, on a state-by-state, or even county-by-county, basis. For lack of clearer guidance, most jurisdictions have, according to University of Colorado Law School Professor Mark Squillace, based their positions on the 1979 Supreme Court case, *Leo Sheep Company v. United States* [see note 23]. . . . The de facto ban on stepping from public land, to public land, over an intersection with private, hits sportsmen and—women—hardest in Montana and Wyoming. There, access to 724,000 and 404,000 acres respectively is lost behind such corners." Mathew Copeland, "Cornered: Western Sportsmen Trapped by Arcane Regulation Prohibiting Public Access at Corner Crossings," *Outdoor Life*, August 10, 2015.
21. Michael E. Zimmerman, "Was an Easement by Necessity Impliedly Reserved in the Checkerboard Land Grants: *Leo Sheep Company v. United States*," *Public Land and Resources Law Review*, 1, 1980, 112.
22. In 1927 the Texas Supreme Court decreed in *State v. Black Brothers* that the doctrine of necessity does not apply to governments in the same way it applies to private landowners. In this case the State of Texas sued for and obtained an easement across land owned by the defendant, a private individual. On appeal, the Texas Supreme Court refused to recognize the Texas claim to an easement based on necessity, concluding that the application of this rule was limited to situations "where the grantor was another than the Federal government." While the Texas court had always emphasized that strict necessity is the basis for granting an easement, the same necessity does not exist in the case of the state as in the case of the individual landowner. As long as the state holds title to reserved land it can, "in the exercise of the power of eminent domain . . . obtain any and all reasonable rights of way."

In a 1957 decision, *Simonson v. McDonald,* the Montana Supreme Court agreed with *Black Brothers* and reversed its 1912 decision in *Herrin.* The court ruled that because the government has the power to condemn land, it doesn't need a right-of-way that's grounded in necessity. In this interpretation the court recognized and endorsed the idea that in condemning private property the state was required to compensate the owner for his loss.

Although *Herrin* was subsequently overruled by *Simonson,* the "Herrin rule" was reinstated in 1965 after *Simonson* was overruled by *Thisted v. Country Club Tower Corp.* (Addressing contractual matters at an eleven-story condominium apartment building rising above the Country Club golf course in Great Falls, the details of this ruling had nothing to do with sheep but everything to do with the retention of easements by necessity in the transfer of property.)

23. "In Carbon County, Wyoming, some Union Pacific Railroad land had passed to the Leo Sheep Company. The Seminoe Reservoir, used by the public for hunting and fishing, is situated to the west and south of these sections and cannot be reached without crossing private land. Controversy began when Bureau of Land Management (BLM) officials received complaints that Leo Sheep Company and other private landowners were either denying access or were charging a fee to cross their land. After attempts to negotiate failed, the BLM cleared a road across Leo Sheep Company land and posted signs inviting the public to use it for access to the reservoir." Leo Sheep Company sued. The United States District Court, District of Wyoming, upheld the company's claim that the United States had, in clearing the access road, unlawfully entered their land. The Court of Appeals for the Tenth Circuit reversed that decision. The United States Supreme Court held in favor of the company, holding that an implied easement could not be inferred from the Union Pacific Act of 1862, and that no easement by necessity existed because the government retained the power of eminent domain. Michael E. Zimmerman, "Was an Easement by Necessity Impliedly Reserved in the Checkerboard Land Grants: *Leo Sheep Company v. United States,*" *Public Land and Resources Law Review* 1 (1980): 112–13.

24. Henry Sieben was born in Germany, immigrated to Illinois with his family as a young boy, and came to the gold fields of Montana in 1864. Small and wiry, lacking any formal education, he prospected and worked as a farm laborer scything hay in the Madison Valley. He then picked up freight that had been off-loaded from steamboats onto the Missouri River docks at Fort Benton and hauled it in ox wagons to Helena and Virginia City. He turned his played-out beasts onto the open range and fattened them before selling them to butchers. Seeing that more money could be made with cattle than with freight, he began ranching. In 1870 Henry and his brother Leonard bought 160 head of cattle in Utah and trailed them to their ranch in the Chestnut Valley near Cascade, Montana. In 1871 the brothers went back to Utah and brought another four hundred head

to the valley. They added sheep to the enterprise when their younger brother, Jacob, joined them. The brothers bought twenty-two hundred Merinos near Red Bluff, California, and Jacob trailed them to Montana. Henry Sieben eventually acquired two enormous ranches totaling some 115,000 acres of land along the Missouri River, one on Little Prickly Pear Creek south of Wolf Creek and the other at the headwaters of Adel Creek near Cascade. He was a co-founder of the Montana Woolgrowers Association, and founded the Montana Children's Home. Although elected to the National Cowboy Hall of Fame, Sieben never owned a pair of cowboy boots. His family continues to operate the Sieben Ranch Company today. His great-grandson is the former United States senator and U.S. ambassador to the People's Republic of China, Max Baucus.

9. WOOL MANIA

1. In 2011 the National Park Service recognized Free Speech Corner at Higgins Avenue and West Front Street, adding it to the National Register of Historic Places. "Missoula Downtown Historic District Expands," *Missoulian*, April 27, 2011, 1.

2. Clemens P. Work, *Darkest Before Dawn: Sedition and Free Speech in the American West* (Albuquerque: University of New Mexico Press, 2006).

3. Michael Punke, *Fire and Brimstone: The North Butte Mining Disaster of 1917* (New York: Hachette Books, 2006).

4. "IWW Threatened to Destroy Crops," *Ronan Pioneer*, July 27, 1917, 7.

5. The dam was named for Samuel T. Hauser, a governor of the Montana Territory from 1885 to 1887. He made a fortune in banking, mining railroads, ranching, and smelting, but nearly lost it all during the panic of 1893. Reinventing himself, Hauser decided to get in on the ground floor of the new hydroelectric energy industry. In 1894 he formed the Missouri River Power Company and was permitted by Congress to build a dam two miles below Stubbs's Ferry on the Missouri. Steel pilings were driven thirty-five feet into the gravel riverbed; steel sheets were attached to the pilings and the upstream face was covered with reinforced concrete. Both ends were anchored to the bedrock walls of the canyon. Triangular masonry footings topped with concrete supplied the foundation for the upstream face. A layer of volcanic ash called bentonite, which absorbs water and expands, was deposited in a layer twenty feet deep along the upstream riverbed to discourage seeping. On the day the dam broke, water pressure undermined the footings, which gave way. The pilings and sheeting were not the cause of the breach.

In April 1910 the United Missouri River Power company filed a lawsuit against the Wisconsin Bridge and Iron company of Milwaukee, which designed and engineered the dam, asking for a judgment of more than $3.5 million. "Millions Are Asked in Hauser Dam Case," *Anaconda Standard*, April 16, 1910, 1. But Hauser's company never collected, because the engineering firm withdrew its agents from Montana, thus escaping the jurisdiction of the Treasure State's courts. "Meyers Introduces Bill at Request Of Galen," *Butte Miner*, January 26, 1912, 3.

6. Larry Swindell, *The Last Hero: A Biography of Gary Cooper* (New York: Doubleday, 1980), 12.

7. "No Damage in the City," *Great Falls Tribune*, April 16, 1908, 1.

8. "General Donovon Was Drowned," *Great Falls Tribune*, April 22, 1908, 5.

9. "Checks Are Distributed," *Anaconda Standard*, January 28, 1908, 7.

10. "Dam Is Gone," *Great Falls Tribune*, March 18, 1909, 1. In its exclusive coverage of the incident the *Tribune* accused the dam company and the two Helena daily newspapers, *Helena Independent* and the *Montana Daily-Record*, of hiding the truth. "Owing to the suppression of facts in connection with the case by the press of the capital and the officials of the Helena Power & Transmission company, which owns the dam, full details concerning the second catastrophe to the Hauser Lake dam and the power plant have not been learned here." In fact, neither Helena paper ever mentioned the washout.

On March 29, 1909, the *Tribune* editorialized again, on page two, about the coverup, admitting, however, that its report was based on interviews with eye-witnesses who may have inflated the degree of damage. "The public have [*sic*] a right to legitimate news," the *Tribune* wrote. "It is not always to the advantage of big corporations that they should have it. Often in an endeavor to keep such news from the public they suffer far more than they would if they had never tried to conceal the truth. Many large corporations have learned the fact. . . . Most railroads now follow that rule. Some corporations like the Hauser Lake Dam company try to conceal these facts, and even lie about them to the newspaper men. In such cases they have no just complaint if the facts as stated are inaccurate."

11. Amalgamated Copper, which bought 75 percent of United Missouri's electricity and owned a significant portion of its corporate bonds, began buying its power from Hauser's rival, the Great Falls Power Company, owned by John T. Ryan. Hauser sold his interest in United Missouri to Ryan, who in late 1912 merged United Missouri River Power with the Butte Electric and Power Company, Billings and Eastern Montana Power Company, and Madison River Power Company to form the Montana Power Company. Montana Power took over not only United Missouri's Canyon Ferry Dam and Hauser Dam but the abandoned Holter Dam as well. "Montana Power Earnings Show Great Business Growth," *Electrical World*, April 28, 1917, 817.

12. "Scotten Gets Lot of Beans," *Great Falls Tribune*, October 10, 1917, 5.

13. "Another Great Development Dream Is Now Rapidly Becoming a Reality," *Great Falls Tribune*, October 29, 1916, 20. The company's photographer, M. L. DeLong, developed and printed images of the dam's progress. He also filmed and developed reels of motion pictures.

14. "Wolf Creek News," *Helena Independent,* June 15, 1920, 8.
15. The American system of grading wool was developed in the early 1800s when coarse-wooled English sheep were being bred in France to fine-wooled Spanish Merino sheep to produce the Rambouillet breed (see chapter 8, note 3). The wool grade is defined as the percentage of Merino blood carried by the animal, whose quality of wool was influenced by both its health and its age. The grades or fiber diameters were expressed as fine, 1/2-blood, 3/8-blood, 1/4-blood, low 1/4-blood, common, and braid. Today, these terms are not as exact as the trade would prefer, and the spread within a grade is too broad to suit the purposes of wool processors. So the American wool industry adopted the Micron System. This is a system in which individual fibers are accurately measured using the micron as the unit of measure, which is one-millionth of a meter or 1/25,000 of an inch. Fineness is expressed as the mean fiber diameter. "Grading of Wool," Textile School, March 13, 2018, www.textileschool.com/194/grading-of-wool.
16. "War Profiteers Put Out of Business by Penwell," *Great Falls Tribune,* July 7, 1918, 25.
17. Lewis Penwell was born in Diamond City, Montana, in 1869. The "city" was a raucous gold mining camp thirty miles east of Helena high up in Confederate Gulch, which was named for soldiers captured in Missouri by Union forces and released on their promise to give up Dixie and board a steamboat headed up the Missouri bound for Montana. Penwell was an attorney, a politician, and a sheep rancher. In 1913 he was a member of a group of investors who bought the *Helena Independent* newspaper, and he became president of the company. By 1915 he was the owner or part owner of twenty-five Montana ranches on which 105,000 sheep were shorn. In 1916 he bought the lease for San Clemente Island, the southernmost of the Channel Islands in the Pacific Ocean east of Los Angeles, noted as the site of a prehistoric community and a nineteenth-century base for smugglers. The Penwell Company paid the federal government $300,000, which included twenty-five thousand head of sheep, pedigreed European stallions, plus draft horses and mules. Penwell sold the sheep, which had survived the island's paucity of fresh water by crowding into caves during the day to avoid the sun, emerging to graze at night. He then shipped in twenty-five thousand Hampshire Down and Rambouillet ewes, which were shorn in 1918, their wool contributing to the war effort. "Lewis Penwell Buys Big Island Ranch in Southern California," *Butte Miner,* April 12, 1916, 6.
18. "Says Wool Shortage Fear Is Groundless," *Anaconda Standard,* April 26, 1918, 10.
19. "Profits for Wool to Go to Growers," *Helena Independent,* August 11, 1918, 2.
20. "People knitted not just at home but at work, at church, on public transport, in the theater, and while waiting for trains and sitting in restaurants. Female life-guards in Southern California, covering for men who had gone to war, brought their knitting to the beach. A sitting grand jury in Seattle knitted socks. In 1915 the New York Philharmonic Society had to issue a plea for audience members

to refrain from knitting, as it disrupted performances. Men who had not gone to fight also contributed. There are accounts of Red Cross members teaching firemen to knit, train conductors knitting between stations, and inmates at Sing Sing knitting in the prison yard, serenaded by mandolin players. Men were encouraged to knit at work during their lunch hours, and wounded soldiers knitted from their hospital beds." Anika Burgess, "The Wool Brigades of World War I: When Knitting Was a Patriotic Duty," *Atlas Obscura,* July 26, 2017.

21. "More Sheep, More Wool, More Food," *High Point (NC) Enterprise,* August 3, 1917, 7.

22. The Navy League of the United States, founded in 1902 with the support of President Theodore Roosevelt, is a nonprofit civilian educational and advocacy organization that supports the Navy, Marine Corps, Coast Guard and Merchant Marine.

23. "Knitting Enthusiasm Sweeps Great Falls," *Great Falls Tribune,* January 6, 1918, 13.

24. "Butte Firemen Will Knit Soldier Socks," *Butte Miner,* June 4, 1918, 6.

25. "Gatley Urges Respect for Germans' Culture," *Daily Missoulian,* September 24, 1917, 2.

26. "No Wool Left for Your Suit," *Conrad Independent,* September 19, 1918, 2.

27. "Used Wool Shortage Scare Used to Promote Sale of Shoddy Clothes for U.S. Soldiers," *Billings Gazette,* January 6, 1918, 1.

28. In 1901 William H. Clinkenbeard opened a photography studio on Central Avenue in Great Falls called the Progressive Art Company and later, the Studio La Grande. He specialized in posed photographs, using "all the latest scenery, fancy posing chairs, most expensive instruments," according to one of his newspaper ads. To advertise the studio, he set up a stereopticon on the sidewalk. This device combined two different images to create for the viewer a three-dimensional effect. He also organized art exhibits at his studio featuring the work of local painters, such as Charles M. Russell. In 1903 he announced that he was seeking a patent on a coating for prints he called "silk finish," which he claimed made it possible to clean the print without damaging it. He told a newspaper that "sufficient capital" is all that is required to thoroughly establish the value of the invention as an important addition to the art of photography. "Silk Finish Photos," *Great Falls Tribune,* April 12, 1903, 3. A month later he filed for bankruptcy. Two photographers quarreled after vying to buy the fixtures of his studio during a sale administered by the trustees. One photographer threw the other one down a flight of stairs and was arrested. "Thrown Down Stairway," *Great Falls Tribune,* July 20, 1903, 8.

10. THE WATER BELOW AND THE AIR ABOVE

1. Except for bison, in 1924 Montana was still home to an abundance of fish and game. But the generous limits set by law would be reduced over the years in

response to habitat depletion. The bag limit for ducks shot in the Pacific Flyway—the western half of the state, which includes Lewis and Clark County—had been reduced from twenty in 1924 to seven in 2019. And the forty fish per day limit that was allowed Lewis and Clark anglers in 1924 had been reduced in 2019 to five trout of various species. However, if an angler wished to drive to a different habitat in the afternoon after a morning of trout fishing, he or she could take five bass, for example, ten channel catfish, or ten salmon.

2. Montana Code Annotated, 70-16-101. Rights of owner in fee—above and below surface. The owner of land in fee has the right to the surface and to everything permanently situated beneath or above it. The Latin expression is "*cujus est solum, ejus est usque ad coelum et ad infernos*," translated as "whoever owns the land owns the property all the way to heaven and all the way to hell." While a landowner new to Montana might believe that this law grants him unrestricted domain, in a 1946 case, *United States v. Causby*, the Supreme Court ruled that the ancient heaven-to-hell doctrine "has no place in the modern world." Thomas Lee Causby, who owned a chicken farm outside Greensboro, North Carolina, claimed that noise from low-flying aircraft taking off and landing at a nearby military airport caused several of his birds to lose their minds, run amok, and kill themselves. The problem was so severe, Causby claimed, that he was forced to abandon his business. He sued the federal government for illegally taking his livelihood. A lower court agreed. The Supreme Court ruled that although Causby could not claim airspace in which high-flying aircraft traveled, it also ruled that, "if the landowner is to have full enjoyment of the land, he must have exclusive control of the immediate reaches of the enveloping atmosphere." It directed the government to pay Causby for his loss.

3. "Damage by Trespasser; Suit to Determine Rights of Ranch Owner," *Butte Miner*, October 3, 1924, 4.

4. Nineteen twenty-nine was a typical year for lawyer Toomey. He represented a family whose relative had been buried in a family plot at the Odd Fellows Cemetery in Helena, discovering later to their horror that the managers had dug up the woman's corpse and dropped it in another grave. Toomey asked for a judgment of $25,000. "Brief Is Filed in Odd Fellows Cemetery Case," *Helena Independent*, May 8, 1925, 5. He also represented a Chinese national named Won Cue, who was accused of heroin and cocaine possession. "Acquit Won Cue of Drug Charge after Four Hours; Chinese Is Found Not Guilty," *Helena Independent*, November 17, 1929, 6. That same year, he defended a woman accused of murdering a World War I veteran with a shotgun. She was convicted of manslaughter and served less than a year in the state penitentiary "Negress, Who Shot Townsend Veteran, Moves to Spokane," *Helena Independent*, October 26, 1929, 10. Montana newspapers of the era routinely identified people who weren't white by their race or nationality.

5. "Trespassing Case under Advisement by Supreme Court," *Helena Independent,* October 25, 1925, 5.

6. "Hunting and Fishing Privilege Dealt with in Court Decision," *Butte Miner,* November 25, 1925, 1.

7. "Trespassing Case under Advisement by Supreme Court," *Helena Independent,* October 25, 1925, 5.

8. "Hunting and Fishing Privilege Dealt with in Court Decision," *Butte Miner,* November 25, 1925, 1.

9. "Want Trespass Case Appealed," *Billings Weekly Gazette,* December 1, 1925, 3.

10. "Trespassing Law Not for Anglers Says Montana's Chief Justice," *Billings Gazette,* March 28, 1926, 4.

11. Louisiana adopted the Napoleonic Code, which differs from English common law in mostly minor ways, but stresses clearly written and accessible legal language. A consequence of the French Revolution, it replaced the labyrinth of laws that evolved under feudalism.

12. The Civil Code of 1895 in section 1291 codified the rule that "the owner of the land, when it borders upon a navigable lake or stream, takes to the edge of the lake or stream at low-water mark." The 1895 legislature, in the new civil code, claimed the state as owner of "all land below the water of a navigable lake or stream." The 1895 legislature, in adopting the Political Code of Montana, defined public ways as "navigable waters and all streams of sufficient capacity to transport the products of the country are public ways for the purposes of navigation and transportation." Robert N. Lane, "The Remarkable Odyssey of Stream Access in Montana," *Public Land and Resources Law Review* 36, article 5, 76.

13. Lane, "Remarkable Odyssey."

14. Lane, "Remarkable Odyssey."

15. Dennis Mike Curran was born in Butte, Montana, in 1917 and attended Ohio State University before going to work in the construction business. He made and lost several fortunes in the oil industry. His company laid the last American-built pipeline across Iran before the Shah was driven from power by the Islamic Revolution. Whenever Curran was flush he bought land along the Dearborn River. His largest acquisition was the Rock Creek Ranch, which he bought from Brian O'Connell. The Rock Creek Ranch increased Curran's holdings to more than seventy-thousand acres along the final seven miles of the river. In 1980 a coalition of sportsmen and recreationist sued Curran after he began denying access to floaters and sportsmen who wanted to camp overnight on the banks of the stream. Curran claimed they damaged fences, scattered garbage, and injured livestock. He was accused of destroying a floater's raft by running over it with his pickup. "We're not a public campground," Curran told a newspaper.

In a sweeping landmark decision that helped make Montana's laws safeguarding stream access the strongest in the nation, District Judge Gordon Bennett ruled against Curran. "The key points of the district court's decision are that members of the public have the right to float and recreate in non-navigable streams, that they may wade and use the banks up to the ordinary high-water, and that these rights are founded in statutory language." (Lane, "Remarkable Odyssey," 80. In 1975 Judge Bennett made a ruling in the *Herrin v. Herrin* divorce settlement that the Supreme Court would overturn.)

Later, on appeal, the Montana Supreme Court held that "under the public trust doctrine and the 1972 Montana Constitution, any surface waters that are capable of recreational use may be so used by the public without regard to streambed ownership or navigability for nonrecreational purposes." The public trust doctrine is an ancient principle holding that the "sovereign" (or the state) holds in trust for public use some resources as shoreline between the high and low tide lines, regardless of private property ownership.

In 1983 a federal judge threw out Curran's legal challenge to the Montana Power Company's efforts to secure an easement across fifteen miles of his land in order to upgrade a natural gas pipeline built in 1931.

After Curran died in 2002 from Alzheimer's disease it was announced that he had bequeathed $1.4 million each to the College of Great Falls, the Great Falls Public Library, the Mayo Clinic, and the McLaughlin Research Institute in Great Falls, whose mission is to improve human health through genetic research.

11. IN THE GREASE

1. "American Industry in the War: A Report of the War Industries Board" (Washington DC: Government Printing Office, 1921), 71.
2. "Wool Situation Not Encouraging," *Anaconda Standard*, October 25, 1920, 9.
3. "Report of the Federal Trade Commission on Methods and Operations of Grain Exporters, Vol II" (Washington DC: Government Printing Office, June 18, 1923), 34.
4. "Potato Prices Drop 90 Percent," *New York Times*, May 27, 1921, 6.
5. Both brands were extremely rare in Montana. Most people who could afford a car—and were willing to put up with rural roads that weren't much more than ruts—bought a Model T. In 1919 Holly paid $4,500 for his Cadillac; the Franklin Sedan cost $2,500, and the Model T $750. Holly bought the Franklin for two reasons: First, it was powered by a unique air-cooled engine, which meant that unlike a water-cooled engine it would not freeze in Montana's frigid winters or overheat in the summer because of a failure in the cooling system. Second, the Franklin offered a certain snob appeal. According to a 1916 ad "The typical Franklin owner is a successful man who thinks for himself. . . . He sees in the Franklin the best use of his money—and his whole habit of life has taught him to seek efficiency."
6. The unpopular presidential incumbent, Woodrow Wilson, was replaced on the Democratic ticket with an obscure congressman from Ohio named James

M. Cox. The Republicans had hoped to throw Teddy Roosevelt into the fray, but he died in 1919 from a blood clot in his lungs. They settled on Warren G. Harding, Ohio's senior senator. Foreshadowing a GOP presidential candidate, a century later, Harding played on the nostalgic yearnings of Americans for "the good old days" before the war, when it was perceived that the United States had been free from foreign entanglements and "progressive" political ideas, such as a federal income tax and banking system. Harding's advocacy of protective tariffs on imports was one way to court this America-first isolationism. He won by the largest margin in American history. The GOP not only wrested control of the Senate from the Democrat by a 59–37 margin, it increased its already sizable majority in the House. (In Montana one congressional seat stayed in GOP hands and the other one, held by the Democrats, was flipped to the Republicans by a wide margin. However, one of the few counties outside the South that voted for Cox was Mineral County in Montana.)

7. "Ewes Worth $20 Each," *Great Falls Tribune*, May 11, 1922, 5.

8. "Keeping Money at Home," *Helena Independent*, July 6, 1911.

9. The Woodmen of the World (WOW) was founded in 1890 in Omaha, Nebraska, by Joseph Cullen Root, a lawyer and businessman. This was an era that lacked government safety nets, compelling Americans down on their luck to take charity and handouts. Inspired by a sermon describing "pioneer woodsmen clearing away the forest to provide for their families," Root aimed to create a fraternal order that "would clear away problems of financial security for its members." Because the death of a husband often meant poverty for the wife and children, WOW sold low-cost life insurance policies in addition to providing an exclusive club for men.

   A physical legacy of the organization are headstones poured from concrete in the shape of a tree stump. This was an early benefit of Woodmen of the World membership, and forty-five thousand of the headstones are found in cemeteries nationwide. The program was abandoned in the late 1920s because it was too expensive. The headstones included a depiction of WOW relics and symbols of the organization. These might include a stump or felled tree, a maul, a wedge, an axe, or a Dove of Peace with an olive branch.

10. Link and Haire also designed Cellblock No. 1 of the Montana State Penitentiary in Deer Lodge, the Elks Building in Missoula, and the Rundle Building in Glasgow (see chapter 2).

11. Wags wondered whether Fletcher erected the fence to keep out Holly's sheep, or to prevent Holly's sheepherders from discovering the family still. That previous April Fool's Day Fletcher; his wife, Jessie; and their twenty-two-year-old son, John Jr., were arrested by federal agents for moonshining. This was a violation of the Volstead Act, which was passed in 1919 after the Eighteenth Amendment ushered in Prohibition. Part of a still was found at the ranch, where Fletcher

the elder was arrested, along with a quantity of whiskey. The remainder of the still was found concealed in a culvert fifteen miles south along the Little Prickly Pear Creek. Mrs. Fletcher and her son were arrested at the Gans Block, a seedy, forty-two-room boarding house in Helena. Agents seized and later sold John Sr.'s Ford Model T, a full set of tires, and one mud chain. They also sold John Jr.'s seven-passenger Hudson Speedster Touring Car, a full set of tires, and a tool kit. The Fletchers' rides were confiscated by the Internal Revenue Service because they were used to transport liquor. After posting a $200 bond Fletcher the elder tried to hide his vehicle in a draw behind one of the Scratch Gravel Hills outside Helena. He was sentenced to ninety days in the county jail. His wife and son were fined $50 each.

Prohibition was a spectacular failure, especially in hard-drinking Montana, where most people were from Irish and German stock. For the Fletchers, the money they made selling moonshine far outweighed the fines they paid and the jail time they served. Fletcher Sr. was arrested again in spring 1925, fined $200 and sentenced to sixty days in jail. On Christmas Day of that year the liquor business turned deadly. Under the headline "Drunken Row among Moonshiners Ends in Killing," the *Helena Independent* reported that the body of a carpenter named John Billstrom was discovered by a hunter tracking a mountain lion on a ranch owned by the Fletchers, in remote Skelly Gulch west of Helena (December 28, 1925, 1).

Billstrom had been killed with an axe, which "cleaved his forehead open six inches." When Sheriff Jim Barnes arrived in the area he went first to a cabin, where he discovered two men operating a fifty-gallon still in a nearby shed. A third man, a Romanian sheepherder named Joe Sass, was asleep in the cabin next to a double-barreled shotgun (see chapter 8 for more about "Romanian blood lust"). A trail of blood led to Billstrom's body. A shallow grave had been dug next to the cabin, into which a pick and shovel had been tossed. The moonshiners apparently grew tired of the work and instead dragged the body by a rope a quarter mile downslope through the snow, where they deposited it behind a hill. At trial the coroner exhibited Billstrom's skull—stripped of flesh, hair, and organs—in order to show the jury the extent of the fatal injury. The jury was subjected to another unpleasant experience when a large chuck of plaster fell from the courtroom ceiling onto their laps. The air in the crowded, overheated courtroom grew so foul that the judge considered having it "fumigated" after the end of each session.

One of the moonshiners was convicted of second-degree murder, another of violating the Volstead Act. Although it was probable that Joe Sass wielded the ax after being ordered to do so by the others, he was exonerated in exchange for turning state's evidence against the others. He also pleaded innocent to violating the Volstead Act. Sheriff Barnes and his men destroyed several barrels of mash they found at the cabin, plus a barrel of sugar. On New Year's Eve, Mrs. Jessie Fletcher was arrested as she poured a glass of moonshine for a customer at her home on Jefferson Street in Helena. She tried to smash the bottle, and thus the evidence, but a federal agent stopped her in the act. She was fined $125.

12. "Farm Bankruptcies," *Billings Gazette*, September 12, 1927, 10.

13. Clarence W. Groth, "Sowing and Reaping: Montana Banking, 1910–1925," *Montana* 20 no. 4 (December 1970): 28–35.

14. Henry Ford and Samuel Crowther, *The Great To-Day and Greater Future* (New York: Doubleday, Page, 1926), 269–81.

15. "Wool Pool Is Sold at 41 Cents," *Helena Independent*, May 23, 1922, 5.

16. After dynamite was discovered in several buildings around Lawrence a local undertaker was accused of planting the explosives in order to implicate the IWW. He was fined $500 and released without a day in jail. In May of 1913, Wood appeared in a Boston courtroom, charged with a conspiracy involving his payment of a large sum of money to the undertaker shortly before the dynamite was found. "On Trial for 'Plant' in Lawrence Strike," *New York Times*, May 20, 1913, 8. Ernest Pitman, a Lawrence building contractor who had done extensive work for the American Woolen Company, confessed to a district attorney that he had attended a meeting in the Boston offices of Lawrence textile companies, where the plan to frame the union by planting dynamite had been made. Pitman committed suicide after he was subpoenaed to testify. With no witness to testify against him, Wood was exonerated. Eight jurors voted him innocent, and four wanted to convict. "Wood Found Not Guilty by Jury," *Boston Sunday Globe*, June 8, 1913, 2.

17. "Striking against America," *Helena Independent*, August 30, 1920, 4.

18. "William M. Wood . . . Kills Self," *Daily Missoulian*, February 3, 1926, 1.

12. UNDER THE SWAYING PALMS

1. Montana, however, would remain predominantly rural until the 1950s, when the majority of the population lived in Butte, Billings, Great Falls, and the state's smaller cities. *Montana: 2010 Census of Population and Housing, Population and Housing Unit Counts*, CPH-2-5. U.S. Census Bureau (Washington DC: Government Printing Office, 2012), 1.

2. In November 1916, three years before the ratification of the Eighteenth Amendment, Montana voters approved a referendum for the statewide prohibition of alcohol. Montana's influential and well-organized branch of the Women's Christian Temperance Union had led the effort to ban the manufacture and sale of liquor. The law, which went into effect at the end of 1918, reflected the new power of Montana women, who won the right to vote in 1914. Not all Montana women supported prohibition. Many of them rightly saw it as an unenforceable overreach by government that would lead to a rise in crime. And some women,

such as Jessie Fletcher (see chapter 11, note 11), saw it as a chance to make a buck.

3. The Montana Club was started in 1880 as a private poker game for prominent men who didn't want to sully themselves gambling in saloons. It was formally founded in 1885 by 130 lawyers, bankers, and magnates from the mining, livestock, and timber industries whose stated mission was for "literary, mutual improvement & social purposes." They met from time to time in various venues to schmooze and make deals. One of these founding members was Wilbur Fisk Sanders, one of the original Alder Gulch vigilantes who lynched and strangled at least forty-six alleged road agents. In his book, *Immortal Hero, New York Times* op-ed writer Timothy Egan presents strong circumstantial evidence that Sanders assassinated Thomas Francis Meagher, governor of the Montana Territory, who disappeared mysteriously in 1867 from a steamboat docked in Fort Benton. Upon his appointment, Meagher had enraged Sanders and his vigilante thugs, calling them "ill-bred bigots." Sanders, Meagher's political rival and a perennial but unsuccessful Republican candidate for the Territory's nonvoting congressional seat, responded in a letter to a supporter: "We must put a quietus on the doings of this pretender."

In 1893 club members footed the bill to build a massive five-story stone edifice that served as their "clubhouse." It was erected on the spot where gold was first discovered in 1864. The many national celebrities who visited the club included Mark Twain and soon-to-be vice president Teddy Roosevelt, who stayed there in 1900 as a guest of U.S. senator Thomas H. Carter of Montana. This was a year before President McKinley was assassinated in Buffalo, New York, propelling Roosevelt into the White House.

In April 1903 the building was largely destroyed by a spectacular fire that started on the seventh floor. The horse-drawn fire wagons dispatched to the scene could do nothing more useful than hose down one of the three safes that were still too hot to touch even days after the inferno died. Because of a quantity of coal that had been deposited next the boiler in the basement, the ruins smoldered for days.

In May, Helena police announced that a fourteen-year-old named Harry Anderson admitted to starting the fire. "Young Negro Boy Burned the Club," a headline in the *Great Falls Tribune* announced. Small and quiet, dressed in knickerbockers, Harry calmly confessed, sparing the police the task of forcing a confession through "the sweating processes," according to the *Helena Independent.* They promised the boy that his punishment would be no harsher than a stint in reform school. Harry, who worked in the club as an elevator boy, said he had set a fire on the club three days previous to the disaster, and also claimed responsibility for torching two downtown barns. He said the reason he set the fires was because he "liked to see the fire horses run and to help the firemen work." In fact, Harry was on board one of the fire wagons that arrived at the inferno. His father, Julian Anderson, had no idea his son was an arsonist. Julian also worked at the club, at the time as a waiter and later as a bartender, serving the membership for sixty years. In 1955 he was honored with an invitation to the club's annual stag party, where he was applauded for his hospitality and his superb mint juleps.

While the ruins were still smoldering, donations and insurance claims were cobbled together for the financing of a new building. Cass Gilbert was hired as architect. An early proponent of skyscrapers, Gilbert would go on to design the sixty-story Woolworth Building in New York City. He chose to retain the granite arches that withstood the club's collapse, and designed skyward from there, employing an eclectic Italian Renaissance style featuring a brown terra cotta façade and a Mission-influenced roof. One of the other details he held over from the original 1885 building, which the 1893 club replaced, was the tiled floor of the main entryway, which is adorned with aristikas (swastikas flipped horizontally). In etched glass above the floor is signage that explains that in many cultures the aristika was a symbol of good luck.

Holly was a member of the Montana Club for only one year—1922. During that period, he failed to pay a cent in dues. Among the more responsible of the 450 members were two prominent pioneers whose accomplishments had directly affected Holly—Samuel T. Hauser and Arvin M. Holter, the dam builders.

4. "Wild Sheepherder Stands to Answer a Serious Charge," *Helena Independent*, June 29, 1926, 2.

5. "Earthquake Smashed His Hands and Cold Freezes the Stumps," *Helena Independent*, December 21, 1927, 5.

6. "Ranch Hands in Fatal Accident," *Helena Independent*, September 16, 1929, 1.

7. "Herder Commits Suicide as Camp Tender Looks On," *Helena Independent*, August 5, 1930, 10.

8. Herrin family myth holds that Holly was deeply indebted to a bank after borrowing money with low interest rates in order to buy the ranches of neighbors who would have lost everything if not for his generosity. There is no evidence to support this belief. Family myth also holds that an officer of this bank masterminded the confiscation of Holly's assets. And that he was able to do so because he was sleeping with Mary Ellen. The marriage unofficially ended when Holly caught them in bed together. Again, besides the coincidental sale of the Herrin ranches in 1930 to the Wolf Creek Live Stock Company and the collapse of the marriage that same year, there is no documented evidence to support these beliefs, which are based on undated notes prepared by Jena Herrin from interviews with Wayne and Gordon Herrin, Holly's grandsons.

9. "Harlan [*sic*] J. Herrin, Prominent Sheepman, Dies," *Independent Record*, February 20, 1946, 5.

13. FOR THE LOVE OF THE GAME

1. In 1911 Tom Herrin was a nineteen-year-old sophomore. There is no evidence he was ever awarded a diploma. This was not unusual; at the time, less than 6 percent of all Americans were high school graduates. The first descendent of Daniel's to attend college (and graduate) was Harland Sanford Herrin, his grandson.

2. "Holter Dam Ball Team Victorious," *Helena Independent,* July 10, 1910, 7.

3. "World Record for Strike-Outs," *Helena Independent,* September 23, 1912, 7. As was the custom, newspapers identified ballplayers by last name only.

4. "Troubles in City League," *Helena Independent,* July 8, 1912, 7.

5. Although the marriage license claimed Marie was eighteen, she was actually seventeen and had agreed to marry Tommy when she was sixteen, requiring the couple to ask for her father's permission.

6. The Helena Senators played their final four years in the Union Association against teams such as the Boise Irrigators, the Murray (Utah) Infants, the Salt Lake City Skyscrapers, the Butte Miners, and the Great Falls Electrics. See "1914 Union Association," Stats Crew, accessed May 31, 2021, www.statscrew.com/minorbaseball /l-UA/y-1914. At the time, Minor League teams were independently owned. The farm system in place today was invented in 1919 by St. Louis Cardinals executive Branch Rickey, who also broke Major League Baseball's color barrier when he hired Jackie Robinson in 1947 to play first base for the Brooklyn Dodgers. "Rickey's farm system idea was a strategy for saving money. Instead of bidding against other major-league teams for minor-league players, Rickey wanted to grow his own. After World War I, when the minors were in a financial slump, Rickey put his strategy into effect. In 1919 the Cardinals acquired controlling interest in teams at Houston and Fort Smith; by 1939 the Cardinal empire included 32 minor-league teams and about 650 players." Kevin Kerrane, "How Branch Rickey Invented Modern Baseball," Deadspin, November 15, 2013, https://deadspin .com/how-branch-rickey-invented-modern-baseball-1458137692.

7. Family lore has it that Tommy didn't like his stepmother, Mary Ellen, and chose to live with Mary Theresa Sanford. There's no documented proof of this animus. It's likely he chose to live in Helena instead of the Holter Lake ranch because of the city's schools and its sports opportunities.

8. While the food Marie crafted was elegant and memorable, she remained thin and petite to the end of her eighty-eight years.

9. In February 1943 an explosion in an eight-thousand-foot-deep shaft at the Smith Mine #3 killed seventy-four men. It was the worst mining disaster in the state's history. A decade later, coal extraction in the Bear Creek area had dwindled considerably and finally ceased in the 1970s.

10. "East Helena Is Given Trimming," *Helena Independent,* June 28, 1915, 6.

11. "The Doll Shop," *Helena Independent*, April 28, 1912, 11.

12. "Lucky Thirteen Enlist at Falls," *Helena Independent*, April 21, 1917, 3.

13. "Lieutenant Harold Joyce of Helena Killed In Action in France," *Independent-Record*, September 28, 1918, 1. During the war, Montana's young men were drafted based on a state population of 940,000, when in fact its true population was less than 550,000 (no one has ever explained the discrepancy). As a consequence, Montana sent forty-thousand soldiers to war, nearly double the quota of any other state. K. Ross Toole, *Twentieth-Century Montana* (Norman: University of Oklahoma Press, 1972), 255.

14. "Harold H. Joyce," *Helena Independent*, September 28, 1918, 4 "Seventy-nine Montanans were convicted under the state law, considered the harshest in the country, for speaking out in ways the authorities deemed critical of the United States. In one instance a traveling wine and brandy salesman was sentenced to seven to twenty years in prison for calling wartime food regulations a 'big joke.' One man was pardoned after the war. On 3 May 2006 Montana Governor Brian Schweitzer pardoned the other seventy-five men and three women. 'I'm going to say what Gov. Sam Stewart should have said,' Schweitzer said, referring to the man who signed the sedition legislation into law in 1918. 'I'm sorry, forgive me, and God bless America, because we can criticize our government.'" "Pardons Granted 88 Years after Crimes of Sedition," *New York Times*, May 3, 2006, A20.

14. NO LONGER THE LAZY CROP

1. The previous year, baseball fans worried that the game would never return to Montana on a professional level. "Before the great war upset the world," the *Helena Independent* editorialized, "baseball in a professional way was played in Helena. It had a more or less unsatisfactory existence, partly because the management was bad and partly because the patronage was poor. . . . It is time that Helena took an interest in baseball, but whether it is possible to rejuvenate the greatest of American games is a question."

2. *Report of the Chief of the Weather Bureau*, 1919–20 (Washington DC: U.S. Government Printing Office, 1921), 211.

3. "State Land Sells Readily," *Glasgow Courier*, June 6, 1919, 1.

4. According to Rogan, he met the plant wizard in 1912 and begged him for one potato to use as seed. Burbank initially refused but finally relented when he discovered that Rogan was an Irishman who doted on spuds. He removed one of these potatoes from a glass case and handed it to Rogan, who tenderly wrapped it in tissue and took it back to Montana. In 1914 he claimed to have sold two carloads of Sacramentos. "The public is still yelling for more," he trumpeted.

5. "Work of the County Farm Bureau Is Told by County Agent W. W. Skuse," *Helena Independent*, June 2, 1918, 6.

6. "No War at State Fair," *Helena Independent*, September 12, 1925, 1.

7. "Decision of Judge Poorman in Toomey Case Upheld by State's High Court," *Helena Independent*, April 17, 1926, 1.

8. "Multitudes Cheer Col. Lindbergh, at State Fair," *Helena Independent*, September 7, 1927. Following Lindbergh's appearance, a woman called the Helena police department, demanding that officers be dispatched to find her car, which she had misplaced in welter of four-thousand vehicles parked on streets and fields surrounding the fairgrounds. The officer advised her to wait until everyone else drove away before looking for her car again. Earlier in the day Lindbergh had flown from Butte to Great Falls. Because of his schedule he didn't have time to land in what boosters of the era called the "Power City," but he buzzed low over the downtown. At the intersection of Third Street and Central Avenue he tossed out a canvas pouch tied with an orange streamer. The pouch, which contained a message to the people of Great Falls promoting the increased use of airplanes to deliver the mail, hit Ingeberg Myhr on the shoulder. Myer, the owner of a women's apparel shop called The Peacock, was uninjured. She promptly delivered the satchel to the mayor, who read Lindbergh's message to the gathered throngs. "Famous 'Flying We' Greeted by Great Falls," *Great Falls Tribune*, September 7, 1927, 1. The "Flying We" was Lindbergh's description of the spiritual connection he claimed to have had with the Spirit of St. Louis. Painted on the propeller of the monoplane was an aristika—the left-facing swastika that is a universal symbol of good luck often adorning the aircraft of early aviators.

9. "Flathead Indians Will Appear at State Fair," *Helena Independent*, August 25, 1927, 5.

10. "Theaters: The Marlow Theatre," Helena as She Was, accessed December 30, 2019, http://www.helenahistory.org/marlow_theatre.htm.

11. The Orange Crush Bottling Company manufactured Coca-Cola, Canadian Club Ginger Ale, Becco Beer, and Orange Crush, which it produced by combining carbonated Lissner Mineral Water with a syrup produced from vats of orange juice delivered by rail directly from California groves. Marcus Lissner was a Prussian Jewish merchant who built the International Hotel at the corner of State and Main in Helena in 1869, after he arrived in Montana in 1864 and began mining in Alder Gulch. The site of the hotel was also the source of Lissner's spring water, which at one time was shipped in tank cars to the Eastern Seaboard. Orange Crush also manufactured lime and lemon crushes. Jewish Museum of the American West, www.jmaw.org/lissner-jewish-montana/, accessed January 14, 2020.

15. HOW TO PROSPER WHEN TIMES ARE DARK

1. Although it caused no deaths or injuries, the 1925 quake was felt throughout the Northwest, from Seattle to Wyoming. The three hours of intermittent shaking,

which included four aftershocks, caused a significant amount of masonry damage, however, and brought down rockslides on railroad tracks in the Three Forks area, stranding three trains loaded with tourists. Almost every business in Three Forks was damaged. The school was destroyed, and patients were moved out of the hospital onto the lawn. During the quake, a jury in the Missoula County courthouse deliberating charges against a man named George Kolvick demanded to be freed from the locked jury room; their demand was granted. After they returned to consider their decision, they quickly declared Kolvick guilty of selling alcohol. He was sentenced to ninety days in the county jail.

The 1925 quake was the beginning of a thirty-five-year cycle of seismic disturbances in Montana, which included the 1935–36 earthquakes in Helena and the devastating 7.2 quake that killed twenty-eight people in the Yellowstone Park area and created a new body of water—Earthquake Lake (usually called Quake Lake).

2. "Herrin Dairy Has Fully Accredited Herd," *Helena Independent*, January 15, 1933, 8.
3. "Herrin's Dairy; Our Name on Every Cap," ad in *Helena Independent*, September 8, 1935, 5.
4. "Modern Cooler for Milk Installed by Tom Herrin Dairy," *Helena Independent*, June 2, 1938, 6.
5. Opponents of raw milk, such as the National Milk Producers Federation, continue to cite safety concerns about bacteria. Advocates cite raw milk's health benefits, claiming that heating milk destroys vitamins and milk's natural antipathogenic capabilities. Each side questions the scientific basis for the other side's position.

   Montana allowed the sale of raw milk from regulated and regularly inspected dairies until 1998, when this trade was halted by the legislature. Milk industry lobbyists cited a salmonella outbreak in 1980 that sickened eighty-three people, sending some of them to the hospital. The Missoula County Health Department traced these cases of food poisoning to raw milk from King's Dairy in Missoula. A young goat that visiting children petted was found to be harboring salmonella, and was destroyed, but it wasn't clear if the goat was the source or a victim of the disease.
6. Lactose intolerance is an unpleasant condition experienced by adults as a result of the deficiency of an intestinal enzyme called lactase, which aids in the digestion of lactose, a milk sugar. Symptoms include diarrhea, bloating, gut pain, and nausea. Discovered in the 1960s, the condition affects 65 percent of the world's adult population, although there are wide variations among different populations. Northern Europeans, such as the Scandinavians, who domesticated cows and goats early in the Neolithic, tend to be less prone to the condition than people who never kept milk animals, such as Italians and Montana Indians. Mongolians, nomads who drank horse milk for millennia, tend to have fewer problems with milk-based foods than their historically more sedentary Chinese and Japanese neighbors, whose diet does not include milk products.

7. "Earl Hill, 24, Dies as a Result of Car Accident," *Helena Independent*, January 8, 1936, 1.

8. "Helena Boy Dies after Dive into Blackfoot River," *Helena Independent*, August 5, 1936, 1.

9. Home Demonstration Clubs were a program of the U.S. Department of Agriculture's Cooperative Extension Service. Their goal was to teach farm women in rural America better methods for getting their work done, in areas such as gardening, canning, nutrition, and sewing and to encourage them to improve their families' living conditions. Originally intended to "uplift" rural women through professional instruction, Home Demonstration clubs became a way for Montana women to socialize, learn from one another, and serve their communities. "Head, Heart, Hands and Health: Montana Women and Girls in the 4-H Movement. Women's History Matters," August 12, 2014, http://montanawomenshistory.org /head-heart-hands-and-health-montanas-women-and-girls-in-the-4-h-movement/.

10. Carol Van Valkenburg, *An Alien Place* (Missoula MT: Pictorial Histories Publishing Company, 1995), 46.

16. GREENER PASTURES

1. "Father Seeks Son's Marriage Annulled," *Helena Independent*, August 20, 1933, 5.

2. "Herrin Ranch Gets Brief Taste of Bombing Attack," *Helena Independent*, January 13, 1943, 5.

3. Intermountain Union College was established in Helena in 1923 after Montana Wesleyan College and College of Montana in Deer Lodge merged. The school's 150 students were housed in three large brick building near the Montana State Capitol. In 1935 three days of earthquakes brought down the walls of the gymnasium and damaged the other building to such an extent that Harland and his classmates were moved briefly to Great Falls. The administration then accepted an invitation to share the campus of Billings Polytechnic Institute. The two schools merged in 1947 to become Rocky Mountain College.

4. "Search For Boys Being Conducted in Hills," *Independent Record*, November 11, 1944, 3.

5. "St. John's Lutheran Church Scene of Rites," *Independent Record*, April 29, 1951, 11.

6. "Ex-Helena Man Designs 16 Prize-Winning Floats," *Independent Record*, June 21, 1964, 19.

7. "This Is Sweepstakes Winner," *Helena Independent*, May 24, 1941, 1.

8. "Millions Enchanted by Parade's Scenes of Childhood Fantasy," *Los Angeles Times*, January 2, 1971.

9. "Here Are Top Winners in 84th Tournament," *Los Angeles Times*, January 1, 1973.

10. "Murder and Mayhem Jar Parade Route," *Los Angeles Times*, January 1, 1973.

11. "Verdugo Views," *Glendale News-Press*, January 2, 2009, www.latimes.com/socal /glendale-news-press/news/tn-gnp-xpm-2009-01-02-gnp-yamada02-story.html.

12. "City Proud as Peacock over Float Honor," *Los Angeles Times*, January 9, 1977, 424.

17. AN HEIR IS BORN

1. Hannah Alsgaard, "Rural Inheritance: Gender Disparities in Farm Transmission," *North Dakota Law Review* 88 (2012): 347, 348–408.
2. Letter from F. H. McBride, superintendent of the Field Service, Office of Indian Affairs, U.S. Department of the Interior, to Alex Grant Swaney, June 21, 1944. McBride's letter informed Swaney, a Helena saddle club member, of a Blackfeet Indian phrase—"oh-mak-see pass-kan," meaning "riding big dance"—which McBride said "would be a very appealing [name] for your Field Day."
3. "Home in Helena Valley Is Swept by Fire," *Helena Independent*, February 9, 1942, 1.
4. "Winners in Four Places in O-Mok-See Announced," *Independent Record*, June 29, 1961, 15.
5. Keith Herrin Jr., 4-H Club Member's Record, compiled in 1968 and 1969.

18. DARK ACRES

1. "A National Trophy for Pole Benders," *Western Horseman*, April 1964, 49.
2. "Keith Herrin Heads U.S. Saddle Group," *Independent Record*, January 21, 1965, 10.
3. "Horse Wins over Cycle in O-Mok-See Challenge," *Independent Record*, 11.
4. "Colorful Last Chance Stampede Begins Friday Night," *Independent Record*, August 1, 1965, 15.
5. "Faculty Council Raps Federation," *Billings Gazette*, November 19, 1961, 5.
6. Fact Sheet, 1962 Wheat Stabilization Program, United States Stabilization and Conservation Service, 1961.
7. "Wheat Producers Do Have a Choice in Referendum," *Independent Record*, August 26, 1972, 4.
8. "Billie Sol Estes, Texas Con Man Whose Fall Shook Up Washington, Dies at 88," *New York Times*, May 14, 2013.
9. "Bureau of Reclamation Denies Farm Group Leader's Charges," *Billings Gazette*, June 9, 1962, 3.
10. "Western Airlines Convair Breaks through Runway," *Independent Record*, March 24, 1960, 10.
11. "Farm Bureau Opposes Bond Issue," *Independent Record*, May 21, 1960, 3.
12. Advertisement, *Independent Record*, May 26, 1960, 12.
13. Advertisement, *Independent Record*, June 6, 1960, 9.
14. "Voters Overwhelmingly Approve Airport Issue," *Independent Record*, November 6, 1968, 1.
15. "Vendetta against the Airport Bonds," *Independent Record*, November 1, 1968, 4.

16. "Taxpayer Group Issues Statement against Airport," *Independent Record*, October 31, 1968, 5.

17. As an illustration of the popular saying that Montana is just a small town with long streets, in 1975 Gordon Herrin's niece, Laura Herrin, married Sandy and Beth McPherson's son, Thomas.

19. RES IPSA LOQUITUR

1. "Land Use," *Independent Record*, June 10, 1973, 27.

2. J. B. Neilands, Gordon H. Orians, E. W. Pfeiffer, Alje Vennema, and Arthur H. Westing, *Harvest of Death: Chemical Warfare in Vietnam and Cambodia* (New York: Free Press, 1972).

3. "Weed Board Unreceptive to Spraying Criticism," *Independent Record*, May 7, 1975, 7.

4. "Chemical Linked with Miscarriages Banned," *Post Crescent*, April 19, 1979, 27.

5. No. 14404, *Keith W. Herrin v. Molly Burke Herrin*, Supreme Court of the State of Montana. Decided January 24, 1979.

20. THE LAST ACRE

1. "Health Board Bars Attorney from Hearings," *Independent Record*, November 1, 1978, 7.

2. "Weeds Worse than Sprays," *Independent Record*, August 28, 1983, 1.

3. "County Broke Herbicide Law: Officials Resign," *Independent Record*, July 26, 1983, 1.

4. "Herrin Critical of State," *Independent Record*, July 31, 1983, 27.

5. "Roundup Maker to Pay $10 Billion to Settle Cancer Suits," *New York Times*, June 24, 2020, 1.

6. "Weeds Worse than Sprays," *Independent Record*, August 28, 1983, 1.

7. "Rancher Not Blamed by Jury for Accident," *Independent Record*, November 30, 1983, 9.

8. "Hay Stacker Suit Back," *Independent Record*, August 21, 1985, 9.

9. "Witness Recants Story: New Twist in Arson Trial," *Independent Record*, July 10, 1984, 10.

10. "City Approves Permit for Crittenton Home," *Independent Record*, April 8, 1993, 1.

APPENDIX 1

1. "'Dream Ranch' at Wolf Creek One of West's Most Elaborate," *Great Falls Tribune*, November 16, 1947, 35.

2. "Siege of Rieke Plant at Auburn Is in Progress," *Garrett Clipper*, January 20, 1941 1.

3. "Select Board to Adjust Auburn Labor Trouble," *Garrett Clipper*, January 27, 1941, 1.

4. "Rieke 'Dream Ranch' Materializes," *Great Falls Tribune*, November 16, 1947, 38.

5. "Hawaii-Bound Holma Hits Misfortune's Shoals on Holter," *Great Falls Tribune*, November 14, 1969, 20.
6. "Babcock Buys Oxbow," *Great Falls Tribune*, August 26, 1977, 7.
7. "No Subdivision Planned at Oxbow, Says Babcock," *Great Falls Tribune*, February 23, 1978, 5.
8. "Babcock and BLM Finalize Sleeping Giant Land Swaps," *Montana Standard*, March 27, 1961, 17.
9. Doug Swanson, *Blood Aces* (New York: Penguin, 2014).
10. "Conservationists Buy Oxbow," *Great Falls Tribune*, March 7, 1989, 1.
11. "Oxbow History," OX: Ox Bow Ranch, Wolf Creek MT, www.oxbowranchangus.com, accessed August 1, 2020.

APPENDIX 2

1. *Society of Montana Pioneers*, Constitution, Members, and Officers, with Portraits and Maps: Volume 1, 1899.
2. "The Pioneers of Montana," *Great Falls Tribune*, September 24, 1901, 3.
3. Timothy Egan, *The Immortal Irishman* (New York: Houghton Mifflin Harcourt, 2016), Kindle, chap. 21.
4. "May Raise the Limit," *Great Falls Tribune*, September 21, 1903, 8.
5. Diane L. Magnuson and Miriam L. King, "Comparability of the Public Use Microdata Samples: Enumeration Procedures," *Historical Methods* 28, no. 1 (Winter 1995): 27–32.

CPSIA information can be obtained
at www.ICGtesting.com
Printed in the USA
LVHW031542290122
709553LV00003B/361